Sacred Groves and
Local Gods

Sacred Groves and Local Gods

Religion and Environmentalism in South India

ELIZA F. KENT

OXFORD
UNIVERSITY PRESS

OXFORD
UNIVERSITY PRESS

Oxford University Press is a department of the University of Oxford.
It furthers the University's objective of excellence in research, scholarship,
and education by publishing worldwide.

Oxford   New York
Auckland   Cape Town   Dar es Salaam   Hong Kong   Karachi
Kuala Lumpur   Madrid   Melbourne   Mexico City   Nairobi
New Delhi   Shanghai   Taipei   Toronto

With offices in
Argentina   Austria   Brazil   Chile   Czech Republic   France   Greece
Guatemala   Hungary   Italy   Japan   Poland   Portugal   Singapore
South Korea   Switzerland   Thailand   Turkey   Ukraine   Vietnam

Published in the United States of America by
Oxford University Press
198 Madison Avenue, New York, NY 10016

Library of Congress Cataloging-in-Publication Data
Kent, Eliza F., 1966–
Sacred groves and local gods : religion and environmentalism in South India / Eliza F. Kent.
p. cm.
Includes bibliographical references (p.) and index.
ISBN 978–0–19–989546–5 (hardcover : alk. paper)—ISBN 978–0–19–989548–9 (pbk. : alk.
paper)
1. Sacred groves—India—Tamil Nadu.   2. Tamil Nadu (India)—Religious life and
customs.   3. Forest conservation—Social aspects—India—Tamil Nadu.   I. Title.
BL583.K46 2013
294.5′35095482—dc23
2012027027

ISBN 978–0–19–989546–5
ISBN 978–0–19–989548–9

Contents

Acknowledgments

IT IS A daunting task indeed to recognize all the people and institutions who have contributed to a project that has taken more than a decade to come to fruition. First and foremost, I owe a deep debt of gratitude to the residents of villages throughout Tamil Nadu who opened up to a stranger sufficiently to share with me the stories of their gods. Their dedication to maintaining forested shrines in spite of many temptations to put the trees in them to more "productive use" have inspired people around the world, as word of India's remarkable tradition of sacred groves has spread. The conventions of anthropology, which stipulate the granting of "informants" a degree of anonymity through the use of pseudonyms, prevent me from listing each of them here by name. I would also like to express my profound gratitude to the environmental activists, botanists, conservation biologists, and advocates of traditional medical systems in India who warmly welcomed me and good-naturedly endured my many questions. Many of these are accomplished individuals whose publications have informed this project significantly, thus blurring the line between "informants" and professional interlocutors. Special mention must be given to these extraordinarily dedicated individuals: Joss Brooks and N. Loganathan of Pitchandikulam Forest (Auroville), Nanditha Krishna and M. Amrithalingam of the C. P. Ramaswamy Environmental Education Centre (Chennai), and P. Unnikrishnan of the Foundation for the Revitalization of Local Health Traditions (Bangalore).

While in Tamil Nadu, I was fortunate to have the good company and invaluable assistance of a number of skilled field assistants while conducting the research for this study. Many thanks to M. Thavamani, J. Arun Selva Raj, and Charles Asir for sharing in the spirit of adventure on our excursions together and for their creative insights into Tamil culture in all its manifold variety.

My thinking about religion, environmentalism, and the religious meanings of trees and forests in India has been shaped by conversations with scholars spanning many disciplines. It has been a pleasure to talk (and e-mail) through many of the ideas in this book with friends and colleagues, including David Aftandilian, Catherine Cardelús, Christopher Key Chapple, William Elison, Ann Grodzins Gold, John Grim, David Haberman, Pankaj Jain, Timothy McCay, Robert Menzies, Vijaya Nagarajan, Albertina Nugteren, Whitney Sanford, D. Samuel Sudanandha, and Bron Taylor. Scholars working in India at the intersection of folklore, anthropology, and botany greatly enriched my understanding of sacred groves while setting a high standard for gracious hospitality should they return the favor by coming to the United States to write or do research: I would especially like to mention M. A. Kalam of the University of Madras, M. D. Muthukumaraswamy of the National Folklore Support Centre (Chennai), M. Kannan of the French Institute of Pondicherry, and M. D. Ramanujam of the Centre for Post-Graduate Studies (Pondicherry). Meika Loe has been a fellow traveler in so many ways, not least of all through the process of writing a second book. It is a pleasure to express my gratitude for her patient reading of numerous drafts and for the ways she pushed me to write for a broader audience.

Parts of the book were presented at the South Asia Program Seminar Series at Cornell University, the South Asia Seminar Series at the University of Texas at Austin, the Brooks Lecture Series at SUNY Cortland, Wesleyan University's Department of Religion and Program in Asian Studies, and the Humanities Colloquium at Colgate University. I'm grateful to the conveners of these series for inviting me and to the participants at these diverse venues for helping me to clarify and deepen my understanding of complex phenomena.

Portions of the material presented in this book are drawn from articles published earlier, and they are reprinted here with the kind permission of the publishers. Portions of the introduction and chapter 1 appeared in an article in *Worldviews: Global Religions, Culture and Ecology* 13, no. 1 (2009), © Koninklijke Brill NV, 2009. Chapter 2 appeared as part of a special issue on the religious meanings of trees and forests in India in the *Journal for the Study of Religion, Nature and Culture* 4, no. 2 (June 2010) © Equinox Published Ltd., 2010. Similarly, chapter 3 contains material from "Fierce Gods and Dense Forest: Sacred Groves in Coromandel," coauthored with

M. P. Ramanujam, which was published in *Indian Folklife* [Chennai, India] 26 (July 2007).

At Colgate, I've been fortunate to have the intellectual, moral, and financial support of an outstanding liberal arts college. My colleagues in the Department of Religion are second to none. I benefitted from sharing my research on Tamil sacred groves with the students in two iterations of RELG 420: Religion and Enviromentalism in South Asia, in the spring of 2005 and 2008. At various stages, student research assistants have completed huge amounts of Internet research and bibliographic assistance in short amounts of time, especially Abhinav Maheshwari, Anand Kapur, Utsav Adhikari, and William Sánchez. It seems there is nothing on the Internet they cannot find.

Many of the above-mentioned individuals have read and commented on earlier versions of the chapters in this book, whether conference paper, article, or chapter draft. In addition, three anonymous reviewers provided valuable feedback on the manuscript at a crucial stage of the project. Having gladly acknowledged my debt to these generous and careful readers, I alone am responsible for any errors in fact or interpretation that may have crept in despite their diligence.

I'm also pleased to acknowledge grants from numerous organizations that made this book possible: the American Institute of Indian Studies and the Colgate Research Council provided vital support for field research during several extended trips to India, and the National Endowment for the Humanities provided support for that increasingly rare yet crucial ingredient for scholarship—time to think and write.

My parents, Keni Kent and Maggie Kent; my brother, Roger Kent; my uncle and aunt, Edward L. Strohbehn, Jr. and Heather Ross; my stepsister Aine Kelly and stepmother Carole Kelly; and my mother- and father-in-law, Audrey Smolen and Charles Shopsis, have all been excellent conversation partners through every stage of this project and have motivated me to press on with their enthusiasm for every small accomplishment. Finally, it is my greatest pleasure to acknowledge the support of my partner, Mari Shopsis, and our children, Philip Rodrigo Shopsis-Kent and Alice Rose Shopsis-Kent. It has been such a delight to discover the pleasures of the woods anew with you, again and again. This book is dedicated to you.

Note on Transliteration

TAMIL WORDS WERE transliterated following the University of Madras Tamil Lexicon. Note that according to this system, "c" is pronounced "s," and "ḻ" is the unique Tamil letter linguists refer to as the voiced retroflex approximate, which is pronounced somewhere between "l" and retroflex "r." For reading ease, Tamil personal, caste, and place names are given with diacritics at first mention but then rendered without diacritics using the most widely recognized Anglicized forms. Most non-Tamil Indian words have been transliterated without diacritics, using the standard Anglicized forms where possible.

Map

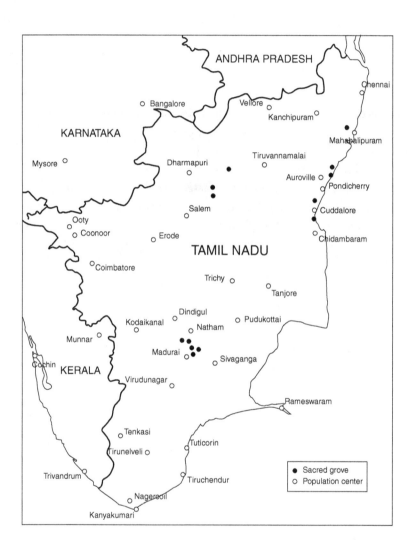

Sacred Groves and
Local Gods

Introduction

IN RECENT YEARS, environmental nongovernmental organizations (NGOs), botanists, specialists in traditional medicine, and anthropologists in India have shown enormous interest in the pan-Indian phenomenon of "sacred groves," small forests or stands of trees whose produce is set aside for the exclusive use of a deity. With the deepening of the global environmental crisis, many Indians concerned about the effects of deforestation have claimed the sacred groves of India as an ancient indigenous ecological tradition. Known by a variety of different names in different parts of India—in Tamil, they are called *kōyilkāṭu* (literally "temple-forest") and *cāmitōp* (lit. "god grove") or are referred to more simply in spoken Tamil as *kāṭṭle irukkiṟa kōyil* ("the temple that is in the forest")—the beliefs and practices surrounding forested shrines also show considerable variation, as does their floral composition, their size, and their embeddedness in concrete relations of property and patronage.[1] Indeed, when one closely examines the phenomena across India, it seems sacred groves in different regions share little in common beyond the fact that their maintenance leads to the conservation of pockets of abundant and diverse flora and fauna in areas otherwise denuded by deforestation.

The German forester Dietrich Brandis, first General Inspector of Forests, is credited with identifying the phenomenon of religiously motivated forest conservation in India with the term *sacred grove*. In his 1897 review of indigenous forestry, he wrote, "Very little has been published regarding sacred groves in India, but they are, or rather were, very numerous. I have found them in all provinces.... These sacred forests, as a rule, are never touched by the axe, except when wood is needed for the repair of religious buildings or in special cases for other purposes."[2] As Brandis's wording suggests, there has always been a pall of doom surrounding sacred groves, a foreboding sense that they are on the brink of extinction.[3] Given the realities of food and land shortages in India, it is indeed remarkable that the practice of protecting stands of trees or small forests endures. Sacred groves have survived not only the intense deforestation initiated by the British but also the surge of deforestation that accompanied independence. Today, they are threatened by population growth, rising demand for firewood, greater access to electricity for irrigation, and thus the ability to put more land under cultivation. In addition, as the mostly non-Brahman residents of communities that maintain forest shrines become integrated into wider social networks, people's exposure to new religious ideas is changing the way they think about and behave in the groves. Yet in spite of all these factors, patches of forest protected by religious taboos exist all over India—in the thousands. This book seeks to understand why.

Madhav Gadgil, a senior Indian environmental historian, established one of the key ideas that brought attention to India's sacred groves in the 20th century, namely, that they provide an ecologically significant refuge for species.[4] In 1971, he returned to Maharashtra after doing graduate work in mathematical ecology at Harvard University and conducted fieldwork with his former professor, V. D. Vartak, on sacred groves in the hilly catchment area of Panchet Dam, not far from his old hometown of Pune.[5] Gadgil drew on the work of evolutionary biologist G. F. Gause to help explain the ecological potential of what appeared to him to be extraordinary remnants of the climax forest that once covered the region. Gause's experiments with protozoa demonstrated that in an environment where no limits were placed on the population of either prey or predator, one could prevent the extinction of prey species only by providing them with an area inaccessible to predators, from whence they could repopulate and colonize other areas.[6] Sacred groves, he argued, essentially provide such shelter to plants and animals from human use, serving as a kind of *in situ* seed bank for native and medicinal plants. By restricting or regulating the use of forest products, the taboos surrounding sacred groves limit the overutilization of species by human beings. The groves provide additional ecosystem services in offering habitat for pollinating birds and insects, recharging and stabilizing the underground water table, acting as a windbreak, and helping to prevent soil erosion. In addition, one frequently finds in sacred groves trees that are themselves considered sacred, such as the banyan and the pipal. Gadgil and Ramachandra Guha have observed that many such sacred trees are "keystone species" that provide habitat, nesting material, and food for a myriad of animals and birds.[7] Given all these ecological benefits, Gadgil and others regard the sacred groves as an exemplary system of "traditional community resource management," where natural resources held in common are conserved for the long-term benefit of the community. However, unlike the reserved forests maintained by the Indian government's Forest Service the ideology at work in the groves is not that of scientific natural resource management but of religion and custom.

Gadgil's influential characterization of sacred groves represented them as relics in both a botanical and a cultural sense. They not only preserved remnant patches of old-growth forest that used to cover the subcontinent; they also harbored primitive forms of religiosity that had been long superceded by Brahmanical Hinduism, Buddhism, Islam, Christianity, and other more modern religions. J. Donald Hughes and M. D. Subhash Chandran have refined this historical understanding of sacred groves to generate a broadly applicable model. Drawing on a comparison of sacred grove practices in India and the ancient Mediterranean world, they argue that the "practice of honoring sacred groves" began among hunter-gatherer people in Paleolithic times.[8] Bound by animistic belief systems in a web of spiritual relationships with their biophysical environment, primal hunter-gatherers approached animals and plants with reverence and a sense of kinship, killing them only when necessary. In forested areas, Hughes and Chandran hypothesize, where agriculture began with slash and burn methods, the first sacred groves stood out from the surrounding land as areas spared from the fire.[9] As the population grew and forests were further cleared for agriculture, peasant farmers continued the practice of honoring the groves that had begun with hunter-gatherers, associating the groves with gods who normally protected the growing crops but who could be provoked by transgressions of their space into inflicting famine and disease. Rounding out this historical narrative, Hughes and Chandran speculate that while sacred groves in urban areas were incorporated into temple-based worship in cities and became cultivated temple orchards and gardens, those in rural areas remained as enduring fragments of the original forest ecosystem.[10] The botanical and cultural claims undergirding this theory of sacred groves are intertwined: The primitive simplicity of the forms of worship found in groves anchors the flora in a bygone time when tribal peoples supposedly lived harmoniously with nature, just as the presence of endemic species in groves that remained when the surrounding areas were converted to fields or grazing land lends force to the notion that the religiosity practiced in groves has ancient origins.

Since the first publication of Gadgil's theories about sacred groves in 1975, scholarly and popular interest in the groves has grown by leaps and bounds. There have been numerous conferences in India bringing together botanists, ecologists, and environmental activists to share information and best practices for managing sacred groves.[11] Restoration projects have sprouted up all over the country, funded by federal and state government agencies, as well as by local and international environmental organizations like the World Wildlife Fund for Nature. Projects such as these entail, I would argue, more than just utilitarian goals. In the face of criticism from abroad, and deepening concern from within Indian society about the pace and direction of India's development, they also communicate an inspiring utopian model of society, according to which the failures of the recent past can be reversed by developing more culturally sensitive methods that draw on the best elements from the ancient indigenous past, updated for the present. Yet environmental discourse surrounding sacred groves in India tends to represent the groves as a vanishing tradition, part of a heritage of ancient wisdom that is being eroded as Indian society becomes more industrialized, educated, materialistic, and imbricated in global networks of commerce and information. In the 1970s, Gadgil was already beginning to call for a national program that would preserve sacred groves in the face of both increasing land pressure and the diminishing strength of traditional religious beliefs. He wrote, "It is, therefore, imperative to survey these sacred forests and properly assess their role in nature conservation so that these forests may continue to be preserved *even if the religious beliefs associated with them weaken and may disappear.*"[12] The argument that Gadgil makes here has great appeal. There is evidence that forested shrines preserve, in some regions, the only existing patches of indigenous forest.[13] Yet the rhetoric of the vanishing tradition can be used to sanction top-down appropriation of the effective local ownership of sacred groves. Critics like Meera Nanda, Emma Mawdsley, and Mukul Sharma argue that the romanticized, essentialized vision of tradition that accompanies much of the rhetoric about sacred groves feeds into a resurgent and militant Hindu nationalism, which glorifies the supposed centrality of Hinduism to India's national character in a way that antagonizes others.[14] In addition, this rhetoric has had a profound pragmatic effect on sacred groves in some regions of India.

In Maharashtra (the state in which Gadgil conducted his pioneering research), the state government has been particularly active in asserting control over village-level forests, sacred groves included. With the passage of the Maharashtrian Private Forests Acquisition Act of 1975, vast amounts of forest, much of it held in tribal villages in the hilly regions of the state, were transferred to the state at the stroke of a pen. The rationale for the law was the premise that local people were unable to properly conserve or protect forests and that state intervention for the "purpose of attaining and maintaining ecological balance in the public interest" was necessary.[15] However, as Indian anthropologist J. J. Roy Burman has demonstrated, the effect of this act and similar subsequent state measures was an increase in temple-building and felling of trees in sacred groves acquired by the state. A related trend was their subsequent afforestation with economically valuable species through Joint Forest Management initiatives which tended to diminish the extent to which people regarded the groves as holy.[16] A 2003 amendment to the federal Wildlife Protection Act of 1972 was meant to obviate such excesses by providing a mechanism for the legal recognition of community involvement in the protection of habitat for fauna and flora. Government-owned land that was not inhabited or already a national park or state wildlife reserves could be designated a community reserve, which guaranteed both local control of the land and its protection through the management and oversight of a committee of community representatives.

The most recent formulation of Indian national forest policy, the Intensification of Forest Management Scheme (IFMS), inaugurated in 2009 as part of India's 11th Five-Year Plan, includes a new provision for the protection and conservation of sacred groves. The Scheme provides funding for projects that will, among other things, create management plans for all the sacred groves in each Indian state. One of the expected outcomes of the central government's policy, as it is implemented over the next several years, is the creation of a state-by-state inventory of all sacred groves with "details of their location, area, people involved in protection, cultural and religious beliefs associated with these sacred groves."[17] In addition, funds will be made available for "improvement works," which include "i) labeling of important species and signage, ii) cultural operation, iii) improvement of footpaths, iv) laying of eco-trails for education purposes, v) protection measures."[18] Such a vision for sacred groves may well capitalize on the environmental education potential inherent in this distinctive variety of traditional community resource management, but it has the potential to make more visible, public and park-like forested shrines that up to now have been largely secluded places, with access closely controlled by local communities. IFMS documents repeatedly stress the importance of working with local communities as management plans are created. "It may please be noted," states the Operational Guidelines for the IFMS, "that as far as possible in all activities of works the people associated with a particular sacred grove would be involved in planning, execution and monitoring of the work programmes."[19] But, as is often the case in India, whether or not the collaborative, cooperative spirit of these laws and policies is achieved when they are actually implemented depends a great deal on local political conditions.

What Is Sacred about Sacred Groves?

Until recently, much of the scholarly discourse surrounding sacred groves focused on their environmental aspects and tended to generalize broadly about the religious beliefs and practices surrounding them. Lack of careful, sustained attention to the religious aspects of the groves has led to simplistic views of devotion in these groves as a form of nature worship (thus testifying to the inherently ecological nature of Hinduism) or as gross superstition (thus testifying to the primitive or backward nature of Hinduism, particularly village, non-Brahman Hinduism). One can see the first approach at work in Vandana Shiva and Gadgil and Guha's sweeping and somewhat inflated claims about sacred groves, as when Shiva writes, "Sacred forests and sacred groves were created and maintained throughout India as a cultural response for their protection.... All religions and cultures of the South Asian region have been rooted in the forests, not through fear and ignorance but through ecological insight."[20] Such characterizations of the relationship of indigenous people to forests relies on what Kay Milton has called the "myth of primitive ecological wisdom," which rests on a set of assumptions regarding indigenous people's innate ability to live in an environmentally sustainable way in harmony with the environment. Some indigenous people have started to use this discourse themselves in contests over control of water and land.[21] But as Amita Baviskar and others have argued, bourgeois environmentalist views of tribals and rural people as inherently ecological places them in an uncomfortable position, where their efforts to secure decent ways of life are supported only if they conform to the image of the "tribal" close to nature.[22]

The second set of assumptions regarding the religiosity associated with sacred groves, characterizing it as grossly superstitious and backward, has dominated discussions of sacred groves in Tamil Nadu. For example, in his ground-breaking survey of the sacred groves of Tamil Nadu, M. Amrithalingam describes the animal sacrifices that take place in the groves as "particularly gory and cruel, involving live impalement, throwing animals from heights, tearing them apart with bare hands, biting live animals by the devotees." He continues, "It is unfortunate that little has been done to educate people about the cruelty of this form of worship."[23] So long as government agencies and NGOs regard the religiosity surrounding sacred groves as a variety of superstition, destined to be superceded by either a more refined religious sensibility or rational, secular thought, it is difficult for communities who maintain forested shrines to enter into equal partnerships with them. Sometimes the religious convictions of environmentalists themselves lead them to disparage, or seek to reform elements of, local religious practice that they find distasteful, particularly animal sacrifice. The impulse to reform seen in the work of some environmental NGOs has multiple sources. At one level, it is part of a centuries-long vector of religious change in the direction of assimilating local religious practice with pan-Indian Brahmanical modes of religiosity. Sanskritization, the adoption of Brahmanical norms, rituals, and beliefs by upwardly mobile non-Brahman groups, is a long-standing pattern in South Asian religious history.[24] At another level, unspoken assumptions about religion held by many environmentalists may also contribute to the discomfort some feel in the face of the rituals of possession, exorcism, self-mortification, and animal sacrifice that are regular features of the worship found in sacred groves.

In her comparative study of religious environmentalism in Britain and India, Emma Tomalin demonstrates the ways in which the conceptualizations of both nature and religion in international religious environmentalism (such as found in World Wildlife Fund for Nature and Association for Religion and Conservation initiatives) are shaped by the specific history of modernity in the West. First, thanks to the influence of Romantic poets, writers, and philosophers such as Henry David Thoreau, Ralph Waldo Emerson, and John Muir, nature tends to be viewed as valuable in itself.[25] Undisturbed nature (i.e., wilderness) is especially valuable as a zone of redemption, a crucial antidote to the moral and material pollution of industrialization. Second, complex processes of secularization in the modern West have produced an attenuated understanding of religion (compared to, say, medieval Europe or Puritan America). Tomalin argues that the emphasis in modern forms of religiosity is on the "transcendent" at the expense of the "pragmatic," so that religion, or, more precisely, "faith" (the deeply felt, personal and interior response to the sacred) is required in order to lend meaning to existence but not to contract a marriage, distribute property, or settle disputes. I would add that a third characteristic of modern religion, which derives from the specific history of Protestantism, is the expectation that faith best finds expression in the realm of ethics, where it guides individuals toward more enlightened behavior and restrains their baser impulses. The historical development of religion in modern India has not proceeded in exactly the same way as it has in the West. To compress a long and complicated history, traditional religion exercises much more influence over the daily lives of people in India compared to the secularized denizens of the West. Moreover, the Indian state's policy of religious secularism does not so much limit state intervention into the "private" realm of religion (as in the United States) as insist that the state support all religions equally. Just as with the idealized "wall" between religion and the state in the United States, the Indian ideal of a state equidistant to all religions has been imperfectly realized in practice. But seeking to implement that ideal has resulted in extensive governmental involvement in religious affairs—from state management of "public" religious institutions (such as popular, and wealthy, Hindu temples) to the state's adjudication of religious personal law. Nonetheless, as a result of the rise of Hindu reform movements in the 19th century and of transnational guru-led sects in the 20th, one finds many of the above-mentioned Western assumptions about religion among urban Indian elites. As Sudhir Kakar has written, today "the West" is less a geographical region than a state of mind. Bourgeois, urban-based Indian environmentalists often embrace modern Western assumptions regarding nature's redemptive value and the deeply personal, faith-based nature of religion. Therefore, it is no surprise that some of them view the embodied norms, rituals, and narratives, and the often deeply pragmatic discourses that surround sacred groves as strange and even morally questionable.

In a context in which policies are being designed and implemented about how best to preserve these ecologically significant patches of forest, some of which are guided by incorrect or unconsciously normative assumptions about religion, it seems especially important to listen carefully to what the people who have protected the flora and fauna surrounding sacred groves over time have to say about them. Confounding simplistic representations of the religious beliefs and rituals surrounding sacred groves, close study demonstrates that local practices regarding sacred groves are at once more imaginative and pragmatic than previously thought.[26]

Religion and Change in Tamil Sacred Groves

From the summer of 2001 to the winter of 2006–2007, I conducted four separate research trips to India. The increasing complexity of life as a midcareer academic made staying for long periods difficult, but breaking my field work up into several journeys over a long period of time meant that I could survey forested shrines in several regions of Tamil Nadu, sometimes returning to the same site year after year to record changes. My fieldwork methodology consisted of visiting villages in the company of a field assistant, who was himself often known to the people in the village as a relative or coworker. I had the pleasure of working with several field assistant-collaborators. Sometimes we would work simply as a pair, other times, we would arrive with a small entourage including driver, translator, local contact person, and even family or friends of one of the latter. Although one might think that traveling in a crowd like this would make fieldwork difficult, it heightened the sense of fun and adventure. In addition, though it had some drawbacks, swooping into a village midday with a car packed with people signaled to local residents (rightly or wrongly) the urgency and importance of my visit. I rarely had difficulty gaining access to people willing to talk about forest-dwelling gods in the area. Though some groves I visited only once, others I returned to multiple times, to follow up on leads or conduct interviews with different people. These interviews were digitally recorded, then painstakingly transcribed into written Tamil in notebooks and translated into English by myself and field assistants. At such times, members of my "entourage" of helpers and collaborators were of vital importance: glossing key Tamil terms with local usage, elaborating on the significance of festivals, myths, motifs, rituals, and details of daily rural life described so fleetingly in the course of the interview. Without this assistance, it would have been impossible for me to take up the more solitary work of organizing these experiences and narratives into written form and interpreting them through the lens of contemporary scholarship, historical records, colonial accounts, and my own insights and impressions.

There were definitely drawbacks to the field methodology that forms the basis for this research. I hope that someday someone will be able to conduct a deep ethnography based on long residence and close association with village residents who maintain a forested shrine. If I arrived in the heat of the day, residents were sometimes away—working in the fields or offices. When I turned up without making prior arrangements, as I often did, I could not anticipate whom I would speak with, whether the recognized leaders of the village, women, or young people sitting idly at home during a school vacation. Depending on their social location, people obviously had different perspectives on the meaning, value, and

ose of forested shrines. In some cases, the unpredictability of my field
methodology worked to my advantage, as I was able to speak with people
who might otherwise not have been authorized to give an account of the
village deities. However, this unpredictability, and my own ignorance of
the local sociology of specific villages, also could get me into trouble. One
time I arrived in a village with a friend and driver but without a local contact person who knew the village directly. After conducting a couple of
lackluster interviews and leaving my contact information, we returned to
the rural development institute where I was staying. Later that evening,
I was astonished to see a crowd of angry Tamil men, in formal white dhotis
(an ankle-length men's garment wrapped around waist) pour through the
compound gate, demanding to know who was planning to build a temple
in their village. It turns out the people we had spoken with earlier in the
day were members of a family whom village leaders were shunning for
some transgression, and the dominant members of the village were furi-
ous at the thought that this upstart family was now creating alliances with
complete strangers. It was due only to the patience, tact, and discretion of
my hosts that the men left mollified, reassured that I was just conducting
research on temples, not seeking to build one; they demanded only that
we return to their village later to get the true *varalāṟu*, or myth-history,
about the village and its deities. The frightening incident brought home
to me one of the central findings of my research: The forested shrines
beloved by environmentalists and botanists for their conservation values
are, to the people who maintain them, very powerful sites. Among other
things, they are the homes of gods who are themselves sources of power
and protection, sacred centers that organize status relations among the
community and serve as vital living conduits to the past.

On the basis of this fieldwork, conducted over six years in four districts of Tamil Nadu, I argue that several elements of the prevailing theory of sacred groves are incorrect or at least do not apply well to Tamil
sacred groves. First, the religiosity surrounding sacred groves is not
primitive, nor does it revolve around the worship of nature, ancestors,
or, in most cases, mother goddesses; rather, it is an integral component
of village-based non-Brahmanical Hinduism that organizes space, time,
and village society in complex, fascinating ways. Second, the absence of
datable textual references to sacred groves makes it difficult to determine
accurately in which historical era (or eras) the practice of maintaining
sacred groves actually arose.[27] If the practices, beliefs, and mythology surrounding Tamil forest-dwelling deities are anchored in any time period, I

would argue it is not the era of Paleolithic hunter-gatherers but rather the politically decentered 18th century, when the Tamil country was effectively ruled by local chieftains. These chieftains (the *pāḷaiyakkārars*, "poligars," or Little Kings so famous in Tamil historiography) collected revenue, settled disputes, and protected the residents of their domains from cattle thieves but, if not adequately compensated for such protection, might very likely appropriate the cattle themselves. However, even to speculate about origins risks generating a perception of groves as unchanging, which is the third aspect of Gadgil's original characterization that has not held up under scrutiny. Far from being pristine patches of relict forest untouched for millennia, sacred groves show extensive disturbance. In the present moment they are changing rapidly as residents of communities that maintain forest shrines become integrated into wider social networks and gain exposure to new secular and religious ideas, transforming the way they think about and behave in the groves. Roads and environmentalists, I would argue, are particularly important vectors of change.

In the scholarly discourse surrounding sacred groves, change is almost always lamented. According to Gadgil's view of sacred groves as pristine remnants of ancient forests preserved by vestigial forms of animism, change in beliefs leads to destruction of the groves. In an important article, Hughes and Chandran gave precision to this theory of decline by identifying Sanskritization as the major factor leading to the degradation of forested shrines. As local forest-dwelling gods become identified with deities from the pan-Indian Sanskritic tradition (Vishnu, Shiva, Parvati, etc.), communities build physical temples for them in the groves. But over time, the sacrality once associated with the forest is transferred to the icon of the deity, and neglect or destruction of the surrounding forest ensues.[28] Hughes and Chandran here identify a pattern widely observable in Tamil Nadu. Another trend they document is that the presence of a nearby road often determines whether a forested shrine will undergo this process of development (or degradation). Yet, though roads often have a deleterious effect on the health of the forest associated with a sacred grove, they do not always or necessarily lead to irreversible destruction. Besides connecting communities to new markets, they also create opportunities for higher education and the influx of new ideas—sometimes democratizing ones that erode traditional boundaries and hierarchies. I have observed, especially in the coastal areas of northern Tamil Nadu, that roads have led to some degradation of forest ecology, but they have also put villagers in touch with environmentalists and NGOs bearing new ideas about the value of the forests in their care. The encounter between environmentalists and villagers, however, is often complicated by their very different religious worldviews. Environmentalists can, wittingly or unwittingly, promote the very Sanskritization that Hughes and Chandran correctly identify as a significant factor in the decline of the forests associated with sacred groves.

Chapter Outline

Each chapter of this book is grounded in detailed descriptions of the beliefs, myths, and rituals surrounding Tamil sacred groves which are drawn from fieldwork carried out between 2001 and 2007 in villages near Madurai, Tiruvannamalai, Pondicherry, and Chennai. The sequence of chapters not only traces a rough trajectory from southern to northern Tamil Nadu but also a continuum from the relatively pristine groves around Madurai, to those that have undergone more extensive intervention from temple authorities and environmentalists alike, to a grove created from the ground up by a Chennai-based environmental NGO. Because they constitute valuable property held in common by a group, sacred groves cannot be looked at in isolation from social and economic conditions. Each chapter begins with a discussion of the environmental history of the region and illuminates a constellation of analytically distinguishable but interrelated factors that affect the ecological condition of the grove.

The first chapter begins with a brief discussion of the place of sacred groves in the cultural imagination of North America, focusing on the celebration, even sacralization, of undisturbed nature by 19th-century writers and activists such as John Muir. These ideas have deeply informed environmental thought and practice in the West; but a rather different set of relationships between civilization and the forest, nature and the sacred, and violence and fertility obtains in Tamil sacred groves. I then turn to analysis of groves in Dindigul district, north of the renowned pilgrimage city of Madurai. The groves here are found in mostly single-caste (Ambalakkarar or Muttaraiyar) villages where they are owned and managed collectively by a patriarchal kin group that also organizes annual village festivals. These festivals ritually represent the groves and the deities who reside there as dangerous and liminal, as contrasted with the village center, where the more benevolent village goddesses reside. Here the villagers' constant vigilance has been fairly effective at limiting human overuse of the groves' flora and fauna. Moreover, they have largely left the forested shrines in their verdant condition, not even building in them the structures commonly found in sacred groves elsewhere. In part the relatively undisturbed nature of sacred groves in this area is due to the availability nearby of forest produce for fuel, construction materials, and animal fodder, but it is also due to the tight cohesiveness of the communities. The taboos that protect the boundaries marking a community's forested shrine are closely related to those rules that govern the community itself. As a result, the health of the forest provides a visible index of the community's ability to enforce its own rules and maintain discipline among its members. Superficial treatment of the religiosity surrounding sacred groves has limited our ability to see what is sacred about these sites from the point of view of the people who actually maintain them. Contextualizing the reasons for tree protection given by residents of villages in the Madurai area in the broader cosmology and social history of Tamil Nadu, I suggest an interpretation of Tamil sacred groves as places where people now living very much as settled and moderately prosperous farmers connect with vital aspects of their communal identity as former hunters and warriors.

In Tiruvannamalai, the focus of the second chapter, the groves I visited were maintained by a community living in the foothills of the Kalrayan mountains of western Tamil Nadu, the Malaivazhmakkal Gounders. Their animistic religiosity led to their being classified as tribals in the 19th century, but their rituals and beliefs are a complex blend of non-Brahmanical local religion and devotion to Vishnu in his incarnation as Lord Rama, known and revered throughout India as the hero of the epic, the Ramayana. The groves here are in the process of being "cleared" or "cleaned" (in spoken Tamil, *cuttamā ceyntirukkiṟatu*) as part of the self-improvement efforts of upwardly mobile members of this community. Thanks to the construction of tar roads over the past twenty years, villages in this area are increasingly connected to regional centers, creating new opportunities for education and employment. These roads have also been vectors of new ideas about religion and what it means to be a sophisticated, civilized person. Young people in the village view the taboos surrounding the shrine as old-fashioned. While such taboos imply a deity who could be anywhere within the grove, young devotees prefer to see the god as localized in the main icon, which is housed in colorfully decorated concrete temple buildings. Upwardly mobile Malaiyalis have come to see the relatively simple structures of forest shrines, or the absence of structures altogether, as a sign of neglect or disrespect to the god and a troubling signifier of the community's backwardness. The construction of built structures in the groves can thus be seen as a manifestation of community self-assertion made possible by newfound access to education and political power. Such ambitions sometimes come into conflict with the Tamil Nadu Forest Department, which has sought to implement its own ideas about how the community should develop. It is not only the construction of roads that have led to the clearing of sacred groves: in different parts of India, Joint Forest Management schemes sponsored by the Indian Forest Service have also, perhaps inadvertently, led to their conversion to agriculture.

The social and religious trends visible among Malaiyali villages in Tiruvannamalai, including declining commitment to the taboos surrounding sacred groves and resistance to heavy-handed state-sponsored social forestry initiatives, led some environmentalists to seek new ways to support the conservation of village forests. In the third chapter, I consider the dramatic upsurge of interest in sacred groves seen in the 1990s. This arose because of a variety of factors, including disillusionment with large, bureaucratic, state-driven development campaigns and a corresponding attraction to local grassroots initiatives. After describing and assessing the claims made in these debates, I make an argument for the ecological significance of sacred groves, especially in heavily populated areas such as Pondicherry, where my fieldwork took me after Tiruvannamalai. With its proximity to the global city of Chennai, the whole Coromandel Coast is developing at a rapid rate. Yet many communities in this area are quite loyal to their forested gods, who often function as lineage deities (*kulateyvam*) for families whose members have migrated throughout Tamil Nadu and the world. For most of the year, the sacred groves that shelter these deities enjoy a kind of benign neglect, their forest produce off-limits to human use or regulated by customary rules; however, at festival time they attract hundreds, even thousands, of devotees, who return to fulfill vows, petition for help, and carry out other transactions with the lineage gods who protect them long after they have left the physical site of their ancestral village. After a brief description of the environmental history of the Pondicherry region, I then employ the insights of forest ecologists to investigate the conservation value of groves in this region while also examining the religious and social factors that both support and undermine their continued survival.

As sacred groves gain fame, and the catchment area from which they draw pilgrims expands, one often sees an increase in development of the built structure of the shrine at the expense of the forest. One could argue that the culmination of the process of Sanskritization in a grove is when a temple becomes a stop on public pilgrimage routes. The third chapter ends by describing the efforts of the priests and trustees of a large, well-documented sacred grove, Puttupaṭṭu, outside of Pondicherry, to promote the grove as the birthplace of the popular regional deity Ayyappan, assimilating him to the traditional village guardian Ayyanar (Aiyannar). In addition, this grove has attracted the attention of an NGO associated with Auroville, a neo-Hindu intentional community of Indians and foreign nationals, which has sought to raise people's consciousness about the value of the grove through environmental education campaigns.

The environmental education effort launched from the Puttupattu temple is the focus of chapter 4. Environmental education and sacred grove restoration campaigns constitute another important vector of new ideas about the relationship between religion, nature, and a new factor— health. Cosponsored by a group of Aurovillians and a Bangalore-based NGO, the Foundation for the Revitalization of Local Health Traditions, the environmental education campaign at Puttupattu sought to raise people's consciousness about the value of the forest that surrounds the Ayyanar-Ayyappan shrine, reframing it as not merely the backdrop for the adventures of a god but valuable in its own right as a treasure house of medicinal plants. In the first section of this chapter, I discuss the history of Auroville to demonstrate how environmental concerns came to occupy center stage in a community founded as a laboratory for cultivating human unity and enspiriting the material world. I then turn my attention to the history and career of one environmentally minded Aurovillian, Joss Brooks, who, in a manner somewhat parallel to Auroville's founders, has built a complex environmental education and restoration organization, Pitchandikulam Forest, out of humble beginnings. Seeds gathered from Puttupattu and other forest remnants in the 1970s and germinated in Pitchandikulam's nurseries have now grown into towering trees, which, though interspersed with a fair number of exogenous species, constitute a significant patch of restored forest. Thirty years after the establishment of Pitchandikulam, Joss Brooks and others sought to conserve and protect the tropical, dry, evergreen forest in Puttupattu. My investigation into this endeavor illustrates the challenges involved when Hindus of such different kinds work together under the banner of sacred grove restoration. Though in many ways Aurovillians try to avoid imposing their cosmologies or values on local communities, cultural differences and varying expectations surrounding forested shrines have made enduring partnerships difficult. As mentioned previously, religiously motivated environmental projects in

India entail more than just utilitarian needs. I conclude this chapter by reflecting on typologies of environmentalism advanced by other scholars and considering the specific role of religiosity in contemporary environmentalist projects—whether that of the local people, which environmentalists want to harness and direct toward the goal of sustainability, or the religiosity that inspires environmentalists to become activists in the first place and sustains them through the inevitable challenges and setbacks they encounter in implementing their projects.

The fifth chapter continues the investigation of religious environmentalism surrounding sacred groves through a close study of a grove near Chengalpattu that was planted by a Chennai-based NGO, the C. P. Ramaswami Environmental Education Centre (CPREEC). Begun in 1993 at the peak of national interest in sacred groves as sites for community-driven forestry initiatives, by 2001 the Centre had thirty-two sacred grove restoration projects underway. In these projects, the CPREEC helped select the site for reforestation with villagers and supplied soil-testing and plant material. The one stipulation the CPREEC made was villagers could no longer sacrifice animals in forested shrines restored with its help. I begin the chapter by describing the history of the CPREEC and its founder, Dr. Nanditha Krishna, the charismatic great-granddaughter of Dr. C. P. Ramaswami Aiyar, a reform-minded Tamil Brahman statesman. Through an analysis of the sacred grove restoration campaign materials and two project sites, I argue that, like many other scholars and activists interested in India's sacred groves, CPREEC seeks to promote expressions of reverence and gratitude for the natural bounty promoted by the divine while adopting an evolutionist stance toward some of the other "traditional" ritual practices associated with the groves, particularly animal sacrifice. I then engage scholarly debates about the degree to which the language and metaphors of religious environmentalists converge with ethnic chauvinist Hindu nationalism by focusing on the rationale and meaning of the CPREEC's ban on animal sacrifice in the groves that it partnered with local communities to restore. Tamil sacred groves in Tamil Nadu are generally dedicated to forest-dwelling deities who are worshipped primarily by non-Brahmans and who require regular animal sacrifice. The CPREEC, on the other hand, is guided by the reform-minded Brahmanical values of its founder. Given this discrepancy, it is hard not to see the ban on animal sacrifice as an attempt to impose Brahman values on non-Brahman groups. Moreover, I argue, in the context of the rise of

Hindu nationalists to political power in the 1990s and their efforts to craft a homogenous, unified "Hindu" identity, the CPREEC's imposition of this condition for the receipt of assistance resembles moves by Hindu nationalists to penetrate social services agencies as a means of spreading their ideology. I thus show that neither the Dravidian heartland nor the environmental movement is immune to the influence of political Hinduism, contrary to popular and scholarly views.

The study of Tamil Nadu's rich tradition of sacred grove preservation suggests that a paradigm shift is necessary in order to fully appreciate its true value—both its ecological value, measured in terms of the ecosystem services sacred groves provide or the conservation significance of the plant species they harbor, and its cultural value, which is immeasurable. Sacred groves may not be the pristine, remnant patches of ancient forest ecosystems that their proponents once imagined them to be, but they have shown remarkable resilience, enduring and adapting through an era of unprecedented social change. Similarly, the restoration projects designed to capitalize on the sacred grove phenomenon have not yielded the results their organizers anticipated. And yet, close examination of these projects' successes and failures demonstrates that religion can be a potent force motivating people to persist in spite of uncertain outcomes.

Fierce Gods and Dense Forest

SACRED GROVES NEAR MADURAI

Introduction

Today I took an excursion with Lakshmi and Ponnusamy three kilometers up the wooded slopes of the Sirumalai mountains northeast of Madurai to the forested shrine of the village guardian deity, Manjalmalaiyandi (Mañcaḷmalaiyāṇṭi). We parked our car at a small tank where a bright blue kingfisher perched on a boulder and walked along a dirt path until it disappeared amid the shrubs and rocks. Ponnusamy, who seems to have a relative in each of the villages in this region of Tamil Nadu, soon located a guide for us, a seventy-year-old grizzled shepherd, who swiftly led us along a creek to Manjalmalaiyandi's sacred grove. Crossing the stream one last time, we finally spotted the thick stand of trees sheltering the deity. A moustached guardian deity (*kāvalteyvam*) with popping eyes, Manjalmalaiyandi sat majestically on an open-air concrete platform. Stacked under the surrounding trees were rows and rows of moldering votive terracotta warriors, horses, and dogs standing in mute testimony to the deity's power and his devotees' gratitude (figure 1.1). Among Manjalmalaiyandi's powers is the ability to grant the boon of children. Dozens of cloth "cradles," weighed down with fist-sized stones, hung from the branches of the tree growing over the shrine, placed there by couples trying to conceive. They swung gently in the breeze alongside brass bells brought by grateful parents. After asking dozens of questions, we worshipped, and the priest distributed *vibhūti* (sacred ash) in a slip of paper, a recycled political flyer adorned with the face of M. Karunanidhi (then Tamil Nadu's chief minister). Then a remarkable thing happened: The

FIGURE I.I Votive offerings at Manjalmalaiyandi shrine, Valayapatti

other woman in our party, Lakshmi, who had been trying for years to conceive, said that she would give the deity's power a try. The priest and the shepherd told us that if we had any more questions, we should ask them now, because once we did this, we had to leave the shrine and descend the mountain without stopping. With great determination, Lakshmi took hold of a large rock and hammered at the end of her sari until she made a small tear. She ripped off about six inches of the cloth. Taking that strip, she tied it around the tree branch and placed in it a small, round stone. Playfully, she struck the cloth as if to swing the cradle, and we were off. (Field notes, December 17, 2005)

Environmental discourse in the United States has typically depicted protected forests as tranquil, verdant natural shrines, such as the Cathedral Grove of Muir Woods and the Mariposa Grove in Yosemite, which inspired John Muir to call these stands of giant sequoia "God's First Temples." In one of Muir's early essays, he elaborated on this metaphor in dramatic prose, exulting in the beauty, grandeur, and even holiness of undisturbed nature: "The sunshine falls in glory through the colossal spires and crowns, each a symbol of health and strength, the noble shafts faithfully upright like the pillars of temples, upholding a roof of infinite leafy interlacing arches and fretted skylights."[1] The beauty and serenity of these charmed spots were best enjoyed at leisure, according to Muir, when one had left the cares of the workaday world behind and could operate according to the more graceful tempo of the natural world. Muir's passionate devotion to groves of old trees captures several elements of Western environmental discourse—its postmaterialist concern for "wilderness," natural areas untouched by human occupations, its view of undisturbed nature as itself sacred, and its positing of a stark distinction between the sacred and the profane. As Emma Tomalin and others have argued, if there is a religious thread that runs through such discourse, it lies in the legacy of Romanticism's celebration of the restorative, redemptive qualities of nature, which was itself a reaction to the horrors of the industrial revolution.

Many of these understandings of both religion and nature need to be set aside in order to understand Tamil sacred groves properly, in the sense of comprehending what they might mean to the villagers who maintain them. First, as the vignette from my field notes above suggests, forested shrines in India are sites for both political expression and the articulation of deeply felt pragmatic need. Second, sacred groves in Tamil Nadu are not vast wildernesses but small patches of forest. They range in area from one-half to three hectacres (about one to seven acres).[2] Some sacred groves stand out as verdant patches of forest in the midst of dry grazing lands (figure 1.2), while others are nestled in the valleys of the surrounding hills. These latter groves tend to merge into the forest reserve lands that they border, although local residents (and Forest Officers) know their boundaries well (figure 1.3). Typically, sacred groves in Tamil Nadu are not marked with fences or clear boundaries, nor are there usually clear images in their centers. Rather, people know they are entering such an area only when they are asked to remove their sandals, just as they would before entering a Hindu temple or home. The trees typically found in these groves represent a range of species, including *kāñciramaram* (strychnine tree, *Strychnos nux vomica*), *vēppamaram* (neem or margosa tree, *Azadirachta indica*), *ālamaram* (banyan tree, *Ficus benghalensis*), *usilamaram* (bitter acacia, *Albizia amara*), *nāvalmaram* (black plum tree, *Syzygium cuminii*), *karppūramaram* (eucalyptus, *Eucalyptus globules*), *puḷiyamaram* (tamarind tree, *Tamarindus indica*), and *karuṅkālimaram* (red cutch, *Acacia chundra*). While some of these trees are useful to humans for their fruit or medicinal qualities, most have limited economic utility and many have religious associations, which could explain why they are not cut down.[3] Thus the

FIGURE 1.2 Sacred grove near Sikupati

FIGURE 1.3 Entrance to sacred grove of Manjalmalaiyandi, Valayapatti

third difference is that while the trees and plants that grow in sacred groves are set aside from *ordinary* usage, they are utilized in a variety of regulated ways. To some extent, the setting aside of sacred groves resembles the crucial distinguishing characteristic of the sacred according to early-20th-century sociologist of religion Émile Durkheim—that the sacred *does not touch* that which is profane, that is, that which is connected to commerce, productivity, and the ordinary exigencies of life. But one should not exaggerate this "setting apart" when considering how well the Indian example fits the prototype established by Durkheim (who, like Muir, conceptualized his view of the sacred in the context of the industrial revolution). A few questions directed at the villagers who actually maintain these groves instantly establishes that its produce is used, but in a limited fashion. The fruit that falls in a grove is auctioned off, dry branches can be collected, and sometimes green branches are lopped for goat fodder. Government entities can even route roads and electrical wires right through the middle of a grove and people will still say, "Everything in it belongs to God." Understanding how sacred groves are used, what they mean, and why they are set aside as sacred precincts of specific deities is the main aim of this chapter.

Rural citizens in India rely on the natural resources of forests for their everyday subsistence. The trunks, branches, and leaves of trees are used for firewood, medicine, animal fodder, and housing materials. In addition, one must consider the value of the land itself in a densely populated area, where every small tract of potentially arable land is put under the plow. What motivates people to sacrifice such benefits in order to maintain these diminutive scraps of undeveloped forest? In this chapter, I provide two different ways of considering the meanings that people in villages in one region of Tamil Nadu attach to these forested shrines. First, I describe the answers that people whom I have interviewed in villages north of the great pilgrimage center of Madurai provide when asked why they do not cut the trees in sacred groves. Their answers are quite straightforward when regarded from the perspective of local cultural and religious assumptions. In addition, though, I believe there are subtler, less easily articulable reasons why it is important to maintain forested shrines for gods who must reside far from the village center. While the first approach adopts a more emic point of view, the second takes a more critical perspective, contextualizing discourse about sacred groves in the history of the region to uncover very old paradigms that inform present-day beliefs and practices. Thus my second method for arriving at a sense of the meaning of these sites is to examine four mythic narratives that feature the fierce forest gods who typically preside over Tamil sacred groves in order to argue that the villagers' commitment to these groves is bound up with their commitment to the gods who reside there. These deities embody values and qualities that stem from the community's partly mythologized past as fearsome warriors or brave hunters. While Durkheim's positing of an absolute dichotomy between sacred and profane does not apply well to the Indian context, in this argument I find confirmation of his well-known understanding of religion as "first and foremost a system of ideas by means of which individuals imagine the society of which they are members and the obscure yet intimate relations they have with it."[4] But, like most societies, that of Tamil Nadu is not simple but complex, not homogenous but variegated, not unitary but fragmented and split. The forest gods so central to the tree-protection practices that sustain these fragments of indigenous forest represent a part of Tamil village identity that is often disavowed but from which people derive considerable vitality: the fearsome warrior-king who bends human and divine rivals, and even nature, to his will. As I demonstrate through an analysis of the environmental and political history of the region, this archetype does not come out of some shared human collective consciousness but out of the concrete history of this community in this place.

In my research I have found very little in the stated beliefs and practices of people who maintain these groves that could be seen as evidence of an "ecological" ethos, if by that we mean exhibiting a "reverence" for nature. On the contrary, the men and women with whom I spoke came across as hard-headed pragmatists, who seek to draw liberally on all the resources available to them—social, material, and supernatural—in order to thrive in a difficult environment. And yet it seems to me that there is a profoundly ecological ethos embedded in the religious cosmology that their beliefs and rituals articulate, which rests on an awareness of being ensconced in a dense network of relationships with a wide range of beings such that if one affects one element, one affects all others. Moreover, the cosmological framework that supports the protection of trees in these villages contains much that defies conventional thinking about "folk" Hinduism in Tamil Nadu. Far from being a crude form of superstition, the religiosity surrounding these shrines exhibits great complexity and historical depth. Forest gods in Tamil Nadu, I argue, are closely modeled on the *pāḷaiyakkārar*s (or poligars) of the 16th to 18th centuries, fierce local chieftains who formed alliances with, and sometimes defied, generations of rulers seeking to subdue the region. Evidence for this is found in both the iconography of the deities and their human and animal entourages and in the mythology surrounding them. Before describing that religiosity in greater detail, it is important to provide some background information on the environmental and historical context in which the sacred groves in this part of Tamil Nadu find their meaning.

Sri Azhagar Koyil: The Environmental and Political History of a Sacred Center

Among the sacred groves I have observed and visited since the summer of 2001 are nine located in an area about three miles northwest of Madurai, a major pilgrimage destination, a growing center of commerce, and the second largest city in Tamil Nadu. The villages in which one finds the richest tradition of maintaining sacred groves are located in the Melur taluk of Madurai district and the Natham taluk of Dindigul district, to the east and west of the Natham road that connects Madurai to the market town of Natham (figure 1.4). In the valleys that splay out from the ridges of the Azhagar hills (to the east) and the Sirumalai and Perumalai hills (to the west) are dozens of villages bound together into a single cultural region by their common orientation to Tirumalirunsholai (Tirumāliruṅcolai, lit. "the grove of Tirumāl or Vishnu"), a temple dedicated to a local form of the pan-Indian deity Vishnu, Sri Azhagar (Śri Aḻakar, the "beautiful Lord"). Tirumalirunsholai is a geographical and spiritual center of great antiquity located at the base of a forested mountain, and there are references to it dating back to the time of the Āḻvārs, Vaishnava saints of the 7th to 10th centuries CE. However, the deity who is equally if not more important to local people than Sri Azhagar is his *kāvalkkārarteyvam* (guardian deity), Sri Patinettampadi Karuppasamy (Śri Patineṭṭāmpati Karuppucāmi, lit. "the dark god of the eighteen steps"), about whom we will learn more shortly.

We can gain some sense of the environmental history of the region by considering the changing conditions of the hills and plains surrounding Sri Azhagar's temple. According to a somewhat eccentric history of the temple (Tam. *talapurāṇam*, Skt. *sthalapurāṇam*) written in English in 1942, the site has been known through the ages by many names. Its location in a shola (*cōlai*), a grove made cool and beautiful by the presence of many trees, vines, and herbaceous plants, is indicated by its formal name,

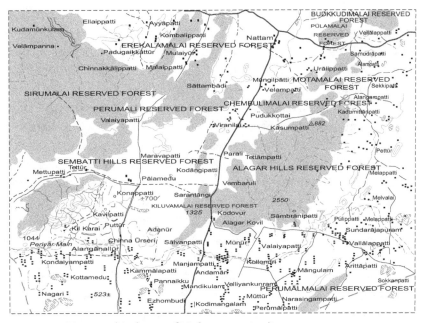

FIGURE 1.4 Topographical map of Natham area (cut?)

Tirumalirunsholai. The Vaishnava Alvar saints refer to it in their poetry as Tirumālkunṟam ("hill of Tirumal"), Irukunṟam ("two hills"), and Tēṉ Tirupati ("southern Tirupati," referring to the most important Vaishnava temple in south India, the famous hilltop shrine to Lord Venkateswara in what is now southern Andhra Pradesh). Beneath the dense tree cover, a vast sponge-like network of roots retains rain water, which in turn feeds many natural springs. One of these, Sri Noopura Ganga, is considered a goddess tantamount to the Ganges, and water from this spring is carried from the summit of Azhagar mountain to the temple at the base of the hill, for use in all the Azhagar temple rituals.[5] Even today, water from this spring is central to the religious rituals of people in the surrounding villages.[6] The mountain is also home to a Murugan temple, Pazhamudhirsholai, which is one of the six principle Murugan temples in Tamil Nadu.

Azhagar mountain enjoys distinction even as far back as the 5th century CE, when it was cited in the Jain epic, the *Silappadikaram* by Ilango. Describing "Vishnu's mountain" as a cool oasis in a landscape parched by summer heat, where "deer stand and cry aloud thirsty and panting for water," Ilango notes the existence of three pools that bestow miraculous gifts on those who bathe there.[7] In the medieval and early modern period, Azhagar Koyil was an outpost of Madurai-centered king-doms in the sparsely populated but strategically important territory north of the capital and was patronized by Vijayanagara, Nayaka, and Mughal rulers. In fact, the ruins of the fort of Tirumalai Nayaka (r. 1623–59), the most famous of the Madurai Nayaka kings, are still visible today in the modern town of Azhagar Koyil. With steady increases in population, however, came considerable impact on the landscape. First there were the effects of frequent warfare in the region between Mughals and Marathas, Nayakas and Vijayanagara overlords. Political instability led to the disrup-tion of agriculture in many places. It is likely that in this region, as in the northern plains of Tamil Nadu, untilled land turned to thorny jungle.[8] Second, the rising population along with their herds led to unsustainable levels of tree cutting for firewood, fodder, timber, and so forth. When mature forests in this area—with their tall trees and relatively sparse undergrowth—were cut for lumber and fuel wood, they were replaced by dense but short secondary-growth forest known by the evocative term "scrub jungle."

To the degree that the Azhagar temple itself was one of the main land-owners in the area, changes in its management also had profound envi-ronmental effects. With the decline of Nayaka rule in the 18th century, the temple passed through various hands as Mughal and British rulers vied for control of the area. Under East India Company rule, British administrators assumed many of the functions of traditional Indian sovereigns, including serving as the chief patrons of Hindu temples. This was not motivated so much by religious tolerance as by strategic realpolitik. Temples were cen-tral nodes in what Arjun Appadurai and Carol Breckenridge call a "redis-tributive network" of both tangible and intangible resources and as such were key sites for the constitution and legitimation of political author-ity in early modern south India.[9] Temples possessed vast tracts of lands held in the name of the deity, the produce from which was shared among the many people who provided service to the deity at the temple's center. Tirumalirunsholai was no different, and much of the land surrounding the temple was effectively owned and managed in the name of Sri Azhagar. However, in 1801, the British District Collector of Madurai, Thomas Bowyer Hurdis, sought to reorganize the functioning of the temple in his capacity as chief trustee.[10] In a major departure from tradition, Hurdis assigned per-manent ownership of temple lands to people who had previously enjoyed only usufructory rights in exchange for the services they rendered to the temple. This move was consistent with British ideas that social stability was fostered better through private ownership of land rather than collective sharing of its use-value, and it laid the groundwork for further radical changes in the administration of the temple and its properties.

The temple was managed by the District Collector until 1817 and then by the Board of Revenue from 1817–63. Finally, control of the temple was transferred to the Temple Committee (a precursor of the Hindu Religious and Charitable Endowments Administration Department) under Act XX of 1863.[11] It was in the course of the latter transfer of management that things became really confused, and the temple lost control over considerable property. A particularly hard blow was the transfer of the forested hills surrounding the temple into the hands of the Forest Department in 1886. The historian of Azhagar Koyil, K.N. Radhakrishnan, offers a plaintive description of this loss:

> Another equally important item of property which we have lost very recently, is the famous "Sri Alagar's Hills" otherwise known as "Then Thiruppathi." These hills were till 1886 in our absolute possession and enjoyment. But by some grievous error the Government annexed these Hills. The enjoyment of Sri Alagar's Hills by the Devastanam [the Temple] has now practically vanished except in respect of a few items as per G.O. No. 2111 Ms. Development, dated 25–8–1939.... How the Temple Administration also failed to advance their claim to these Hills when the Government attempted at annexation remains a mystery.[12]

Representatives of the colonial administration naturally had a different point of view on the transfer of the Azhagar hills.

W. Francis writes in the *Madura District Gazetteer* that prior to their coming under the control of the government in 1886, the forests on the full ten-mile range of the Azhagar Malai were almost completely denuded by the lack of protection. He writes, "On all these hills the growth (which is all deciduous) was cut to ribbons in the days before conservation began. In 1871 it was reported that almost every stick had been cleared as far as the base of, and for a considerable distance up, the slopes of the Sirumalais."[13] By 1914, Francis was able to report that due to conservation practices introduced in the late 19th century, the southern slopes of the Azhagar Malai ridge, facing Madurai, were showing "notable" improvement. Nowadays, the forests covering the Azhagar hills, which are managed by the Dindigul Forest Division, are quite dense and thick.

Today, a paved road leads from the main temple to Sri Azhagar at the base of Azhagar mountain through dense forests to the summit, passing numerous holy sites along the way—from the famous Pazhamudhirsholai Murugan temple to a termite mound shrine tended by an entrepreneurial couple. At the summit, the road ends at a large shrine erected around the Noopura Ganga spring, which is perpetually crowded with pilgrims who walk or drive up the slope to bathe in its waters. Environmentalists have taken advantage of the site's popularity to raise awareness among the visiting pilgrims about the value of the cool, dark forest that surrounds them. As mentioned before, the land is controlled by the Dindigul Forest Division, and it has partnered with a Bangalore-based nongovernmental organization, the Foundation for the Revitalisation of Local Health Traditions (FRLHT), to cultivate endangered plants indigenous to south India, especially those with medical uses, in a nursery located behind a gate at the base of the final slope up to the spring (figure 1.5). Trees alongside the steep slope leading up to the spring are marked with the FRLHT's trademark yellow against green signage, bearing mottos such as "Every plant has medicinal value," and "Kaṇṭaṅkattiri [a thorny plant that bears yellow flowers] cures asthma." In October of 2005, I spotted a stall set up at the foot of the steep stone staircase leading to the spring at which a somewhat sleepy young man sold plant-based medicinal remedies prepared by women's empowerment self-help groups in the area.

FIGURE 1.5 Entrance to FRLHT medicinal forest at Azhagar Koyil

Chapter 4 describes in greater detail the efforts of this nongovernmental organization to connect the preservation of sacred groves with the revitalization of local health traditions here and in other parts of Tamil Nadu.

People of the region

One of the reasons Azhagar Malai has attracted so much devotional, political, and (more recently) environmental interest is the way it stands out from the surrounding landscape as a green and cool oasis in the midst of a dry and in places virtually desolate land. This territory has long had a reputation for being an ungovernable wasteland and has been regarded as the abode of thieves and bandits. This set of assumptions is reinforced on the one hand by the belief held by many Tamils that people and the land they inhabit mutually reinforce each other's character and on the other by colonial constructions of so-called criminal castes.[14] As with other groups who inhabited the dry, rain-fed, and forested areas of Tamil Nadu, as opposed to the rich, river-fed lands that have traditionally formed the religious and political centers of Tamil culture (e.g., Tanjore with the Kaveri River), the ecological marginality of the people in this region corresponded with their political and social marginality.

In the villages I visited to the east and west of Natham road northeast of Madurai, two caste communities (*jātis*) were associated with forested shrines: Kallars and Valaiyars. Before describing these two, it is important to set aside notions of the "caste system" in which individual castes constitute the immutable "building blocks" of traditional Indian Hindu society. Rather, communities organized according to caste are better conceptualized as the result of ongoing cultural processes that can achieve a certain stability over time to the extent that they are reproduced by individuals who have internalized the codes, norms, rituals, and values that instantiate "caste" at a particular moment in time but that are also subject to change—sometimes radical change—as the winds of history shift.[15] Like most other *jātis* in contemporary India, Kallars and Valaiyars practice endogamy and thus maintain community boundaries and traditions to some extent over time. They are also involved in diverse projects of self-improvement meant to allow their members to thrive in the modern world. Sometimes these projects entail molding themselves into universalistic, or at least nationalistic, visions of upright citizenship: getting an education, wearing pants instead of dhotis, organizing politically to create new or influence existing political parties, or participating in pilgrimages or guru movements with a modern sensibility

[margin annotation: caste in this context]

or style. Yet sometimes advancing in modern India means retaining clear connections to one's past and to more particularistic forms of identity. As Pamela Price has argued, the advent of a fully centralized, bureaucratic state in the 20th century has not altogether obviated earlier, particularistic forms of community that arose out of the segmentary state formations of the early modern era. In the ruling polities of the 16th through the 18th century, authority and power, honor and prestige were distributed in a highly decentralized way, such that various domains of power wielded considerable autonomy even as they were connected to a more encompassing political order through relations of patronage and protection. Contemporary political life in Tamil Nadu, and the religious realm with which it remains closely allied, shows the traces of these earlier forms of community at every turn.[16] The memories, rituals, myths, and modes of being that are associated with the forested shrines maintained by Kallars and Valaiyars are one such form of particularistic association, which has endured long beyond the broader political formations in which it arose. Yet, like all forms of identity production, it is capable of being invested with new meanings over time, even as it retains some connections to bygone days.

One illustration of the dynamic nature of the relationship between caste identity and memory so integral to sacred groves is that the names that I have used to designate the two communities most involved in the maintenance of forested shrines, Kallar and Valaiyar, are rarely used today by the communities themselves as terms of self-reference. While they have a certain use-value to the extent that they can be traced through the writings of 19th-century British observers (such as W. Francis, Edgar Thurston and K. Rangachari, among others) and are recognized by academic scholars, government registries of castes, and local residents, they both carry negative associations linked to the community's traditional occupation and can be taken as terms of contempt.

Kallar literally means "thief" and is related to the community's traditional occupation as wielders of violence in the service of chieftains or kings.[17] Indeed, by all accounts it does appear that for roughly three centuries the Kallars of Tamil Nadu had a fearsome reputation. A numerous caste, with branches and subcastes extending from their putative native country west of Madurai to northern areas around the cities of Melur, Putukkottai, and Tanjore, Kallars were known as a martial group who offered protection to other castes, particularly from thieves and cattle-raiders. Like many groups in early modern India, they were involved in a variety of different occupations, especially herding and farming, but they were known primarily for their role as village watchmen, or *kāvalkāran*. According to a local system of policing, called *pāṭikāval*, Kallars would be paid an annual fee to serve the village. As such, they were responsible for protecting herds and property, overseeing the harvesting and distribution of the produce of the land, and maintaining law and order. If there were thefts under their watch, they had to make good for any losses themselves. But if a community decided to do without their policing and protective services, the Kallars could forcefully seize compensation for themselves, leading in part to the colonialists' view that this policing system was no better than a form of blackmail and the Kallars a wild and predatory tribe, preying on the hard work of the noble peasants. We should be cautious, however, before too quickly endorsing the view the British had of groups who explicitly contested their rulership. Viewed from within local categories and norms, the kavalkkarars operated in many ways like kings, albeit over diminutive territories: They provided protection from harm using their skill at arms and exacted "taxes" for such service.[18]

Known also as Moopanars (to signal their historical relationship and contemporary political alliance with several other Tamil *jātis*), the community's preferred caste title "Ambalakkarar" means literally "people of the *ambalam*" or village center, where affairs having to do with justice and corporate decision making are conducted.[19] Historically, rather than being led by a single hereditary chief, the Ambalakkakars prided themselves on their ability to make corporate decisions, quasi-democratically, through the gathering of all the men at an assembly held at the village center. Arguably, in the 17th and 18th centuries it was the Ambalakkarars' ability to coordinate their efforts that allowed some lineages to parlay their hired-gun status as protectors of communities into recognition as the established sovereigns of small kingdoms, or palaiyakkarars.[20] Palaiyakkarars (known as poligars in British sources and "little kings" in more recent historiography) were drawn from Kallar lineages, along with other martial groups and Telegu-speaking "northerners," and were distributed in a vast network throughout the dry zones of southern India.[21] When they wished, these headstrong independent figures could be thorns in the sides of other rulers with regional aspirations. In one of the earliest pieces of colonial ethnography on the Kallars, Thomas Turnball wrote in 1817,

> During the feudal system that prevailed among these Colleries [Kallars] for a long time, they would on no consideration permit the then Government [the Madurai-based Nayakas] to have any control

or authority over them. When tribute was demanded, the Cullers would answer with contempt: "The heavens supply the earth with rain, our cattle plough, and we labour to improve and cultivate the land. While such is the case, we alone ought to enjoy the fruits thereof. What reason is there that we should be obedient, and pay tribute to our equal?"[22]

Such independence and willingness to defy authority led the British to classify some subcastes of Kallars as "criminal tribes" and to seek to subdue this refractory group. Under this designation, Kallars were subject to a combination of intense police surveillance meant to contain them and social reform measures designed to civilize and domesticate them.[23]

In addition to their so-called traditional occupation as village watchmen, the Ambalakkarars were also farmers. In the dry villages of the Melur taluk, they made their living from rain-fed land, *vānampārtta pāmi* (Tamil, lit. "land that looks towards the sky [for rain]"). However, in 1885, construction was completed on the Periyar Dam, located about ninety miles (150 kilometers) west at the headwaters of the Vaigai River in the Western Ghats. Since that time, irrigation water has allowed agriculturalists in the region to boost production substantially.[24] With the development of agriculture came the conclusion of a centuries-long process of "settling" for the supposedly criminal Kallars in the Melur and Natham region.[25] According to local residents, for many decades farmers in the area mostly grew *payir*, a collective name for crops grown on good soil (rice paddy, cotton, sugar cane, sorghum, etc.). But since 1990 many farmers have turned to the more lucrative cultivation of fruit trees and flowers. Many Ambalakkarar villages are now filled with jasmine flower gardens and mango and coconut orchards, the produce of which is exported throughout the region and the world. Even though much has changed in the life-worlds of the Ambalakkarars over the past 100 years, one is struck by their attachment to their traditional identity and to the community's coherence. The present-day corporate solidarity of the caste is reflected by members' attention to the innumerable marital, kinship, and ritual ties that bind together all eighteen Ambalakkarar villages in the region— "eighteen" being less a numerically accurate than an auspicious number.

The preferred caste name of the second community in this region well known for its maintenance of sacred groves is *Muttaraiyar*. As with the Kallar-Ambalakkarars, today they generally avoid the older caste title, *Valaiyar*, which relates to their past as hunters of small game (mice, rabbits, squirrels, doves, etc.) in the region's forested peripheries. Yet Valaiyar-Muttaraiyars also at times affirm their connection to that past, for example in the annual hunt that marks a high point in the annual celebration of Muttaraiyar village deities, the *tiruviḷa*. At this time, men in the village go to the forest and string a net (*valai*) between two rocks or trees and then beat the bushes to chase animals into the net (as they did in days long ago as "beaters" for the king). Success in the hunt is taken as the deity's *sukam* (lit. "well-being," here "blessing"), granting permission for the festival to continue.[26] In his voluminous ethnohistory of nearby Pudukkottai, Nicholas Dirks writes that in precolonial Tamil Nadu Valaiyars were ranked just above the untouchable Paraiyar and Pallar castes.[27] On the one hand, they were stigmatized for their proximity to the disordered realm of the forest and never obtained the right to control land or provide protection, which were the established avenues for gaining power and prestige in premodern Tamil country.[28] On the other hand, their knowledge of the forest allowed them to serve the king in the hunt, a ritually very important royal occupation, and their ability to survive on the forests' bounty, when necessary, allowed them to maintain a fragile autonomy in the emerging social formations organized around royal polities in the dry land regions of Tamil Nadu. Unlike Pallars and Paraiyars, who resided in the *ceri* physically separated from but socially connected to the village streets dominated by higher castes, the Valaiyars resided in their own villages and sometimes served as priests in the temples of forest-dwelling gods.

Valaiyar-Muttaraiyars in the Azhagar hills region between Natham and Madurai have, like the Kallar-Ambalakkarars, benefitted materially from the availability of irrigation water thanks to the Periyar Dam. In addition, they have, like many lower castes in the decades since independence, sought to advance their claims to higher status by adopting new names and new mythologized histories.[29] At the same time, to maintain benefits accessible to them under the modern Indian state's policies of positive discrimination for historically oppressed groups, they must highlight their current poverty and lack of education so as to be classified as a most backward caste (MBC). As anthropologist D. Samuel Sudanandha has described, the mobilization under the name of Muttaraiyar of a number of castes spread over a large area—even into Andhra Pradesh—entailed the production of a new history that meets both these needs.[30] The pan-south-Indian Muttaraiyar Sangam (lit. "association") has been one of the principal actors promoting a revised history of the community, according to which they were descended from the Kalabhra royal lineage of ancient India. The ancient Muttaraiyars (*muttu* = pearl, *raiyar* = king), it is said, ruled beneficently after conquering the last of the Chola kings and then ruled as vassals or chieftains of Pallava and Pandya kings when the latter came to prominence. As a way of combating the present-day stigma associated with their traditional occupation as hunters of small game, Muttaraiyar activists urge their fellow caste-mates not to eat mice or engage in demeaning labor (such as clearing away leftover banana leaf-plates at weddings or other special functions).[31] Interestingly, I did not hear much about these claims to kingship or social uplift campaigns in my conversations with Muttaraiyars, but anecdotes about their service to kings in a mythologized past were frequent motifs in the *varalāṛus* (or myth-histories) they shared about their village and the deities associated with them.

The medieval past that Muttaraiyar activists draw on is a murky realm of evidence, the history of which consists of copper plates and stone inscriptions on which the names of Chola, Pandya, and Pallava kings can be rather flexibly interpreted to meet present-day requirements. The early modern past—from the end of the Vijayanagara period to the Nayaka period—can be narrated with a bit more certainty. I would argue it is this era that comes alive in the mythology and iconography of the village deities who serve in so many ways as anchors for the identity of Muttaraiyars and Ambalakkarars alike.

This connection to a mythologized historical past is evidenced in the iconography of shrines. In the region around Madurai, a sacred grove's main presiding deity is often represented an-iconically, with a stone or weapon. Therefore, the most visually salient feature of a shrine is the array of offerings left by devotees, which creates a visual tableau invoking the sense of the past (figure 1.6). The terracotta figures gifted to the shrine in fulfillment of vows are all, in one way or another, helpers or assistants to the deity. The animal forms almost invariably include horses, the primary vehicle of kings and warriors; in addition, one sometimes finds elephants, which, due to the expense of maintenance, were the exclusive prerogative of kings. I was long puzzled by the frequent presence of votive dogs at forested shrines until I learned that these are crucial helpers for hunters tracking and chasing game and thus suitable offerings for deities modeled on "little kings," for whom hunting was an important ritual occasion. The sense that these deities originate from the poligar era is most vividly projected, however, by the human figures (figure 1.7). Of course the shrines' bodyguard *vīraṉs* (lit. "heroes") are not dressed in modern Tamil style but rather are equipped with a range of costumes and hairstyles associated

FIGURE I.6 Tableau of votive offerings, Sikupati

with this era. With chests bared, or adorned only with a garland, and with their sturdy thighs wrapped tightly in short leggings tied above the knee to permit maximum mobility, a *vīraṉ*'s capacity for violence is concentrated visually in two iconic forms: the sharp sword or bill-hook raised above his head and his bristling moustache. While the thick, curling moustache is still a signifier of powerful virility (and perhaps potential for violence, judging by the extent to which this style is adopted today by police officers and village "big men"), the hairstyles of the *vīraṉ* figures are clearly antique. Typically, they wear their long hair to their shoulders or in a bun on the side of the head (see *vīraṉ* on far left, figure 1.6). The side-bun fashion is most iconographic of Madurai Veeran, a deified folk hero from the Kallar community, whose ballad is set in the time of Tirumalai Nayakar.[32] Tamil film-makers employ similar hairstyles and costumes in period dramas to convey a sense of historical realism—as in the M. G. Ramachandran hit, *Madurai Veeran* (1956), based on the folk ballad, and the Shivaji Ganesan vehicle *Veerapandiya Kattabomman* (1959) about the eponymous poligar chieftain whose resistance to British authority is remembered by some as the first Indian rebellion. Though produced many years ago, these films have a lively afterlife not only on Saturday afternoon television but also,

FIGURE 1.7 Terracotta votive *vīraṉ* offerings at Manjalmalaiyandi shrine, Valayapatti

today, on YouTube, where beloved songs and speeches are excerpted and uploaded by fans. I am not certain how much attention directors of Tamil historical dramas have given to the accuracy of their representation of period-era costumes and hairstyles, but the wild popularity of Tamil cinema suggests that, whatever their accuracy, they are probably the primary vehicles of people's visual associations with the past.

One could argue that the archaic hair- and dress styles of the *vīraṉ* figures at forested shrines simply evoke a generic "Tamil past" and ambiguously reference Chera, Chola, Pandya, Pallava, or Nayaka eras. To be sure, individual viewers no doubt locate the figures in the past according to their own knowledge, interests, and familiarity with the traditions surrounding

the deity. For example, one might expect that Muttaraiyar activists ke[
educating people about the glorious Chola-era royal ancestor Perumpι̣ṭṭu̱κυ̱
Muttaraiyan would locate a deity and his entourage as arising in the 7th
or 8th century CE. However, as I argue shortly, the mythological narratives
that describe how forest-shrine deities came to a particular village refer
to a segmentary mode of political organization that reached its apogee
in the Nayaka period (16th to 18th centuries CE), when the *palaiyakkarars*
exercised the greatest influence. Sometimes the reference to the poligar
era is explicit, as in those myths that grant a starring role to Tirumala
Nayakar, the most famous of the Nayaka kings based in Madurai, who for-
malized the Palaiyakkarar system inherited from the Vijayanagara empire.
Sometimes it must be inferred from the way relationships between gods,
or between gods and humans, echo the decentralized forms of political
power prevalent at this time, when Nayakas exercised nominal rule over
the region but in fact revenues were generated and protection offered by
palaiyakkarars. Before turning to these myths, it is important to gain an
understanding of the broader cosmological themes that lend meaning to
Tamil sacred groves and the deities who preside over them.

Shelter and Shade: The Beliefs that Limit Exploitation of Sacred Groves

In Tamil Nadu, a clear and widely recognized reciprocal relationship exists
between trees and sacred places. Where there are more trees, people
assume the presence of a god. And where people believe a god resides,
one finds a taboo against cutting his trees. This is not because the trees
themselves are considered sacred but because they belong to the deity,
and it would be disrespectful to cut them down. Stories about the divine
punishment meted out to transgressors act as deterrents against casual
encroachment and enable the community to police the sites more aggressively.[33] For example, in Usilampatti, an older woman named Chinnakkal
told a story about a wealthy man who came and cut trees in a sacred grove
dedicated to two goddesses, who were sisters. Though his father warned
him not to do it, he did it anyway. First he lost his money, and then he
lost his sight (interview, December 15, 2005, Usilampatti). In addition, the
fact that these areas are not normally accessed by people from outside the
community makes them easier to police.[34]

Generally, the community (in cooperation with the deity) enforces
taboos that limit the use of forest produce within sustainable levels. For

example, communities sometimes auction off the right to collect the fruits of the black plum or tamarind trees, with the agreement that a share of the proceeds be used to celebrate the gods' or goddesses' annual festival (*tiruvila*). These annual festivals are no small affair but rather multiday elaborate and expensive productions with massive displays of electric lights and fireworks, as well as colored posters advertising the festival posted far and wide. To fund them, communities typically collect a certain amount of money (100 to 500 rupees) from each household in the village and then supplement that fund with any revenue generated by the temple itself or by lands owned by the temple.

As mentioned earlier, analysis of the iconography in and mythology surrounding the forested shrines for Karuppasamy, Ayyanar, and the occasional village goddess suggest they represent a link back to the 16th- to 18th-century poligar era. Taking their imagery and ritual vocabulary from the days of Nayaka kings, when the Kallars were at the height of their independence and the Valaiyars roamed the forests with their game bags and *aruvāl* (Tamil bill-hook, or machete), the groves offer a space where these heroic roles as warriors and hunters can be remembered and forged anew. The shrines' verdant settings, with its dappled crepuscular light filtering through the trees, provides an important backdrop for rituals that narrate the migration into this region of people and the gods who protect them. It is possible that the groves themselves, with their towering trees and dense undergrowth, recall elements of the natural landscape that have disappeared along with the rough-and-tumble lives of the past.

However, this interpretation is not one that Ambalakkarar and Muttaraiyar villagers themselves ever explicitly articulated to me. Rather, the reasons they gave for why they protect the trees within the precincts of forested shrines were much simpler and more direct. To understand even these reasons, and thus the significance of the groves for the communities who maintain them, one must consider them in light of several aspects of Tamil religion and culture. In the following, I describe and explain the most common answers that people throughout Tamil Nadu, from Madurai to Chinglepattu, gave when my field assistants or I asked them why they did not cut the trees in these areas. In the next section, I delve deeper into the cultural meanings and social relations embedded in sacred groves through a close examination of four narratives featuring the fierce forest gods of the Madurai region, which are in many ways representative of Tamil village religiosity. In both sections, when representing the direct speech of the people I interviewed, I translate colloquial spoken

Tamil into English. Where the significance of a literal translation is not clear, I have added words in brackets that attempt to clarify the speaker's meaning.

First and foremost the groves are sites where gods reside; thus they are temples, although they may not contain any structures at all. One notable trend discernible in forested shrines over time, first analyzed by J. Donald Hughes and M. D. Subhash Chandran, is that as a temple "Sanskritizes" or modernizes, the built structures in the grove gain more importance and sacred value than do the surrounding flora, leading to environmental degradation in those groves that have been built up over time.[35] However, most of the groves in the Madurai region had no permanent built structures in them; in some groves an open-air structure with a tile roof supported by four wooden posts covered the terracotta votive offerings left by devotees, but the most common built structure was a temporary shed made from palmyra leaves, which typically decomposes in two or three years. In the absence of built structures, the most straightforward meanings people give to the flora of a sacred grove is that the tall trees protect forest-dwelling deities from rain and the heat of the sun, just as built temples shelter deities who stay in the village. An elder in the village of Azhagapuri said, "The reason trees are made to grow in the temple is that the temple should be good [healthy]. It should be cool inside. It should look beautiful.... It's like a house. Because if there is hot sun He will be uncomfortable" (interview, December 12, 2005). This notion that the gods need our care to keep cool is widespread in Tamil religiosity, as evidenced in Brenda Beck's classic 1969 ethnography on hot and cool themes in Tamil ritual.[36] For example, the rituals conducted for Lord Murugan, a major Tamil deity, in the hot season of May and June exhibit this pattern, in that devotees "take on" the heat of the season by walking for miles in processions that led to the deity's main shrine. Here Sri Murugan is relieved of his heat, by having buckets and buckets of cool milk poured over his image. Were he to become excessively hot, his wrathful nature would come to the fore, and the results would be terrifying. If this is true for a god whose nature is predominantly benevolent and protective, how much more so for those deities whose nature is not unambiguously gentle and good?

A related idea articulated by many informants was that the trees are the *alaṅkāram* (lit. "ornaments," "adornments," by extension "beauty," "decoration") of these outdoor temples or of the gods themselves. As suggested by the informant quoted above, the beauty of forested shrines is connected to their health-giving properties of being cool and refreshing, both for gods and humans. As both Ann Grodzins Gold and Albertina Nugteren have explored, a recurring theme in the discourse surrounding trees and forests in India is the connection between beauty and well-being, whether interpreted as health or material bounty.[37] Trees are gracious and generous, not only with the fruit of their boughs but also with their shade, which in such a hot climate has immeasurable value. Other informants seemed to interpret the equation of trees with the deity's *alaṅkāram* as signifying that the trees are the gods' tangible wealth. Again and again, when asked why one could not cut the trees surrounding a deity's temple, people answered that it was "His"—the god's property or wealth (*contam*). To the extent that the produce of the trees is used in a limited way to support the temple festival, with usufructory rights given temporarily to people who compensate the temple with a portion of the land's produce, the trees of a forested shrine do serve as the property of the deity. However, the rules governing this property are not those of modern private property (with one individual having the sole right to use or sell the land) but rather hearken back to feudal times, when the fruits of property held in the name of the king or a god were distributed among various share-holders after a sizable share was appropriated for the enjoyment of the divine or quasi-divine "owner." Ponnusamy, the Ambalakkarar resident of the area mentioned in the chapter epigraph, explained the prohibition against cutting trees in a sacred grove by comparing the trees to the literal *alaṅkāram*, the jewelry and rich saris used to adorn the village goddess (or *amman*, lit. "mother").

> Even in times of great loss, you cannot borrow against the goddesses' jewels, while you can borrow against your wife's jewelry. Your wife's jewelry is for your "own use" [using the English phrase] and that of your relations. God's jewelry is different; if you steal it or use it, you will be punished. Apart from festival times, it is kept in a "dum" box [chest] that requires three keys to open it.

Like the trees of the fierce (usually male) deities who reside in sacred groves outside the village center, the gold and bejeweled necklaces used to adorn the village goddess during worship are her *contam*, her own wealth. And just as the chest holding the jewels of the village goddess can be opened only when all the keys held by different members of the community (or lineage) are present, so does the disposition of the trees of a temple grove require the collaboration of a complex group of individuals, including temple servants (priests, etc.), prominent village or lineage leaders, and the temple management committee.[38]

Moreover, at an aesthetic level, the identification of the trees as the adornments, or jewelry, of the temple or the deity makes perfect intuitive sense. The towering trees do add to the beauty of the spot, clothing the space with cool shade and providing a lovely green backdrop for the terracotta votive offerings or images of the deity frequently found in sacred groves. But at another level, referring to the trees as *alaṅkāram* is a reversal of the usual dichotomy in Tamil discourse between "nature" and "civilization" or culture. *Alaṅkāram* is typically precisely that which is made (*seykai*), crafted, embellished, or deliberately cultivated beyond its natural state, not that which appears or grows spontaneously, or *iyaṛkai* (the Tamil word most frequently used for "nature"). In much Tamil discourse, civilization, the more highly valued of the pair, arises only with the subduing and controlling of nature, whether embodied in women, animals, or the lower gods of the pantheon. But here, the appreciation given to undisturbed flora seems to complicate the usual valuation of the dichotomy.

Beyond these direct explanations of the symbolic meaning of trees found in sacred groves, their significance can be found in the opposition between settled and wild space, which is absolutely central to Tamil village culture. A frequent theme in both folk and classical Indian literature is the opposition between settled and wild space, where the wilderness (*kāṭu*) represents an encompassing yet chaotic realm of danger and fertility, whose resources can be tapped and transformed into the basis of civilization (the *ūr*, village settlement). In the narratives surrounding regional Tamil kings, the royal hunt is a ritual freighted with symbolic meaning, in which rulers demonstrate their power by catching and consuming wild game from the forest, transforming its chaotic, threatening vitality into sovereignty—the epitome of order.[39] Tamil sacred groves and the taboos surrounding them gain meaning within the context of this dichotomy, articulated within Tamil culture as a tension between the *ūr* and the *kāṭu*, the inhabited settled center of a community and the wild, forbidding, but necessary forest that encompasses it. This is not a duality found only among Indians or Tamils but rather recalls similar patterns found in many cultures around the world: the city on the hill in the midst of a wilderness, exile in the desert and settled living in Jerusalem, or the forest and the village of Grimm's fairy tales. But like any archetype, the polarity between the settlement and the forest takes shape through the cultural categories and history of this place, these people, and their progress through time—both recent and long past. In Tamil religious culture, one finds a clear pattern whereby the living space of a village community can be mapped as a series of concentric circles, where each circle is associated with deities whose nature and function corresponds to the zone they reside. From the civilized heart of the village to the village boundary, and from the surrounding agricultural lands with their irrigation tanks to the most encompassing and wild forest zone, deities are arranged in a spatial order such that gods with a wilder, more dangerous character are found farthest from the settled center.[40] It is these fierce, unpredictable, even dangerous gods, whom Eveline Masilamani-Meyer aptly calls "wilderness gods" (perhaps playing off the neologism *kāṭṭucāmi*), that are most frequently found in forested shrines.[41]

In many villages in Tamil Nadu, the physical center of the *ūr* is marked by the *mantai*, a rectangular platform of compacted dirt about ten by twenty feet wide and raised about two feet off the ground. At midday it is often graced by the supine presence of from one to a dozen men, sleeping off the heat in the shade of a tall, spreading tree. But as the social and ritual heart of the village, the *mantai* is also the place where the assembly (composed mostly of men) meets in the cool of the evening to make important decisions—about disputes over property and sexual morality; about when to plant, harvest, and conduct the annual village festival; and about what to do as a village regarding proposals that come from outside. It is also known as the *ambalam*, or central meeting place, from which the caste title "Ambalakkarars" is derived (and also the title "Ambalakkarar," for a hereditary temple priest in Valaiyar-Muttaraiyar villages). Inside the village one finds village goddesses (*ammaṉs*, lit. "mother") and male gods familiar from the pan-Indian pantheon (e.g., forms of Ganesh, Vishnu [Perumal], and Shiva). Village goddesses such as Mariyamman and Mutthalamman have an ambivalent moral quality, with the potential to be either benign or malevolent, as has been amply demonstrated.[42] When pictured in her single form, unattached to a male consort, the *ammaṉ* can be fierce, swift to punish, and thus dangerous, and she is rarely found in the village center in this guise. But in her more "sweetened" forms she is worshipped as the chief protector of the village, responsible for its general health, fertility, and prosperity.[43] In Ambalakkarar and Muttaraiyar villages, at the time of the annual village festival, the community calls the potter to make the figure of the village goddess and gives him a handful of earth (*piṭimaṉ*) from the *mantai* with which to make the terracotta image used in worship.

The *piṭimaṉ* thus contains the energy or *śakti* of the whole village; indeed, it represents the village in metonymic form.[44] In an apt illustration of Durkheim's understanding of religion, when villagers in this region worship the goddess, they really are worshipping a representation of themselves. However, it is important to keep in mind that the fierce gods of the forest are also representations of themselves. While the village mother goddess embodies the values of the settled agriculturalist—stability, fertility, rootedness—the fierce gods who live in the forest embody the warrior and hunter dimension of Ambalakkarar-Kallar and Muttaraiyar-Valaiyar identity.

When asked why some deities live in the forest and others prefer the village center, a person's first answers is typically that the forest gods are *tuṣṭateyvaṅkaḷ*. The Tamil lexicon defines this term as "malignant deity," but locals gloss it as referring to gods that are angry, arrogant, dangerous, or short-tempered, in contrast to the patient and peaceful deities of the village center. People figuratively convey this short-tempered quality of fierce gods by saying that the reason the deity must live outside the village is that he or she "should not hear the sound of the mortar and pestle" (*ural ulak-kai kēṭkak kūṭātu*).[45] A dense signifier of both domesticity and sexuality, this antique tool for pounding the husk off grains of rice seems to reference the deities' aversion to domestic life with all the impurity and drudgery that it entails. It makes a loud, rhythmic noise that is for many Tamils an evocative sound of village life. Nowadays, however, one hears the *ural-ulukkai* less frequently, since electric kitchen gadgets such as the mixie-grinder have come into vogue.[46] The deities' dislike of the pounding underscores the opposition of the deities of the forest to domesticity, which fits their image as unmarried males—either hunters or warriors or both.

The idea that the deity should not hear the sound of the mortar and pestle has an unmistakable sexual connotation as well—something that informants alluded to when they followed the almost proverbial phrase *ural ulakkai kēṭkak kūṭātu* with descriptions of how angry, irritated, and possibly aroused forest deities were by pollution, known in Tamil as *tīṭṭu*. *Tīṭṭu* comes preeminently from things related to sex, reproduction, and death. One should not go to the sacred grove or any temple after having sex, though a simple bath will remove it. Both men and women are saturated with *tīṭṭu* after sexual intercourse. During the period of mourning after a death in one's family, one is forbidden to enter temples as well. After a ritual bath and shave (for men) that removes the death *tīṭṭu*, one can again enter into contact with deities. On an everyday basis, women more than men find their behavior constrained by the taboos governing pollution. A woman should not enter a deity's forest during the days of her menses or for many weeks after giving birth. People frequently reported that in the old days, when the taboos surrounding pollution were more strictly enforced, menstruating women could not even walk past the grove, let alone through it. Whether grazing goats or collecting wood, they had to walk along circuitous paths to avoid the grove and specifically the sensitive deities who resided within it.

In sum, the meanings that village residents directly attribute to the forested shrines and the deities who preside over them cluster around the central dichotomy in Tamil culture between the *ūr* and the *kāṭu*, the village center (epitomized by the *mantai*) and the forest. While all gods are upset by exposure to pollution, the fierce gods who inhabit forested temples are particularly quick to react. The village mother (*ammaṇ*) goddess is more patient and tolerant of the errors of her children, but fierce deities such as Karuppasamy and Ayyanar will severely punish transgressors for even the slightest infraction. One avoids sacred groves and strictly observes the taboos against gathering wood in them to avoid angering the hot-tempered gods. Tamil villagers speak about the trees that provide shade and a cool, leafy backdrop for rituals as the deity's temple itself, or as adornments for the deity. Thus to cut them would be tantamount to vandalizing the deity's palace, or plundering the royal jewels, a crime worthy of swift and severe punishment.

Fierce Gods and Dense Forest: The Poligars Ride Again

In Tamil Nadu there is a holy power (*śakti*). We have to believe that. You are from America so you may not believe because you are sending rockets to the moon. But in Tamil Nadu there is a power above everyone. There is a power above human beings. (Interview with Ponnusamy, December 26, 2005)

More keys to understanding Tamil sacred groves are revealed through deeper investigation into the qualities of the gods who live within them, as exhibited through their relationship with other gods and through the mythic narratives that villagers tell about them. Seen from a Brahmanical perspective, the deities who preside over the groves in this region tend to be near the bottom of the Hindu pantheon and are most often known as guardian deities (*kāvalkkārarteyvam*).[47] The very fact that they serve other gods, whether the *ammaṉ* (village goddess) ensconced in the village *mantai* or a local form of Vishnu presiding over a palatial stone temple, is a sign of the guardian deity's subordination within the divine hierarchy. Deities at the top of the hierarchy are responsible for a larger domain (and thus are recognized by devotees over a wider social and geographical range), their main temples are the traditional political centers of the region, they have more power, their biographies and exploits are recorded in written sacred texts, their worship is more prestigious and often mediated by Brahmans, and they generally concern themselves with the larger issues of life, death, and ultimate salvation.[48] Gods at the lower end of the hierarchy have none of these signifiers of status and power. However, the sovereignty of gods in this hierarchy is always relative and determined by context. So while Sri Azhagar reigns supreme in his own temple across the Vaigai River from Madurai, in a larger context he is subordinate to his sister and brother-in-law in the city, Sri Meenakshi and Sri Sundareswarar, local forms of Parvati and Shiva whose fame draws pilgrims not just from the region but from around the world. In turn, Sri Azhagar commands and is served by his bodyguard deity, Sri Karuppasamy, who in turn has power over the ghosts, demons, and disgruntled ancestors who plague villagers with various afflictions and menace the high god whose temple gate he guards.[49]

This pattern closely mirrors the political sociology of precolonial south India. At this time, political power was relatively decentralized such that local rulers had great autonomy even as they were encompassed within a larger political order and connected to a raja or maharaja through relations of protection and patronage. Like the rulers of old, the paradigmatic feature of deities in temple-based Hinduism is sovereignty, whether their abode is a huge stone edifice or a simple roadside shrine.[50] Just as the gods and goddesses who reside in the grand temples of Chidambaram and Madurai are modeled after premodern kings and queens, so are forest-dwelling guardian deities modeled after the chieftains or poligars (*pāḷaiyakārar*s) of bygone days. As mentioned previously in my discussion of the political pasts of the Madurai region, the poligars ruled over considerable territory through the 16th through 18th centuries in south India. Responsible for restoring lost property, settling disputes, and meting out punishment for crimes, the poligars exercised a monopoly over force, the force involved both in seizing other people's property and in protecting communities against such banditry. If not well paid for their protective services, they could become marauders themselves. All of these features are remembered in the mythology and ritual surrounding the gods associated with sacred groves: Theft, protection against theft, horses, and weapons are all recurring motifs in their iconography and mythology. To enter the imaginative realm of these fierce deities is to enter a world of prerogatives jealously guarded and transgressions swiftly and brutally punished.

The most prominent of these gods in the region north of Madurai is Sri Patinettampadi Karuppasamy (lit. "the dark god of the eighteen steps"). The story of how he came to be Lord Azhagar's bodyguard shares many themes and motifs with the narratives of other village guardian deities, including a vaguely 17th-century setting during the Nayaka period when the poligars enjoyed considerable independence. One local resident tells the story of Karuppasamy this way:

> In Tirumalai Nayaka's time, the temple had three gates—south, east, and north. At that time, eighteen magicians from Kerala came to Tamil Nadu. They had a special lens looking through which they could see far distances and into anyone's house. With that lens, they could see that there was a lot of gold inside the Azhagar Koyil. Then someone came to know that the magicians were planning to rob the temple. But he was only one man; what could he do against eighteen men? Nothing. He ran up the temple tower and rang the bell. When people in the surrounding eighteen villages heard that bell, they came running to help. Seventeen of the magicians tried to hide, but they were killed and their bodies were buried in the steps leading into the temple. The eighteenth, who was their leader, ran away and hid, disappearing into a water tank. When King Tirumalai Nayaka caught him, the magician pleaded for his life saying, "I'm not to blame; someone sent me to do this." So the king spared him and just cut his throat but kept him with his life. He also gave to him the power of the other seventeen magicians and made him the bodyguard (kāvalkkārar) of Azhagar. (Interview with Ponnusamy, December 12, 2006)[51]

In Ponnusamy's rendering of this story, the mighty Karuppasamy begins his career as the leader of a band of thieves whose ruthlessness and impiety are aided by their magical powers. He comes from "Malayalam," present-day Kerala, considered a hotbed of black magic by residents of the villages surrounding Madurai. But when confronted by the power of

Tirumalai Nayakar, here possessing superhuman capacities himself, he is reduced to a quivering coward, casting blame for his actions on others and begging for his life. The mutually constitutive nature of the king and the god's power in this relationship is revealed when we consider the iconography of Karuppasamy, which depicts the deity as a formidable power who wields enormous weapons and requires thick chains to keep him in check (figure 1.8). King Tirumalai Nayaka must be powerful indeed to subdue such a foe with seeming ease.

Karuppasamy's role as a sovereign who acts independently in his own domain is seen in the custom that people take oaths in front of his main shrine, the doors to the Azhagar Koyil.[52] Historian of religion David

FIGURE 1.8 Karuppasamy's weapons at the temple of Lord Azhagar

Dean Shulman sees something ironic in the idea that oaths should be taken in front of a fierce bandit and interprets this as another facet of Karuppasamy's instantiation of the archetype of "dangerous watchman."[53] But Sri Karuppasamy's role as arbiter of truth makes much more sense if we understand him as modeled directly on the *palaiyakkarar*, a deputy sovereign responsible for law and order in his own Lilliputian kingdom. He gains his authority from the maharaja above him, and, as such, his influence is dependent on the latter; but within his own territory he has all the powers of a king.

The next type of god commonly associated with sacred groves in this region are the *veeran* (*vīraṉ*, lit. "masculine hero") fierce male warrior gods frequently found as guardian deities or wilderness deities. Many of the themes of the Karuppasamy narrative recur in their myths: A fierce god-warrior from "outside" is enlisted in the service of a semidivine human king so that his power may be contained and channeled in support of his master. But *veeran*s are rarely if ever fully subordinated; they must be placated, subdued, and wooed, forcefully if necessary. In an extension of the relations of domination and subordination that structure the divine hierarchy, as Karuppasamy is to Azhagar, these *veeran*s are to Karuppasamy (or to his analogue, the other major horse-riding warrior deity found throughout villages of Tamil Nadu, Sri Ayyanar [*Aiyaṉār*], as I discuss in chapters 3 and 4). Some of these stories can also be read as veiled migration narratives that describe the movement of lineages from one part of the region to another, a pattern that is confirmed in the conventional historiography of the region. In the process, they introduce new themes and bring out new emphases. The story of one of these fierce veerans was told by an elderly Ambalakarrar leader, who lived in a dilapidated compound still known for miles around as the "palace" (*araṇmaṉai*), the descendent of the apical ancestor in a lineage of poligars, Lakshmana Sundara Dakshinamurthi Chinnaiya Kameswara Naicker:

> Three hundred years ago, the *veeran* was living in Kuttiyar Kuttu Kammay, near Tiruparakundram [the site of a major Murugan temple near Madurai and stronghold of the Pramalai branch of Kallars]. He used to come to Valayapatti to go hunting. Noticing him, Sri Ayyanar at Valayapatti wanted to use this fellow as a guard. So Ayyanar sent a wild pig to lure him away. After following the pig a long way, the *veeran* shot and killed it. He then divided it into five pieces, which became five villages: Lakkampatti, Valayapatti,

Arasapatti, Pudur, Kotangipatti. Suddenly, dawn came, but the *veer-an*'s horse had gotten stuck in a muddy pool.

The *veeran* seeks the aid of the local lord (the Dorai) and, in exchange for worship, agrees to stay on as the village protector.

> The Dorai then asked the god to tell him his name, but the god replied that only after building his temple would he come to know his name. Bargaining a little harder, the Dorai said, "What will you give the people?" And the Dorai extracted a promise that he would not punish the people too severely for the mistakes that they made, and that he would only use his power over the rain under the strict control of the Dorai. "If I say, stop the rain," said the Dorai, "You make it stop. You should just strike them in the stomach [that is, withhold rain so that they get hungry]. The animals and people should get sick, but without dying. Only after I give the sacred ash, then you should let the rain come. If I think they have repented enough, then you can bring the rain."
>
> The Dorai then said to the people, "You should worship the Sky God [identifying the *veeran* as a form of Indra]." Finally, the god asked the Dorai to build a temple for him, saying, "Three days after you make the temple, you will know what my name is." At that exact time, the stream was flooded with yellow water, as yellow as turmeric water. The god then came to the Dorai in his dream and said, "From now on, you call me Manjalmalaiyandi [lit. "god/ascetic of the yellow mountain"]." (Interview, December 17, 2007, Valayapatti, Dindigul district) (see figure 1.7)

In this narrative, the agonistic relationship between the human ruler and the dangerous deity is even clearer than in the previous myth. The narrative tension of the story inheres in the battle of wills between the two, where the *veeran* appears a little like a dim-witted giant, physically strong but no match for the cunning and determined Dorai. An interesting motif found in both myths is of the god becoming "stuck," whether Karuppasamy in Tirumalai Nayaka's temple tank or the horse of the *veeran* here in the muddy pool. This motif appears frequently in south Indian myths to explain and demonstrate the legitimacy of a divine being's or a people's settling in a particular place.[54] Here, a kind of uncanny supernatural force compels the god to stay in this area, presumably, the *māya* or magic of Sri Ayyanar, who appears in the beginning as an advocate for the village but then disappears, his authority or power fading into the background as the figure of the human Dorai becomes more prominent. The mighty hunter is made vulnerable by becoming stuck, and this reveals an opportunity for the king to create an advantageous relationship. For, besides protection, this god appears to possess other powers—namely control over the rain, obviously a significant resource in this parched region. As the relationship between the Dorai and the *veeran*, now referred to as a *cāmi* (a general term for "god" in Tamil), deepens, the Dorai keeps him on a tight leash, titrating out the *cāmi*'s power over the rain to enhance his own leadership, so that the people are affected, but not fatally, by the effects of drought (just as Tirumalai Nayaka slit Karuppasamy's throat but did not kill him).[55] And though Manjalmalaiyandi is well and truly made a servant of the Dorai in this myth, he also exercises a certain autonomy as he forestalls his domestication for three days, when he finally reveals his name to the ruler. This notion of a power—raw and mighty, under control but not completely—is a good metaphor for the patterns of kingship during the era of the *palaiyakkarars*. Maharajas like the Nayaka kings in Madurai could control the *palaiyakkarars* under them only so far, just as the *palaiyakkarars* exercised authority, but not completely, over the *kāvalkkarars* who collected tribute for them. It also evokes vividly how the hunters, herders, and farmers of this region may have related to the power of nature, especially in the days before the wide availability of irrigation water.

The force of the gods, and indeed the forces of nature in this harsh landscape, can be very raw indeed. Some of the gods who preside over sacred groves in this region are barely differentiated from the "wilderness" out of which they arise and that they call their home. Historians and anthropologists like Nicholas Dirks and Louis Dumont who have studied the Kallars and related castes have generally relied on written sources. Even sources that are essentially oral narratives that have been transferred to print, like the *Maturai Vīraṉ katai*, seek to link the gods in one way or another to Brahmanical forces, whether those of the imperial kingdoms in Madurai or Tanjore or the gods who are associated with them.[56] These texts, like the genealogies that Dirks has illuminated so skillfully, tend to be organized around a process of social advancement—where the Kallars or Maravars are transformed from bandits to kings, from outlaws to legitimate rulers of territory.[57] The narratives I collected from sacred groves in the Madurai region suggest that as we get further away from written sources, the interest in social advancement recedes, and what is left is a struggle for survival. The gods of these myths are totally unreformed and barely tamed; if they relate to those stories of social advancement at all, it is only the very early steps in the process. In another village called Valayapatti, this one east of Azhagar Koyil, a god known as Pillaitinni veeran (*Piḷḷaitinni vīraṉ*, lit. "the hero-god who eats children") resides in a densely wooded glen at the border between neatly tended mango orchards and the rocky, dry slopes of the state-owned reserve forest, its boundary marked by a sandy road and by the command that one take off one's sandals before entering. Pillaitinni veeran's story was told to me in a fragmentary way by an elderly Ambalakkarar priest, who was a fourth-generation servant of the deity. Like many such priests, he claimed not to know the story well. Only the ancestors knew it fully, he said; its details had been forgotten over time. It is also typical of these gods that the rawness of their power is in inverse proportion to the clarity of their personality. Like Sri Karuppasamy, Pillaitinni veeran comes from Kerala, but beyond that we get few details of his life.

In those days, [because of Pillaitinni veeran's presence], the children born to the community kept dying. First, the community tried withholding worship from him altogether. The youngest of a family of five priests worshipped him in order to get a baby, but the baby died. Then, they tried sacrificing a child of the priestly lineage, but still there were no heirs. Then they tried just cutting a finger of a child [in the hopes that the symbolic death would appease the deity]. The child grew up, got married, and had a baby. But, when they cut that baby's finger, the blood ran out and it died. The people once again withheld worship altogether, but when the god came to the priest and demanded it, they performed a street play in his honor. Finally, they went to the temple of Muthalamman [Mūttāllammaṉ, the village goddess] for advice. She took the priest and vanished. They went to the north country, where there were seven or eight babies hanging in cradles. They belonged to the women working in the fields. The priest was given one baby to take care of, and he ran off with it. He and the goddess were chased, but they hid in a banyan tree that the goddess split open with her power. Finally, the priest and goddess made it back to the temple, where she promised the priest that from now onward they would have heirs. She instructed them to sacrifice a black or brown goat, and to make a

young baby's head from it, and then they would have heirs. Once
there were only five [families], now there are 100 families.

By "civilized" standards, this god is clearly pretty horrible. The people
cannot live with him, but they cannot get rid of him. It is only after the
intervention of the village goddess that they figure out a way to worship
him in such a way that their lineage thrives in his presence, instead of
dying off. The narrative flow here is worth noting: The form of worship
becomes gradually more mediated as symbolic substitutes are located for
the human victim arguably found at the base of all forms of ritual sacrifice. Does this mean that the people became more "civilized" as they
discovered that symbolic sacrifice was more effective than the death of
an actual child? Or does it mean that the god became tamed and pacified
over time? Or is it some combination of the two? Again and again in the
mythology of these fierce village deities, a theme arises of the need to
discern how to worship a god. Sometimes, the god is too dangerous, and
nothing can be done but to put it in a box, tie it up tightly with chains and
throw it into a river, in the hopes that some person who can figure out
the nature of the god will find it and worship it. The myth of Pillaitinni
veeran is so fragmentary that one must be cautious in advancing an interpretation, but I wonder if here too we find an indirect statement about
the difficulties of life in this environment—where one has to persevere
before finding the right combination of techniques to survive.
    A slightly less raw form of divinity is revealed in the mythology of
another sacred-grove deity. In this story, the god is not a powerful hunter,
malevolent child-eater, or thieving magician but a young, hot-tempered
girl. Still, one finds some recurring themes: the god's need to prove its
divinity by performing some deed; the need to get permission to settle, to
win a place in this very crowded land; and most of all the complementary
relationship between the god and a semidivine human ruler. This story
was narrated by the elderly hereditary priest of the Valaiyar-dominated village of Sikupati, a powerful man with a piercing gaze, who was regularly
possessed by both of the figures described in this story. Set in the time
of the British, the narrative begins with Azhaginatchiyamman (whose
name was glossed for me as "the Village Goddess who is a prepubescent
girl related to Azhagar") migrating from one village to another, until she
finds herself in the care of a priest or chieftain named Chinnamannan
(Cinnamannan, lit. "little king"). Challenged by the British to prove the
goddess's power, Chinnamannan boasts that he can make a lamp burn

using only water as fuel. But as soon as he makes the claim, he becomes sick with fear and doubt. The priest continued:

> The *cāmi* came and said, "Why are you not taking any food?" "I told them the fire would burn on water, but if it doesn't happen, they will kill me," said Chinnamannan. The goddess told him, "If you are like this [so weak in faith], who will worship me? Okay, you just go, take water from the pot and pour it in the lamp. It will burn." So the Britishers came and saw the lamp burning on water. This happened at Ponamaravati.

The goddess moves on to Sikupati, where Lord Shiva gives her a place to stay on the outskirts of the village, explaining that "they can't have that goddess inside the village because some men will take liquor. Both good girls and bad girls would come to this place [suggesting that the bad ones will have sex with the drunk men and the resulting ritual pollution will offend the deity]. The goddess should not affect anyone [adversely]." Lord Azhagar (Vishnu) also gives her a temple on the mountain, and Chinnamannan himself gives her a temple in the village in exchange for the boon of a child.

> "Both my wife and I are 100 years old," said Chinnamannan, "If you give a male child, I'll give that child for your service [i.e., he will become the pujari, or priest]." So the goddess gave a male child. After that, Chinnamannan asked for another boon, "You have asked for a place in the *mantai*. I'll just go and plant a dry stick on the *mantai*. Let the branches grow all around [so it gives lots of shade]." The Britishers saw this also and gave land for the temple [believing in the power of the goddess]. (Interview, December 18, 2005, Sikupati)

The hierarchy between deity and human is not as pronounced here as in the previous narratives. Rather, the myth suggests a more collaborative relationship between gods and their human interlocutors. At first, the human priest-king, Chinnamannan, appears as the cowardly one, weak in faith and fearing failure. But after becoming convinced of the goddesses' power, and finding a suitable site for the Azhagi's worship (with the help of the high gods of the area), Chinnamannan finds that the goddess is a font of fertility who can bestow the boon of children and even persuade the British to give land. The narrative even suggests that through the give and take between Chinnamannan and Sri Azhagi, she becomes so amenable that a temple can be made for her in the village center itself, albeit one already equipped with cooling shade to mitigate her fierce qualities.

In the villages that support the two other guardian deities I have considered—Manjalmalaiyandi and Pillaitinni veeran—one finds a dichotomy or tension between the male forest gods and the female village goddess, where the goddess is represented as unambiguously benevolent compared to the fierce male deities. In Sikupatti, however, that split between ferocity and benevolence, *kāṭu* and *ūr* (forest and village) occurs within the goddess herself. As the priest's narrative indicates, the goddess has two temples—one in the *mantai* and one on the mountain—for, even as she becomes pacified through exchanges and transactions with the community, the part of her that continues to live in the dense forested shrine outside the village boundary is still quite fierce. As the priest said of her preference for living in the forest, "She is an angry girl [*kōpakkārap piḷḷai*]. She's very pure [*cuttamāṉa teyvam*]. Some good girls and bad girls may come, and she wants to get away from all that." She is also associated with the community's tradition of hunting. Before the annual festival, her image is brought from the forest temple to the *mantai* temple, while the priest goes out hunting for a rabbit with a party of men from the village. When they are successful, they roast the rabbit on a spit before her and distribute the meat to all the houses of the village. Such a successful hunt is an indication that she is pleased with the community and gives permission for them to hold a festival for her. I believe that here we see a good illustration of the divided nature of Valaiyar-Muttaraiyar identity—on the one hand, they are settled agriculturalists, who draw on the goddesses' power to acquire land for cultivation. On the other hand, they are valiant hunters, who draw on other aspects of the goddesses' power to obtain success in the forest. This power—the power of violence—requires a more cautious approach, as instantiated in the taboos surrounding the goddesses' forest shrine.

The proliferation of village deities has perplexed many scholars of south Indian popular Hinduism. In Azhagapatti, for example, although the sacred grove primarily belongs to a local form of Sri Patinettampadi Karuppasami, whose main shrine is at the Azhagar temple, worship there is directed toward five gods: Periyakaruppasamy ("Big Karuppasamy"), Chinnakaruppasamy ("Little Karuppasamy"), Ayyanar, Nondi sami ("the lame god"), and the Kannimar (seven "virgin" or "young lady" deities). Why are there so many deities, some of whom are barely differentiated from each other? There are no doubt innumerable answers to this question, some of which have to do with power relations in the village and the fact that, at village festivals, the most powerful people in the village serve as the honored vehicles of these deities, when the gods descend and speak to their devotees through the entranced village leaders.[58] In addition, I would argue that, at some level, these gods are best understood not as personalities but as powers. In what may seem like an unlikely echo of ancient Vedic religion, these village deities are like the forces of the natural world: They are powers that can be used, and should be used, but with care. Moreover, these village deities are portable, even malleable. They are traded, moved from village to village, divided into parts and distributed, buried, moved away from, and sometimes locked in chests and thrown into a river, in the hopes that someone, with the right touch for worshipping them properly, can tap into their powers and make them do good.

In the layering of meanings associated with the forest deities, I think we can find more clues as to why the people who maintain sacred groves work so hard to do so. There is a great deal of demand for the natural resources that are preserved in the forests—for firewood, fodder for animals, fruits and leaves to use as medicine, not to mention the importance of the land itself in a densely populated area where arable land is the most highly valued form of property. The Ambalakkarars' and Valaiyars' willingness to observe the taboos surrounding the forests, which protect the forest as the deity's own domain, has to do with their commitment to these fierce gods. These gods evoke, I would argue, 200-year-old community memories of themselves. For Ambalakkarar-Kallars, these memories relate back to their ambivalent role as fierce guardians of the area as well as thieves, alternately protective or vindictive, sheltering or terrifying. For Valaiyar-Muttaraiyars, it is life in the forest that is evoked. The rituals of worship involving hunting, possession, prophecy, and the sacrifice of animals allow for a kind of reenactment, and reinstantiation of these important aspects of their community identity.

Conclusion

What are the reasons that people do not cut the trees in these areas? My conversations with residents of villages near Madurai revealed reasons that, as we shall see, were echoed by villagers in all the districts of Tamil

Nadu I visited. First, the trees belong to the deity as his or her own property, sometimes understood more narrowly as the adornments or *alaṅkāram* of the deity. Second, in an extension of this understanding, the forest constitutes the temple of the deity, its home. Third, some gods dwell in the forest because their fierce, impatient, easily aroused nature makes them dangerous, even though their protective strength and vitality is needed by the community. This reason acquires additional meaning when considered in light of the spatial organization of deities in a village, where more tractable, calmer deities such as Ganesh/Vinayakar and the domesticated village goddess are located in the civilized heart of the village at the center and the wilder, more fierce deities are located in the surrounding *kāṭu*, or forest. While the forces of the *kāṭu* are often conceptualized as being "other" to the village and are often associated with marginal, untouchable service castes, in a broader context they also belong to the village in a more inclusive, encompassing fashion. Close readings of the myths and interpretations of the iconography of the shrines suggest another interpretation of the meaning of the gods as well—that they represent a dimension of communal identity rooted in the past, when Kallar-Ambalakkarars were the protectors and little kings of the area and Valaiyar-Muttaraiyars served those kings nobly through their deep knowledge of the forests. Forest-dwelling guardian deities have been variously understood by scholars as demonic beings,[59] symbols of caste relations,[60] and instantiations of the "dangerous watchman" archetype.[61] But no one has, to my knowledge, explored in depth the many resemblances between them and the poligars of old.[62] In this chapter, I have set forth what I believe is an original interpretation of the meaning and identity of Tamil guardian deities, who are closely associated with the phenomena of sacred groves by virtue of their predilection for forested shrines far from the noise and pollution of settled life. But is this argument, then, purely of antiquarian interest? What does it have to do with environmental concern, or the intersection between religion, nature, and culture?

As I mentioned in the introduction, in discourse about sacred groves produced by middle-class urban Indian environmentalists one finds a striking ambivalence toward sacred groves—while their ecological benefits are widely celebrated, many people express disapproval and distaste for the intense and sometimes violent forms of worship that surround the deities who reside in the groves. I would agree that there are, without doubt, aspects of forest gods' worship that are deeply problematic from an egalitarian, progressive sensibility. Because of their fierce nature, and the threat that they will react violently to ritual pollution, untouchables (Dalits) are often banned from their groves, as are menstruating and postpartum women. Moreover, their myths and worship valorize deeply hierarchical relationships based, from one point of view, on frank domination.

Yet I would argue that far from representing something primitive and in need of reform in Tamil culture, one can find a great deal to admire in these deities and in the enduring relationships that communities have formed with them and around them over time. As Laurie Patton has argued with respect to the effort to mine Vedic thought for the resources for an environmental ethos, we should avoid the temptation to whitewash the violence inherent in much thought about nature in the Hindu tradition.[63] The violence of animal sacrifice, for example, may be seen as a way of embracing our place in the biotic community, not pretending to exist somehow outside of or above it. We live, after all, in a rough-and-tumble world where, as the Upanishads put it, everything is either eater or eaten (Brihadaranyaka Upanishad 1.4.6). Similar relationships of dominance and subordination are vividly described and even valorized in the myths of fierce forest gods, as is animal sacrifice. These may not be ideal ways of relating, but it is not clear that human beings can create communities for long without them.

From a historical point of view, the stories surrounding the fierce forest gods of Tamil Nadu have much to tell us about how communities survived for centuries in an unusually harsh environmental milieu, where rain was infrequent and unpredictable and the heat scorched everything. Though one would never wish it, we as a human community may someday once again find ourselves facing similar conditions of scarcity. These narratives illustrate the qualities necessary for survival under such conditions, which are found in people brave enough to engage with the fierce and unpredictable gods of the forest: cunning intelligence and the ability to think on one's feet, improvising solutions and persisting until techniques that lead to human thriving can be found. They also teach us about the need for patience to negotiate over the long haul, giving and taking in response to the forces—divine and natural—in the environment. What is valued here is not harmony in some utopian form, a peaceful Edenic stasis in which "the lion and the lamb lie down together"; rather, the traditions surrounding the fierce gods and their human communities envision a dynamic harmony in the form of a balance of powers attained through constant negotiation.

A Road Runs Through It

CHANGING MEANINGS IN MALAIYALI SACRED GROVES
IN TIRUVANNAMALAI DISTRICT

Introduction

Roads are often seen as villains by environmentalists in the global north, held responsible not only for physical environmental degradation in the form of erosion, habitat destruction, road kill, and the acceleration of development but also for moral degradation in the form of a lazy, wasteful, and self-indulgent "car culture."[1] While radical elements within the green movement in the United States and the United Kingdom have articulated these anti-road concerns most vividly, they are implicit even in landmark environmental legislation such as the United States' Wilderness Act of 1964, which ruled that potential wilderness areas must be roadless. Yet roads are notoriously double-edged. On the one hand, in both the developed and developing worlds, they symbolize freedom of movement and expansive possibilities. On the other, even as roads allow greater access to urban markets, they also thereby generate material incentive to destroy forests for timber and to clear land for agriculture.

In India, roads are not only crucial elements of material and social development, they are also important signifiers of status. In the 19th century, upwardly mobile low-caste communities rioted for access to public roads formerly denied to them because of their supposedly polluting nature.[2] In his Booker Award-winning novel, *The White Tiger*, Aravind Adiga evokes the allure surrounding modern roads in rural India where a bus conductor's smart uniform and shiny whistle represent power, progress, and a way out of entrenched village pecking orders.[3] Similarly, the roads built through rural areas of Tiruvannamalai district have challenged social hierarchy and created new opportunities and aspirations, especially for the younger generation. Yet these same roads, with their democratizing influence, have in sometimes surprising ways also weakened—but not altogether eliminated—the taboos that have historically limited human use of sacred groves.

As I discussed in the previous chapter, the perception of the forest as an abode of forces both dangerous and crucial to the vitality of settled life plays a key part in restraining people's overuse of the forest's flora and fauna. In Tamil villages that maintain sacred groves, this perception often finds expression in gothic tales that describe the affliction meted out by the grove's deity on those who violate the taboos regulating the use of the forest. However, many of the Malaivazhmakkal Gounders, or "mountain-dwelling farmers," a tribal community whose groves I discuss in this chapter, have largely dispensed with such a view. Only fragments of this vision of the forest as a dangerous yet vital realm remain today, just as only fragments of the forests themselves have survived. In its place is a very different vision of nature, one dominated by pragmatism and rationalism, which regards as illogical and old-fashioned the taboos that once established the sanctity of sacred groves and thus helped to protect their forest produce from overuse. Various historical forces have brought about this shift in religiosity. Particularly powerful vectors of change, I would argue, are the tar roads constructed over the past twenty years that now connect Malaivazhmakkal villages to regional centers. While roads provide access to education, employment, and state-based rural development schemes, they also carry new ideas about space, morality, and divinity, which have contributed to the deterioration of temple forests.

The Beauty and Power of Roads

The search for sacred groves that my field assistant Thavamani and I embarked on in the summer of 2004 took us along some of the most remote roads I've ever seen in Tamil Nadu. I got a taste then of how important high-quality roads are to the basic, everyday lives of people in this region. Located far from transportation depots, with their gravel pits and tar-boiling machinery, the roads that connect provincial towns and villages here deteriorate at an alarming rate due to the harsh weather and irregular maintenance. The driver of the rugged Ambassador we used to travel between field sites could in places go no more than 15 miles an hour over the bumpy, rutted roads. Even then, we would pass men and boys pushing enormous loads on the handlebars of bicycles. How different it was to soar along the smooth surface of what is known in India (following British usage) as a "metalled road," a paved road surfaced with tar.

Along both the rutted and smooth roads in the land-locked *taluks* (an administrative division corresponding roughly to a county) of Tiruvannamalai, we found a wide range of forested shrines as well as evidence of a contemporary temple-building boom, fueled by India's expanding economy through the 1990s and 2000s. In search of forested temples in the area around the Sattanur Dam, southeast of Tiruvannamalai in Chengam taluk, for example, we came upon a sprawling complex of shrines and pavilions built into a rocky hillside and shaded here and there by a few scraggly trees. Located far from the small village center of Veeranam (Vīraṉam), the walls and platforms in this mostly open-air complex were all painted the same vibrant turquoise. The temple was patronized, we were told, by a relative of Tamil film music composer Ilayarajan. Its main deity, Ponmudirayar (Poṉmutirāyar, lit. "lord or king of the gold crown"), rocked gently in the shade of a neem tree on a wooden swing, a familiar prop from Tamil movies with a traditionalist or rural setting. Later, after traversing some rutted tracks through the hills, we found a huge, cavernous temple still under construction in the village of Veppoorcakadi (Vepūrcakkaṭi). The clinking hammers of its stone masons are clearly audible on my interview tapes. Set in a garden replete with white marble statuary depicting gods and goddesses from the Sanskritic tradition, it was dedicated to a local goddess known only as "Finance-amma." Her story was that she blessed poor couples on their wedding day by loaning them lavish silk sarees and gold jewelry so that they could celebrate the occasion in grand style. One day, however, a short-sighted bride kept a nose-jewel from the borrowed trousseau for herself. Abruptly, Finance-amma's generosity dried up, although she continues to receive worship from her devotees in the village and surrounding areas. The deity's oral *sthalapurāṇam* offers a compressed morality tale about the sudden changes in fortune made possible by India's leap into free-market capitalism, combined with the traditionally quixotic nature of Tamil village goddesses.

Our guide in these travels was M. Amrithalingam's pioneering 1998 study, *Sacred Groves of Tamil Nadu,* which lists from six to several dozen representative groves in each district of Tamil Nadu according to the taluk, village, presiding deity, and approximate size in hectares.[4] Because Amrithalingam's guide surveyed forty-seven groves in Tiruvannamalai district, this seemed to us an especially promising place to find examples.

However, to our surprise, some of the sacred groves listed turned out to be no more than isolated shrines with a few trees surrounded by eucalyptus plantations. In these instances, it is possible that in the six years' time between the publication of Amrithalingam's study and our visit, the shrine's land had been taken over by the Forest Department and planted with exogenous, income-generating species such as eucalyptus. Eucalyptus was, after all, the favored species employed by Indian social forestry projects that boomed in the 1980s and 1990s.[5] Alternatively, Amrithalingam may have exaggerated the size of the groves, including the area of the Forest Department land that surrounded the shrines in the size of the grove itself. In any event, it was startling to discover in Kilvanakkampati (Kiḷvanakkampāṭi), for example, that where Amrithalingam's book described an eleven-hectare sacred grove dedicated to the goddess Ammacharu, we found only a hero stone encircled by a few neem trees, with rows and rows of eucalyptus in every direction. According to the village accountant, these had been planted in 1975.

Nevertheless, our misadventures led to insight into an oft-described aspect of environmental history and politics in India, for the stories told by residents who continued to worship at these sites revealed decades of tension between themselves and the state-level Forest Department, usually referred to by the English word "Forest." In one striking instance, residents of Ilavampadi (Iḷavampāṭi, a small village in Chengam taluk of Tiruvannamalai district), described how forty years earlier (around 1964), the forests near the village had been owned and controlled by the panchayat, the local governing council. However, at this time, the Tamil Nadu state government was worried that panchayats were not managing the forests well, and so control was transferred from the panchayat to the Forest Department. The Forest Department then began auctioning off the forest, exchanging the right to harvest and sell the trees for a fee. "Like that they cut and cut and destroyed it. They cut the entire forest. They didn't leave a single place," said one resident. Finally, the Forest Department came in with bulldozers to remove the original roots and then planted eucalyptus. In accordance with Forest Department policy, people were allowed to keep the trees immediately surrounding shrines in places where they had historically maintained them. Thus, when I visited, the "grove" dedicated to Ilavampadi's village guardian deity, Śri Vediyappan (Vetiyappaṉ), the forest was gone and Vediyappan's shrine consisted of a simple wooden structure enclosing an ancient hero stone, depicting a moustached warrior with sword upraised (figure 2.1).

FIGURE 2.1 Vetiyappan's image, Ilavampati

However, questions of access to the shrine and what kind of celebrations villagers could hold there remained a point of controversy. Recently, I was told, an angry crowd had formed in response to the forest ranger's order that they not light fireworks at Vediyappan's shrine at his annual festival, lest they set fire to the surrounding trees. Years before, when the villagers wanted to clear a path from the road to the shrine, their plan was opposed by the village headman, who wanted to uphold the Forest Department's order not to interfere with the plantation. To resolve the conflict, the speaker's uncle vowed that if it rained so much that the waters rose to the height of his knee, it meant the god supported the villagers who wanted the road. Miraculously, the next day it rained so heavily the whole area was flooded. When the headman obstinately pressed his case in spite of this sign from the god, he was struck blind.

The Forest Department's historically heavy-handed efforts to support "social forestry" through various schemes has been the subject of considerable scholarship.[6] Critics argue that many such projects privilege already prosperous local elites through their emphasis on planting economically valuable species such as eucalyptus (the pulp of which is sold to paper manufacturers) rather than locally useful species (such as those that would provide reliable sources of cooking fuel). In this way, rather than challenging prevailing social hierarchies that privilege men over women and propertied groups over the landless, they reinforce existing social hierarchies. To the extent that sacred groves are among the types of forests typically managed by local communities, they have been an inviting point of entry for district Forest Department officers eager to initiate social forestry campaigns, with the assumption that the local people's religious sentiments will help protect new plantings. J. J. Roy Burman's field work in Maharashtra indicates that in many sacred groves this has had largely negative results in that afforestation with economically valuable species (which are meant to be harvested periodically) tends to undermine the original taboos on cutting trees.[7] As I discuss later, stories I heard from village residents southeast of Tiruvannamalai suggest this has been the case in Tamil Nadu as well.

The Mountain-Dwelling Farmers

Among the villages in which one finds forested shrines in Tiruvannamalai district are those dominated by Malaivazhmakkal Gounders, a Scheduled Tribe also known as Malaiyāli (lit. *malai* "mountain" + *āli* "people," "ruler"). The Malaiyali villages in the eastern foothills of the Kalrayans typically lie adjacent to Tamil Nadu Forest Department reserved forest lands, where state-based sanctions limit exploitation of the wooded slopes. To get to the villages, one winds through arid plains on often rutted, bumpy roads, compelled to take detours from time to time around dramatic rock outcroppings, passing rain-fed fields and dry, scrubby grazing lands interspersed with low trees. Forested shrines present a striking contrast in this landscape with their towering neem and banyan trees looming like verdant islands in a dry, brown sea.

The rituals and beliefs of the Malaiyalis are a complex blend of non-Brahmanical local religion and devotion to Vishnu in his incarnation as Lord Rama, known and revered throughout India as the hero of the epic, the Ramayana. Religion played a part in the classificatory schemes of the British colonial administration, and it may have been because of the predominance of "animistic features" in their religious discourse that in 1950 the Malaivazhmakkal Gounders were listed in the Indian Constitution among the Scheduled Tribes. According to the oral history of the Malaiyalis, they migrated in the 16th century from Kanchipuram, where they had been soldiers in the employ of the kings of the Vijayanagara Empire. As recounted by Mr. Velu, an educated, land-owning member of the community who worked in the District Collectorate Office,

> They were a forest-dwelling people, who did not eat civilized food like rice, but took their sustenance from the forest in the form of wild pigs, deer and other wild animals. They also did not wear much clothing, covering their bodies with a single cloth. Periodically, the men of the community used to go to the forest to hunt for one or two weeks at a time. Once, the men went hunting and did not return for three months' time. Only their dogs returned from the forest without them. Convinced that their husbands were dead, the women of the community went as a group to a local temple and removed their *tālis* [the Tamil badge of marriage, a yellow cord worn around the neck]. When the women returned home, they found that their husbands had returned. Refusing to dishonor themselves [by engaging in what would have been the remarriage of widows], the men left the village, taking their deity, Kariyaramar [Kariyarāmar, "black Rāma"], with them. Sometimes when it got heavy they would carry Him on their heads. From Kanchipuram, they traveled through many towns breaking coconuts along the way. But they could not stop in any place, because when people saw them—half-naked and fierce looking—they were frightened and they drove them out. In Citteri they stopped. There they fought with the resident hunters to gain their territory, and after defeating them, took their wives in marriage.[8]

Velu's narrative touches on several of the cultural characteristics said to distinguish so-called tribal communities, also known as *adivāsis* (lit. "original inhabitant") from other Indians: forest habitat, dependence on hunting for subsistence, and relatively simple material culture (i.e., clothing). Historians such as Ajay Skaria have argued that distinctions between Hindu castes and so-called primitive tribals was reinforced, perhaps even created, by British scholar-administrators intent on understanding India's enormous social diversity through various classificatory typologies. Initially, racial differences were foremost in creating ethnological categories, and India's tribals were said to be related to other "primitives" found in far-flung reaches of the British empire—the Aborigines of Australia, Negroid Africans, Mongols, and so on. Later, cultural features, including religion, came into prominence. By the 1940s, however, a consensus emerged that centuries of cultural diffusion between Hindus and tribals had made the creation of clear distinctions on that basis impossible, so people were classified as tribal largely by virtue of their habitat (hills and/or forests) and mode of subsistence (hunting and gathering).

The Malaiyalis I spoke with were all settled farmers, but their identity as tribals is very important to them. Indeed, I would argue that, as with the Ambalakkarars and Muttaraiyars of the Madurai region, the Malaiyalis' maintenance of sacred groves is bound up with their maintenance of Malaiyali group identity as a community of warriors and hunters. Even though some Malaiyalis may be ambivalent or uncertain about exactly how to express that tribal distinctiveness without attracting the stigmatized label of "primitive," they are committed to asserting it for very practical reasons: In a long-standing commitment to remedy discrimination against historically oppressed groups, the government of India grants a special legal standing to tribals, with preference given in such areas as admission to public universities and government employment for those considered "backward" and officially listed on the government's "schedule" of such groups (hence Scheduled Tribe).

Malaiyali village festivals and wedding ceremonies help keep alive the community's memory of their ancestors' long march from Kanchipuram and their forceful appropriation of the territory and the women belonging to a community of hunters. Over 400 years, the community has spread over a large area. Not much is known about their lives during the early modern period, but 19th- and early-20th-century colonial records describe them as a relatively prosperous if geographically isolated community. They traded extensively with plains' dwellers, both for goods and for services such as barbers and washermen. But they were not really on the radar of the colonial administration. In the *Madras District Gazeteer* for South Arcot, W. Francis writes of the hills that comprise their territory: "The number of Europeans who have been up the Kalrayan hills from the South Arcot side could apparently be counted [on] the fingers of one hand."[9] Compared to Malaiyalis in the neighboring hills of the Western Ghats, those of the Kalrayans were relatively untouched by colonial forces, such as the creation of coffee plantations that transferred property rights to nontribal and British planters. While their kinsmen in the Shevoray range were pushed into low-wage labor in the coffee plantations, the Kalrayan Malaiyalis were left to the (somewhat milder) exploitation of local masters.[10] Until 1976, the Kalrayan hills were not even effectively administered by the Tamil Nadu state government; rather, taxes were collected and law applied largely by the jagirdars, traditional chiefs who have ruled the region since the 16th century.[11]

Changes in Malaiyali Sacred Groves

Now, after years of relative isolation from the surrounding population centers, the Malaiyalis have become more connected to the wider society in large part due to the construction of a paved road through the region in 1990 and the institution of regular bus service along it. I do not want to reinforce a false stereotype of Indian *adivāsi*s as communities existing in pristine isolation until the 20th century. As their migration narrative and colonial sources testify, Malaiyalis have long lived in contact with plains' dwellers. But it is also obvious that the frequency and intensity of contact is increasing as roads and other forms of communication connect them to larger networks of people, ideas, and commerce. Presently, even the most important senior men in these villages have no more than a primary-school education. However, as a result of nationwide campaigns to educate children of *adivāsi* communities, and the relative ease of transportation to surrounding schools, their sons (and some daughters) are studying to the tenth or twelfth grade and, in a few cases, pursuing their education to the university level.[12] Other signs of advancing prosperity are the many *pukka* concrete houses in the village, along with post-office branches and fields filled with a variety of crops, including new experimental varieties.[13]

Yet the changes wrought by the construction of roads also seem to be eroding the taboos that once protected the flora and fauna of the forested shrines in the region. Most of these are dedicated to the community's lineage deities, *kulateyvaṅkaḷ* (lit. "family deities") who are all forms of the original deity said to have been brought from Kanchipuram. In Attipadi, for example, a Malaivazhmakkal Gounder village of 200 houses, the *kulateyvam* is Adiramar (Ātirāmar, lit. "original" or "supreme" Rāma). Also known as "sixty-broken pot original (or supreme) Rāma," his full name came from a spoiled ritual that took place many years ago. Once, at festival time, the women of the village lit their fires to cook *poṅkal* (a rice pudding consumed at many Tamil ritual occasions) against a long, hard tree root in the temple area. They did not realize this was the body of Adiramar himself in the shape of a massive snake. When the snake rolled over, he smashed all sixty pots at once.

Temples and trees in Attipadi

Adiramar's temple used to be a simple hut made from palmyra leaves located in a small forest of bamboo and other trees that extended for sixteen acres. Construction in the grove occurred in two phases, each of which can be seen as marking a shift in the community's understanding of the relationship between themselves, the gods, and the groves. Apparently, depredations of the village crops by monkeys led to the first phase, which was marked by the construction of the first permanent building on the temple land. We discovered this through a conversation between an elderly male resident, Somasundaram (about sixty to seventy years old), and Thavamani:

SOMASUNDARAM: The monkeys pulled up the groundnut plants... The temple's place is sixteen acres. In all of these sixteen acres, there were lots of bamboo bushes. The monkeys used to go inside and hide. What the young boys did... they made all the monkeys climb up one bamboo. The monkeys were surrounded by men with spears and dogs. Then the men set the bamboo bushes on fire. They all died. All the houses burned.

THAVAMANI: Which houses?

SOMASUNDARAM: The whole village burned. Not even one house survived. Anjaneya [a name for Hanuman, the devoted monkey servant of Lord Rama] himself did that work.

THAVAMANI: Because they killed?

SOMASUNDARAM: Yes, because they killed. Then it [Anjaneya] came and said to them in their dreams, "because you killed my messengers, I have sent this destruction to your village." It was completely burned. That was 1959. At that time, Pūvaśanmukam was the MLA [Member of the Legislative Assembly]. He brought kerosene and rice for the people. After that, we thought we should build a concrete building. But some said we should not build a concrete building. After that we consulted a *jōsyar* [an astrologer]. When we consulted he said, "No problem. You may build."

It is perhaps ironic that the village residents repented for their cruelty in slaughtering Anjaneya's monkey companions not by restoring their habitat but by building a concrete temple, whose beams were made from neem and bamboo trees harvested from the grove. Apparently there was some resistance to that idea from within the village, as the need to consult an outside authority indicates.

Somasundaram himself did not elaborate on why a permanent built structure for the temple was regarded as a suitable offering. But he did, when pressed, explain more about what was particularly unethical about the burning of the monkeys. In the process he revealed, I believe, something of the restraint embedded in people of his generation's everyday orientation toward the natural world. "Why did Anjaneya punish people so severely?" we asked, "The monkeys, after all, were destroying the crops, undoing all the people's hard work?" "If you want to kill one or two monkeys," said Somasundaram, "go ahead. But why should you kill them off altogether? You should not kill them all. If one or two dies, that's natural. But if you willfully beat them all to death, what's that?"

In 1990, between the first and second phase of the temple's history, the tar road was extended to Attipadi. I did not learn why the road was built then, or why it was constructed right through the middle of the lineage deity's domain. Views of tribals as highly religious might lead one to imagine that the local people would protest the road's bifurcation of a sacred place. Accounts of a similar occurrence in a sacred grove in Madurai district in southern Tamil Nadu may shed light on the deity's and the people's silence on this matter. There people explained that the resident deity did not punish or resist road-makers constructing a road through a sacred grove because it knew the road would bring many benefits to the people.[14] It is also possible that by routing the road through communally owned land, the state transportation agency met less resistance than if it had had to appropriate land owned by individuals.

The second phase was ushered in by the deterioration of the first temple, when, after forty years, its wooden supporting beams had been eaten away by white ants. The building was demolished, and, under the guidance of another village headman, Murugan, the temple was rebuilt in 1995 (five years after the construction of the road). This is a simple, single-story, concrete rectangular structure with three separate naves for Kāriyarāmar (lit. "black Rama"), Iḷaiyarāmar (lit. "young Rama," associated with Lakshman, brother of Lord Rama), and Adiramar (the lineage deity of Attipati residents). Its smooth walls are regularly whitewashed and adorned with several colorful murals depicting scenes from the Ramayana in the modern style of calendar art (figures 2.2 and 2.3). The sixteen acres of land belonging to the

FIGURE 2.2 Mural of Lakshmana, Sita and Rama with Kneeling Anjaneya (Hanuman) and image of Anjaneya used in worship.

temple were cleared over time and are now rented out to farmers who cultivate tapioca on the land. They pay a fixed annual rate to the temple, which is used to help fund the temple festival, a grand affair that takes place over the course of several days once every three years.

In an interview conducted with Murugan in the summer of 2004 (he was then about forty-five years old), he described how the community occasionally cut some of the trees from the temple's forest to pay for the expenses of the annual festival but kept the towering banyan and pūṅkamaram (*Pongamia glabra*, Karanja) trees directly around the temple as *alaṅkāram* ("adornments, decoration") for the deity. At one level, this identification of the trees as the adornments, the beautiful jewels, of the

FIGURE 2.3 Concrete *pukka* temple to Atiramar in Attipadi

temple or the deity makes perfect sense. Indeed, one hears of this in many Tamil sacred groves (see chapter 1). The towering banyans do add to the beauty of the spot, creating cool shade and a lovely green backdrop. But at another level, calling the trees *alaṅkāram* is a reversal of the typical dichotomy between nature and civilization or culture in Tamil discourse. As I discussed in the previous chapter, *alaṅkāram* is typically that which is made, crafted, or embellished beyond its natural state, *seykai*, not that which appears or grows spontaneously, or *iyaṟkai* (the most commonly used Tamil word for "nature"). But when we view this phrase in a larger context, we see that over the course of time, in this grove, the god's forested shrine *has* been made into something like a cut jewel, as it has been landscaped and tamed. As Murugan said:

> The trees are *alaṅkāram* to the temple, so we don't cut [them]. When the bamboo forest was here, huge snakes were living in it. Therefore no people would ever go near. Nowadays, as the level of civilization has risen [among the people] ("*nākarikam vaḷara vaḷara*"), we've started to clean up (*cuttamā irukkom*), and we cut those trees, for income.

In Murugan's usage, it is a bit ambiguous as to whether his key phrase "clean up" (*cuttamā*) refers to the community's campaign to remove the vines, bushes, and small trees in the forest's under story, which harbored snakes, or to the Malaiyali's efforts to shed the stigmatized aspects of their tribal identity.

With his thorough-going pragmatic orientation, Murugan represents the snakes in the bamboo as simple, natural dangers. But for many people in the village, the fears that kept them away from the forest were, like the forest itself, many-layered. For them, snakes in the understory or marauding monkeys in the forest's canopy could be instruments of a quick-tempered deity, whether Anjaneya or Adiramar himself. Murugan's campaign to clear the forest in order to "clean up" the temple can be seen as a reduction of those layers so, for him, the grove no longer appears to be the abode of a fierce deity but now is simply property belonging to the temple, property that requires responsible management.

Like the contrast between *serkai* and *iyarkai*, the concept of *nākarikam* ("civilization") evokes assumptions regarding the relationship between nature and culture. Derived from the Sanskrit word for "city" (*nagar*), it has been employed by upwardly mobile communities in post-independence India as a synonym for progress. To develop *nākarikam* means to become more cultured, sophisticated, and worldly, often through the adoption of customs associated with urban, middle-class folk. For example, when low-caste communities start seeking non-kin brides and grooms for their children (and exchange dowry), instead of marrying them to cross-cousins or other kin, people explain the change as a development of *nākarikam*.[15] Similar to the clearing and cultivation of formerly forested temple land, here progress has both a moral and an economic valence, as discovering how to profit from a situation is esteemed over foolishly letting it go to waste.

Tīṭṭu and transgression

In years past, in addition to the concerns about dangerous animals, people avoided the groves for fear of upsetting the resident deity by exposing him or her to pollution, or *tīṭṭu*. *Tīṭṭu* is a central element of local Tamil religiosity, conceptualized as an invisible substance emanating from all sorts of polluting activities, including sexual intercourse, menstruation, death, and decay. It structures not only gender relations but also caste relations, as castes deemed "lower" in the status scale are subject to a variety of prohibitions because of their supposedly inherently polluting nature.[16] People frequently reported that in the old days, when the taboos surrounding pollution were more strictly enforced, menstruating women could not even walk past the grove, let alone through it. Whether grazing goats or collecting wood, they had to walk along circuitous paths to avoid the grove. Even today, in the absence of built structures such as compound walls or a towering *kopuram* (temple tower), the boundaries of sacred groves are marked by the compulsion to take off one's footwear (a potent source or carrier of *tīṭṭu*). As indicated by the stalls for depositing footwear found at the entrance to virtually every Hindu temple, shoes and sandals must always be removed in the presence of a god because they are the lowest and dirtiest garments on one's body.

With the construction of the tar road in 1990 directly through the grove, these taboos now seem outdated and illogical, especially to the village's younger residents. Thavamani and Murugan discussed this:

MURUGAN [speaking of the old days]: In those days, people would take off their *chappals* [flip-flop type sandals] half a furlong away and wouldn't wear them until they got to the village. Now, the road is there, so people walk with their chappals on.

THAVAMANI: So what? Though the road is there, why don't they carry the chappals in their hands?

MURUGAN: [Some] people do that even now. Old people.

THAVAMANI: What about the young generation, aren't they afraid?

MURUGAN: They believe in their heart there is god, but [they think] what harm will we do to the god by wearing chappals?

It is striking that the young people's reported response assumes that *tīṭṭu* does some sort of harm to god, not that a god angered by *tīṭṭu* will harm *them*. Such bravado surely arises from many sources—the cockiness of educated youth challenging the inherited beliefs of their uneducated parents; a changed view of the divine, as residing principally in the "heart" not in a particular place; and perhaps the triumph of a modern form of bhakti, which regards love for God as the most important aspect of religiosity and deems manifold rituals and customs as meaningless.

Separately, Somasundaram also noted the connection between the road and diminishing concern about the taboos keeping *tīṭṭu* from the deity.

SOMASUNDARAM [speaking of the old days]:They'd remove their chappals from where the bus-stand is now. In those days no one rode [the bus]. Even today, when women get their period they also don't go [by the grove]. For five days they shouldn't walk that way on their way home. Thinking, "a *cāmi* [deity] is here," they shouldn't go near. Since the road has come, people think "oh, we can go like that." So they walk along wearing chappals.

THAVAMANI:Isn't it wrong?

SOMASUNDARAM:Yes, it's wrong. Who can tell them? In the town they wear chappals, why not here? But even now, elderly people will not walk wearing chappals.

The logic of the village youth is irrefutable—if people can wear sandals in the bus while they are riding past the grove, why should they take them off when walking by it? And if they can wear sandals in the town, why can't they wear them in this one part of the village? The road brings with it a new notion of space—not the highly variegated one of the past with its invisible but very real boundaries between the sacred and profane but the homogenous plain of secular space. The road, and especially the bus carrying people of all sorts, also corrodes the hierarchies that organized relationships between men and women, low-caste and high-caste, but not without a struggle from the old order, as illustrated in the narratives people told about a sacred grove in a nearby Malaiyali village.

Roads and resistance

In a neighboring village of 300 homes, called Puliyampatti, two Malaiyali men told of the miraculous appearance of Ilayaramar on a road near the site of his old grove. We mentioned to Balaji (about twenty years old), a young relative of the village headman, that we had seen evidence of construction on a new temple by the road, and in response he narrated the following story:

BALAJI: Before, we had a small hut [for the deity]. And there were anthills also. Now, the Saayar bus service goes this way. One day, they didn't light camphor [a basic element of ritual worship at the temple]. As they approached, a *nākam* [divine snake] with seven heads and a huge tail came and raised its hood in front of the bus. It stood on the tip of the tail. The people in the bus got terribly frightened. This was just near the temple. It happened on the bus's first journey. So the owner brought a *cāmiyār* [an oracle] from the Tiruvannamalai area, who performed *pūjā* [worship ceremony] in the temple. After that, the snake didn't appear for a long time. Later, without knowing about the god, a *dhobi* lady [laundress] brought dirty clothes in the bus. The snake appeared and blocked the bus. Since then the dhobis won't carry clothes in the bus. Now they take them by bicycle. But ever since—from when the *cāmiyār* came and did *pūjā*—no one has seen anything.

THAVAMANI: Who is the snake?

BALAJI: The snake is Ilayaramar. Ilayaramar himself appeared in the form of a snake. The snake belongs to those days.

Though the mixing of social strata made possible by modern public transportation has challenged traditional social hierarchies, one can see that the taboos governing pollution around the god's forest are to some extent still operative in restricting the movements of those lowest on the social scale, namely the untouchable dhobis. It seems the sentiments of awe or fear that once kept people away from forested shrines are no longer strong enough to prevent deforestation, but they nonetheless remain, haunting people's consciousness and subtly affecting behavior. As in Attipadi, people in Puliyampatti said that menstruating women would not walk by the site of the old grove and older people would carry their chappals when passing it. Even some young people in the community were said to feel "a little fear" when passing through the deity's domain. However, outsiders and people on motorbikes went by without taking off their sandals. "Nowadays, they walk," Balaji said, "This is the computer-age, so they walk (*kōmpūttar kālam vara vara natakkiraṅke*)".

That anyone maintains the old taboos was a bit surprising, because in Puliyampatti one saw scant evidence of any forest at all surrounding the god's concrete, roadside temple. However, I was told that at one time there were sixty acres of undeveloped land adjacent to the temple. It was unclear to me whether this was unassessed land belonging to the Tamil Nadu government (*porumboke* land) or land held in the god's name (*kōyil māṇiyam*). The story the youths told was that, about twenty years ago, fifteen to twenty acres of this was cleared for cultivation. The remaining forty to forty-five acres was semiforested grazing land, where "there were lots of bushes, trees, creepers, and thorn bushes." This was left open in part to accommodate the crowds that came for Ilayaramar's once-in-three-years festival. However, according to these youths, in about 2002 the government began planting eucalyptus saplings, possibly through a Joint Forest Management scheme sponsored by the District Forest Office. "What the government did, where the temple's land was, they put saplings. All the people became afraid; if the sapling becomes a huge tree we will have a problem. Even if they give a little money to the temple, that money will be spent in a day. And we will not have a place to stand." The village headman then devised a plan to preempt further appropriation of land that the villagers saw as a local resource, which was to clear it and make it available to their landless laborers. What trees were there, mostly *turiṅki maram* (*Albizzia odoratissima* Black Sirissa), were cut and auctioned off. The land was then divided and distributed to the poor, who paid a nominal rent that was used to support the temple festival.

Like the narratives surrounding the fate of forested temple land in Attipati, this account suggests the changing values at play around forests and religion in Malaiyali villages. A desire to help the village's landless residents combined with a fierce drive to protect local autonomy resulted in the clearing of as many as forty acres of semiforested land. I have neither the expertise nor the data to analyze the environmental costs and benefits of this shift in land usage, but villagers clearly discerned repercussions at the social and supernatural level. The young men described how the community had spent 200,000 rupees celebrating Ilayaramar's festival in a grand manner, but even then, the *nākam* did not appear. "We don't know where it has gone off to," said Balaji, a bit sadly.

Conclusion

The relationship between religion and ecology is never fixed but shifts under the pressure of both natural and social conditions. The religious meanings of trees and forests in India have changed profoundly over the course of centuries, as waves of anthropogenic deforestation and reforestation have transformed the landscape. Trees and forests, which seem so sturdy, implacable, and immoveable from an individual's perspective, are from the point of view of centuries as malleable as dough. A stretch of land can change from multistoried, old-growth forest to dense, thorny secondary-growth forest, to savannah sparsely populated by isolated trees or forest patches, to cultivated fields, and, back again to a multistoried forest depending on the felling and grazing habits of humans and their animals.[17] During the period of urbanization and agrarian settlement that took place in the subcontinent over the course of the first millennium CE, extraordinary effort was required to clear the forests of south Asia. The forest then loomed as a scary and forbidding wilderness that harbored deadly predators, animal, human, and supernatural. This meaning lives on in the contemporary moment, partly because of its thorough inscription in both classical texts and regional folklore and partly because conflict between humans and animals in India continues to arise out of competition over scarce habitat and food resources. Consider, for example, the fears surrounding tigers in the Sundarbans and elephants in Jharkhand.[18]

With the triumph of agriculture and the "scientific" forest management strategies initiated during the British period, however, what little is left of the forest in India has been effectively fenced. How much longer can the image of the forbidding forest carry the weight of emotional truth as the actual forest becomes depleted or is converted to monoculture tree plantations, often planted by nonnative species? The lions, tigers, and bears that once terrified traders are all but extinct. The hill-dwelling tribes, who specialized in knowing the patterns of the forests' nonhuman inhabitants and exchanged seasonal surpluses or the skill of their weapons for the products of plains' people, have largely come out of the hills and converted to settled agriculture or wage labor in the cities. Those who remain in the mountains basically subsist today as a beaten-down proletariat, all but indentured to money-lenders and Forest Department officials.[19] In such a context, how can the view of the forest as the terrifying abode of terrifying creatures endure?[20]

Just as it once took a lot of effort to clear the forests of south Asia, now it takes a great deal of effort to maintain them, especially those located so close to human habitation. With the construction of roads in the region bearing new ideas of progress and modernity, sacred groves located close to the village can no longer be true *iyarkai*, nature allowed to grow spontaneously. They can only remain as symbolic forests, which are cut, cleaned, and polished like jewels. There is one significant way, however, in which the actual physical forest continues to connect the Malaiyalis to their lineage deities—and their tribal identity as former hunter-gatherers. In the days leading up to the elaborate village festivals that Malaiyalis hold to celebrate their lineage deities, one essential ritual requires the men of the village to go out to the forest and bag a wild animal. If they do not bring back a wild pig or deer, it is taken as a sign of the deity's displeasure and the whole affair must be cancelled. J.R. Freeman's research on sacred groves in Kerala also describes the centrality of hunting to the religious rituals surrounding these sites.[21] I was told that sometimes Malaiyalis spend weeks at a time roaming the woods of the nearby reserved forest—illegally—to bag that one animal. It may be that this is a hyperbolic expression of the villagers' determination to complete the ritual properly. It is not uncommon to find that the cooperation of animals (whether as victims of a hunt or of a ritual sacrifice) are necessary signs of the deity's consent to be worshipped. But the Malaiyalis' difficulty in finding game may itself be a sign of the degradation of habitat even in the state-managed forests of the Kalrayan hills.

What these narratives from Malaiyali villages suggest is that villagers' frank pragmatism surrounding their temple land, which constitutes a valuable resource to be managed for the benefit of the community, coexists with beliefs surrounding *tīṭṭu* and the capacity of deities to make their will known forcefully. In light of this, I would argue that the Malaiyalis' pre-existing cosmology that envisions supernatural power, fertility, and divine blessing arising from forested areas has not been completely overturned but exists in a diminished fashion alongside new aspirations and visions of the well-lived life. Those of us who are attracted to the romance and beauty of the older generation's worldview (minus, presumably, the gender and caste hierarchies justified by notions of purity and pollution) may feel saddened by its weakening in the present "computer age." When the ecological significance of sacred groves first became widely recognized, scientists advanced proposals to place existing sacred groves under governmental control, which were justified by predictions that the local people would simply cut them down once they lost their old-fashioned "fear and faith" (*bayam-bhakti*) for good. That view is still heard among some Indian biologists and environmentalists who believe forest departments would manage the groves more responsibly for biodiversity. However, the trend in Indian forest management policy since the 1980s has been toward greater cooperation between state forestry departments and local people, with the hope that such projects will strengthen local, culturally based forest conservation practices.

The experiences of villagers in this area—from Vediyappan's devotees, whom I described at the outset, to the Malaiyali villagers in Puliyampatti—suggest that social forestry and, more recently, Joint Forest Management schemes do not always succeed at fostering a sense of common purpose. Here, lack of consultation with locals led to, among other things, annoyance that the planting of eucalyptus saplings in the "empty" spaces of the sacred grove meant there was no place to hold the deity's annual festival. Subsequently, villagers, or some sector of them, took matters into their own hands to convert some forty acres of semiforested land to agriculture.

The 1990s saw an upsurge in the trends described in this chapter whereby villagers cut down the trees sheltering forest gods to create a more "civilized" and safer ambience for worship and where the Forest Department stepped in forcefully to manage land that appeared to be "wasted" or put to inefficient use. Such developments in turn created the conditions under which new ideas for how to preserve sacred groves emerged. According to this new rubric, what outsiders wanted was to inspire villagers to see the value of the trees themselves. Environmental education campaigns organized around sacred groves sought to reframe them as not merely "backdrops" for the adventures of gods but as valuable in their own right as treasure-troves of medicinal herbs or as hard-working elements of the landscape that provided ecological services to the village, such as ground-water retention and habitat for pollinators. One finds a discourse emerging about how people in these villages once possessed deep knowledge about their environment—about the uses of the plants and trees, about their role in a complex ecosystem and water cycle. As forests all over India were stripped or converted to agricultural production or commercial forestry, environmentalists and social activists regarded such knowledge itself as a precious treasure that urgently needed to be preserved.

3

Mixing Botany and Belief

GUARDIAN DEITIES AND THEIR FORESTS
IN THE PONDICHERRY REGION

Introduction

In Ramnathapuram, a village about 15 kilometers southeast of Pondicherry, a small forested shrine stands surrounded by fields on three sides and is bordered on the fourth by a paved road that separates the fields and the shrine from the village proper. A few steps from the road, Madurai Veeran, the fierce deity who guards this diminutive forest along with the adjacent fields and village, sits majestically in state under a concrete building, flanked on either side by rifle-wielding soldiers. Just as many people in Madurai regard deities from Kerala (to the south and west) as masters of black magic, residents of the northern districts of Tamil Nadu regard the red-faced *vīraṉ* (lit. "heroic, masculine" god) from Madurai (to the south and west) as the embodiment of ferocious occult power. His mythology links him to resistance movements against the British in the 18th century, but no one I spoke with could describe exactly how he ended up in Ramnathapuram. In many respects, the *vīraṉ*'s abode is a quite typical Tamil sacred grove insofar as it is dedicated to a guardian deity whom people honor during annual festivals but generally avoid. I was brought to the grove in the summer of 2004, not to worship the deity, however, but to observe a species of tree, known in Tamil as Alandi maram (*Alangium salvifolium*, Sage leaved Alungium), whose seeds serve as food for insect larvae. According to my guide, Dr. N. Loganathan, an eleventh-generation Siddha medical doctor and trained botanist, the only place in the area one could still find examples of this species of tree was in this grove.

Sacred groves interest students of nature because they preserve some of the only examples of relatively intact indigenous south Indian forest, and they intrigue students of culture because they are protected by beliefs and practices that represent poorly understood varieties of village Hinduism. Environmentalists drawn to the potential of sacred groves as sites for revitalizing, or catalyzing, traditional community forest management have long wondered about the link between culture and nature in these sites. How do religious or other cultural beliefs and practices foster conservation of the flora and fauna? How do the ecological or botanical features of an ecosystem affect the beliefs and customs that have grown up around them? Scientific researchers have produced detailed studies of the botanical and ecological features of sacred groves, but they have not, understandably, given as much attention to the religious, social, and economic dimensions of the phenomenon. Anthropologists and historians of religion, for their part, have little understanding of forest biology, and, for them, one dense stand of trees appears to be as environmentally significant as another. By focusing on a region of Tamil Nadu whose sacred groves have been well studied by biologists, this chapter examines the link between ecology and religion by combining the insights of critical religious studies with the careful observations of scientists. By religion, I should note, I mean not the attenuated version of religion that predominates among secularized moderns but the more robust varieties that informs every aspect of people's lives, encompassing the gritty material dimensions of life as well as the longing for meaning and transcendence. Even though in some ways the sacrality of sacred groves derives from their being set apart and protected from normal use, close investigations of specific groves shows how deeply imbricated they are in the changing political dynamics of village society.

I begin by discussing debates among environmentalists, activists, and scholars about the ecological value of sacred groves and the nature and history of the religiosity surrounding them. Contemporary interest in sacred groves was sparked by Madhav Gadgil's pioneering research in the 1970s and was revived in the early 1990s as an inspiring example of community-based ecological conservation that exemplified a "bottom-up," grassroots alternative to the "top-down" social forestry programs driven by the Indian state. Yet the enthusiastic celebration of sacred groves was met almost immediately by skeptical critique at almost all levels, from the sociological and political to the ecological. I would argue, however, that the polarized nature of the debate between enthusiasts and skeptics should not obscure the significant (if limited) ecological value of sacred groves, not to mention their importance as vital and dynamic elements of village-based

Hinduism. By synthesizing the insights of botanists and social critics with my own field research, I hope to see what can be salvaged of Gadgil's now much-criticized representation of sacred groves, especially when applied to the groves in the Pondicherry region.

After sketching the environmental history of the region, I analyze the social and religious factors that have led to the preservation or degradation of three forested shrines near Pondicherry. The groves in this area are particularly intriguing because they have endured over decades, perhaps centuries, in spite of intense population pressure. With its proximity to the global metropolis of Chennai, the whole Coromandel Coast is developing at a rapid rate. Yet many communities in this area are quite loyal to their forested gods, who often function as lineage deities (*kulateyvam*) for families whose members have migrated throughout Tamil Nadu and the world. For most of the year, the sacred groves that shelter these deities enjoy a kind of benign neglect, their forest products off-limits to human use or regulated by customary rules; however, at festival time they attract hundreds, even thousands of devotees, who are drawn back to their ancestral villages by obligations and requests for help from their lineage gods. The region is also home to two highly esteemed centers of environmental science, the Salim Ali School of Ecology at Pondicherry University and the French Institute in Pondicherry, which means that several groves in the area have been systematically studied by botanists for decades.

Some scholars have argued that the ecological condition of sacred groves in India is deteriorating because of people's weakening fear and faith (*bayam-bhakti*); however, a close look at both botanical and cultural evidence reveals a more complex picture in which social and economic factors predominate. I argue that while religious beliefs and practices are changing, other significant factors also affect the ecological condition of sacred groves. These are (a) the nature of ownership, (b) the degree of community solidarity, and (c) the size of the groves themselves. A new dynamic that is significantly altering both community solidarity and the nature of ownership in Tamil sacred groves is the rising assertiveness of formerly untouchable Dalits, who were once categorically excluded from sacred groves (and other Hindu temples) because of their supposedly polluting nature.[1] Newly empowered by education and political influence, Dalits are asserting their rights as full members of village communities. The forested shrines to village guardian deities now constitute important arenas for demonstrations of their claims to higher status.

The challenges and opportunities facing sacred groves today are perhaps seen most clearly in the history of Puttupattu, a grove that has long attracted the interest of biologists and environmentalists. This chapter concludes with a consideration of the changing conditions at this shrine—ecological, social, and religious. As a relatively large forested shrine, it remains in some ways ecologically healthy and self-sustaining, but the temple's physical structure has expanded over the past thirty years at some cost to the surrounding forest. Puttupattu's history is representative of many sacred groves insofar as the construction of a major highway alongside the shrine has facilitated the transformation of the site from a village deity's forested abode into a full-blown temple dedicated to a regionally important deity that attracts devotees from all over Tamil Nadu. What distinguishes Puttupattu is that its extraordinary ecological features have attracted not only pilgrims but also activists, botanists, and environmentalists.

Into the Green Zone: Scholarly Debates about Sacred Groves

The ecological value of sacred groves is the subject of vigorous debate, as is the analytically separable but interrelated issue of the nature and history of the religiosity surrounding sacred groves. The naturalists who first identified the botanical significance of sacred groves hailed them as remnant patches of virgin forest that preserved what were perhaps the last remaining vestiges of the original climax forest. One of Madhav Gadgil and V. D. Vartak's first published pieces on sacred groves was a two-page spread in *The Illustrated Weekly of India* from September 1973. Published just two years after Gadgil had returned to India from graduate work at Harvard, the article, titled "Groves Dedicated to the Gods," dramatically conveyed both the primitive nature of the gods said to dwell in these groves and the groves' ecological significance:

> These deities are generally of an extremely primitive nature: mother goddesses in the form of unshaped stone lumps smeared with red paint, lying open to the sky … But for the believers they are amongst the fiercest of deities; breaking even a dead twig in a sacred grove may result in a serious illness or in violent death. Such strict taboos have led to the preservation in these sacred groves of forest in its virgin condition, relics of the forest that must have once covered much of India.[2]

The main point of Gadgil and Vartak's article is to make known the value of the groves. In addition to emphasizing the groves' preservation of ancient forests in their virgin condition, the authors detail the other ecological services they provide. Their extensive root systems retain rainwater and recharge underground springs and aquifers, and their rich flora constitute in situ medicine chests for practitioners of traditional systems of healing.

Along the way, however, the authors emphasize the antiquity of the phenomenon, which they infer in part from what they see as the clearly "primitive" features of the religiosity practiced in sacred groves. "The deity is generally feminine," they write, "an indication of its origin in early times, when birth was still the most miraculous of all events. The mother goddess never has a male consort, a reminder of the age when marriage in the present form was totally unknown. The red paint smearing the goddess represents of course the blood of sacrificial victims. These victims were no doubt humans in bygone times."[3] Why the focus on the supposedly primitive nature of deities whose appearance and character seem, to Gadgil and Vartak, to bear traces of earlier, now-superceded forms of worship? Emphasizing these qualities certainly amplifies the sense of mystery surrounding these sites, heightening their appeal for the presumably educated and probably urban-based readers of this English-language periodical. But Gadgil and Vartak also have an ecological point to make.

One of the fundamental theories of ecological change posits that every ecosystem is moving through the process of succession toward a single state of equilibrium among animals, plants, soil, and climate that results in remarkable stability across time. As Donald Worster has argued in his history of ecological ideas, this theory of "climax communities" is grounded in an almost metaphysical faith in the development of ecosystems, like organisms, toward a single telos, or perfect expression of their nature.[4] While such a theory has a great deal of explanatory power across the world's ecosystems and is widely held, it also implies that human beings, as disturbers of ecological equilibrium par excellence, are outside of nature. Solutions to environmental degradation, thus, depend on excluding human beings from fragile habitats, except, perhaps, for those "primitives" who are willing to adjust their lifestyles to nature's inflexible rhythms. Gadgil and Vartak's characterization of the religion in these shrines as "primitive" thus helps to account for the grove's preservation. So long as humans remain, in a sense, half-civilized, or "close to nature," they maintain the climax type of forest by not interfering with it. But if they start changing, for example, by converting to a more modern form of religion, like Christianity, Buddhism, or Brahmanical Hinduism, they are likely to evolve out of this "state of nature" and start destroying the forest.

The characterization of the groves Gadgil and Vartak advanced in 1973 and developed in later articles (1975, 1976, and 1981) has had remarkable influence and staying power over the years. Combined with the visual salience of the groves themselves, in landscapes otherwise denuded of flora, the packaging of groves as a symbol of an imagined India's more religious and environmentally sensitive past has made them a favorite topic of Indian mass media.[5] The most extensive coverage of sacred groves can be found in periodicals dedicated to environmentalism, for example, the 1994 feature story on sacred groves in the Center for Science and Environment's fortnightly magazine *Down to Earth*. This set of articles, "The Spirit of the Sanctuary" (January 31, 1994), exhibited many of the features of mass media coverage of the sacred grove phenomenon: a survey approach that compiles brief descriptions of groves from all over India; a reiteration of both the religious and ecological claims made by prominent advocates of groves, especially Gadgil; and a bias toward local, informal institutions in resource management over bureaucratic or governmental ones.

If Gadgil and Vartak's early work exemplifies a trend in Indian environmental writing from the 1970s and 1980s, which laments the imminent extinction of India's vast biodiversity in the face of increasing modernization, the *Down to Earth* special issue is characteristic of a second wave of interest in sacred groves in the 1990s that saw them as paragons of "community participation in environmental management." As Ann Grodzins Gold and others have shown, in the 1990s nongovernmental organizations and funding sources such as UNESCO found themselves disappointed by the inefficiency of the "bloated" postcolonial state and consequently saw great promise in development projects designed to catalyze local energies.[6] Such interest in grassroots environmental action, particularly with respect to forests, converged with the Indian Forest Service's policy shift in favor of Joint Forest Management, as articulated in the comprehensive National Forest Policy of 1988. Present-day inheritors of the discourse around sacred groves initiated by Gadgil and Vartak tend to eschew the preoccupation with the pristine nature of the forest or the supposedly primitive religiosity that protects them but remain interested in the ways in which they believe community participation turns on the precise linkage between cultural practices and ecology of the grove.[7]

As Gold notes, the tide of discourse celebrating the ability of communities to preserve patches of apparently pristine forest in sacred groves against significant odds was met almost immediately with a surge of criticism decrying such assessments as overly romanticized, naïve, and, at worst, deluded.[8] For example, M. A. Kalam, an anthropologist at the University of Madras, analyzed sacred forests in the Kodagu region of Karnataka (formerly known as the Coorg) over a long period (1886–1985) and concluded that it was not "fear and faith," or any religious sentiments, that preserved sacred groves from exploitation. The most significant factor leading to the conservation or destruction of groves was whether they were under the supervision of the Forest Department (which tended to support their conservation) or the Revenue Department (which tended to support their destruction in favor of cultivating more economically valuable species). When economic pressures were high enough, the policing function of the state or the local community weak enough, and the groves accessible enough (by virtue of terrain or the construction of roads), sacred groves rapidly fell to the axe. Most significantly, Kalam found that the Revenue Department interpreted people's inability to defend the groves against encroachment as evidence that they no longer harbored any religious sentiments toward them, which legitimated delisting them from protection and opened the way to coffee cultivation, timber production, and so forth.[9]

Other skeptics have questioned the representation of communities that maintain the groves as inherently ecological. For example, J.R. Freeman's 1999 analysis of sacred groves, called *kavus* in Kerala, takes issue with this view of forest-dwelling tribals and low castes by highlighting the agonistic relationship between humans and nature envisioned in local religion. This is epitomized in the centrality of hunting in the rituals surrounding *kavus*. Such rituals dramatize the necessity of forcefully wresting the produce of the forest from (other) tribals, animals, or demonic godlings.[10] The main target in such critiques seems to be a romanticized view of an internally harmonious village or tribal "community," whose inherent ecological wisdom enables them to live in a sustainable balance with their natural resource base. It is more likely that low population pressure has been a more significant factor. The romanticists' view, it was argued, was uncritically accepted by nongovernmental organizations and academics who looked toward sacred groves as an exemplary form of traditional community natural resource management. The anthropologist Kay Milton has called this tendency to view nonindustrialized peoples as inherently environmentally friendly "the myth of primitive ecological wisdom," and, it should be noted, it is by no means confined to India.[11]

Another important line of criticism explicitly took up the scientific substance of the claims advanced by Gadgil and Vartak about the ecological value of groves.[12] In an important 2006 essay, biologists Claude Garcia and J.-P. Pascal drew on extensive research conducted among groves in the Kodagu region of Karnataka to question the promotion of sacred groves as ideal forms of forest conservation. They conceded that sacred groves in the region they studied had conservation value when "considered as a network" insofar as they preserved species of plants not found elsewhere.[13] But they marshalled evidence about floristic composition to demonstrate that a neighboring state forest, the Brahmagiri Wildlife Sanctuary, had actually been more effective in preserving a broad diversity of tropical species, especially endemic species. In the state-run Wildlife Sanctuary, human interference was more strictly controlled, and the canopy, as a result, was more intact. In contrast, all the sacred groves they studied bore traces of human interference that led to openings in the canopy (rebutting the claim that religious sentiments lead to effective forest protection). Garcia and Pascal's focus is on debunking the widespread characterization of sacred groves as "pristine" and "virgin" remnants of ancient forests in order to challenge the assumption that goes along with this view, namely, that sacred groves should be preserved because they have high conservation value. Moreover, their argument had a political edge as well. By showing that a state-run wildlife refuge harbored more rare and endemic species than the disturbed sacred groves in the area, they challenged those who held up sacred groves as evidence that "the people" equipped with local knowledge could be more effective than state-based schemes guided by science.

Garcia and Pascal's research challenges the assumption that sacred groves merit special conservation efforts because they preserve intact forest. But several of Gadgil and Vartak's other claims regarding the environmental benefits of groves remain, in my view, largely untouched. Depending on their size and location, sacred groves often do have a positive impact on water resources because of their sponge-like networks of roots. Although they may not have much value for wild animals that require large, uninterrupted territories to thrive, flying animals such as birds and insects benefit from sacred groves, as do farmers whose adjacent fields are pollinated by them. As I discuss at length in the next chapter, restoration ecologists, conservation biologists, botanists, and those interested in the medicinal properties of indigenous plants have found sacred groves very useful as seed banks for species not found elsewhere, as Gadgil and Vartak argued they would. In addition, as Garcia and Pascal themselves recognize, the ecological significance of groves varies enormously from region to region. In areas where large swathes of protected habitat exist in the form of wildlife reserves or well-managed state forests, perhaps sacred groves do not have as much value for biodiversity conservation. But in the densely populated plains and coastal areas of Tamil Nadu, where even the state-based reserves are badly degraded, sacred groves have considerable ecological value.

One difficulty that remains unresolved in the debate between advocates and skeptics of traditional community–based conservation, such as that said to characterize sacred groves, has to do with determining the baseline that best represents how an undisturbed forest should appear. Even if a wide variety of different species are found in a particular forest, indicating rich biodiversity, how does one know whether that combination of species is typical of the "intact" forest? This is a problem that raises philosophical as well as practical issues. Given the dynamism of all ecosystems over time, and given the ubiquity of human involvement in ecosystems all over the planet, what combination of organisms, at what point in time, constitutes the "ideal" or "climax" or "undisturbed" formation for that place? In mountainous areas there are sometimes remote forests that have not experienced a great deal of human interference. In densely populated coastal areas or on the plains, it is much more difficult to locate examples of the pristine forest to represent the ideal. Much of the reason that sacred groves in the Pondicherry area have attracted so much attention from botanists is that they do represent some of the best examples of intact forest in the region.

Environmental History of the Coromandel Coast

The districts of Cuddalore and Villupuram were once the eastern edge of the sprawling South Arcot district, but over time they were divided into smaller administrative units. In this densely populated region, every square meter of open land is put to use, whether for agriculture, construction, or active grazing; as a result, the landscape is almost entirely deforested save for exogenous casuarina (*Casuarina equisetfolia*) and eucalyptus plantations.[14] The region has been a center of Tamil civilization—and hence of people making use of natural resources—for centuries. During the Pallava period (4th to 9th centuries) it was part of the Tondaimandalam, a cultural region organized around the Pallava capital at Kānchi (Conjeeveram, Kanchipuram), and connected to the world by oceanic trading networks

that extended from Rome to Southeast Asia. In the 9th century, it
came under Chola rule (9th to 13th centuries), where it became a global
pearl-fishing center, attracting the interest of European explorers such as
Marco Polo. Its main population center today, Pondicherry (Puducherry),
played a role in the 18th-century power struggles between empires in
south India, during which it passed hands between the French and the
English several times before the Treaty of Paris of 1814 made it a French
territory. So Pondicherry remained, a small island of French influence surrounded by areas governed first by the English East India Company, then
the British Crown, and finally the independent Indian nation, until it was
officially made a territory of India in 1954.

The gradual settling and conversion to agriculture in the area took
place over centuries, but a dramatic acceleration of the pace of deforestation began in 1826 when Josiah Marshall Heath, a retired officer of the
Madras Civil Service, founded the Porto Novo Iron Works some 50 kilometers to the south. Such was the East India Company's eagerness to
compete with Swedish iron manufacturers that it not only granted Heath
the exclusive privilege of manufacturing iron using European methods of
smelting, but it also gave him free access to any amount of fuel he needed
from government land.[15] The factory produced large quantities of pig iron
used as ballast in ships bringing cotton and tea to England, but it struggled financially throughout its existence. One problem was its inefficiency.
According to economic historian P. P. Pillai, Heath's plant required 3.75
tons of charcoal to produce each ton of pig iron.[16] "As the jungles diminished," stated the 1908 *Imperial Gazetteer*, "charcoal for smelting had to
be brought from longer distances, and the working expenses became too
heavy to allow of any profit."[17] Even with numerous loans and the take-over
of the company by the East India Company, the iron works failed to make
money. The enterprise finally ceased operations in 1867, after forty-one
years of intensive use of the surrounding forests.

Another surge in deforestation occurred with the construction of the
East Coast Road, which connects the metropolis of Chennai with tourist and
commercial centers along the Coromandel Coast (e.g., Mammalapuram/
Mahabalipuram, Pondicherry, MGM Dizzee World). Given the size and quality of the road (a two-lane, divided toll road), the impact of deforestation is com-
parably larger than that described in the previous chapter on Tiruvannamalai.
Completed in 1998, the East Coast Road connecting Chennai to Cuddalore
was built with assistance from an Asian Development Bank loan as part
of a planned 732-kilometer road from Chennai to Kanyakumari.[18] Other

important factors in the modern-day denudation of indigenous forests in the region have been the ongoing conversion of forested land to agriculture, the creation of eucalyptus and casuarina plantations, and lignite mining in Neyveli. Taken together with the burgeoning population, these factors place considerable stress on the remaining forest cover.

The region was once quite densely forested. Indeed, in a tantalizing reference to what the region might once have been like, the name "Arcot" is said to come from āṟu kāṭu or "six forests," referring to the abodes of six Vedic rishis.[19] Scientists at the French Institute in Pondicherry, particularly the late V. M. Meher-Homji, have conducted pioneering studies of the geological and botanical history of the region. They have found that the soils of the region are generally red ferralitic, a sandy red soil that drains easily but needs considerable manure and mulch to retain fertility. The vegetation in this region is unique. Characterized as tropical dry evergreen forest (TDEF), it thrives in areas with biseasonal rainfall followed by a considerably longer dry season that lasts about six months of the year. TDEFs largely contain hardy, small-leaved evergreen species, many of them with thorns and spines, along with some deciduous species. Such forests are also characterized by a distinctive two- (and sometimes three-) layered structure, with one layer of plants in the 8- to 10-meter range in height (about 26 to 32 feet) and another in the 4- to 7-meter range (13 to 23 feet). Due to deforestation and the steady conversion of forested land to agriculture and grazing lands over the past two centuries, only fragments of TDEFs remain. Aside from state-run reserve forests, the only places they can be found are in sacred groves, where a complex web of religious beliefs and taboos limits human intervention. Elsewhere in the region, natural vegetation has become very sparse; even the 230-hectare (about 568-acre) Marakkanam Reserve Forest has been reduced to a scrub woodland. Most sacred groves, on the other hand, exhibit a two-layered forest canopy structure with considerable species diversity and stand density.[20]

Botany and Belief: Social, Economic and Religious Factors in the Preservation or Degradation of Three Sacred Groves

Interestingly, whenever I talked to people who maintained these forested shrines, ecological issues were usually quite far from their minds. Residents of villages in the Pondicherry who maintained sacred groves generally knew that the forest were interesting to botanists. My interviews almost always included some mention of students, professors, and even foreigners like myself passing through to do "research" (using the English word) on the forest. But generally the priests, village headmen, and ordinary villagers and devotees with whom I spoke did not know the names of many of the plants, nor were they much interested in them. What fascinated them and me as a scholar of religion were the gods who presided over these shady groves far from the village center. As in Madurai and Tiruvannamalai, the deities whose temples or shrines were located in forests were all guardian deities (*kāvalteyvaṅkaḷ, pātukāppu teyvaṅkaḷ*) who were kept away from the village center because of their angry nature. The aversion of these "wicked" gods (*tuṣṭateyvaṅkaḷ*) to ordinary domestic life and the inevitable pollution (*tīṭṭu*) it entails was conveyed here in the proverbial expression that the deities should not hear the sound of the mortar and pestle (*ural-ulukkai*), as in Madurai. The majority of the forest-dwelling gods in this region are local forms of Ayyanar, a horse-riding hunter-warrior god who patrols the boundaries of the settlement at night attended by *veerans*, visually expressive "heroes" whose fierce masculinity is embodied in their massive hands, curling moustaches, and enormous clubs or spears. As in Madurai, the imagery of the forested shrines in Pondicherry region is reminiscent of the 18th-century Poligar (*pāḷaiyakkārar*) era described in chapter 1, when chieftains attached to armed forts governed the area with a kind of rough justice. While they settled disputes and meted out punishment for crimes, they also collected protection money in exchange for not raiding the horses and cattle of the peasants in their domain.

While these deities need to be treated with caution, they are also loyal protectors. At almost all of the shrines I visited, informants reported instances of property recovered and/or thieves punished when the devotees submitted to the deity a *cīṭṭu* (from the English word, "chit," a petition written on a piece of paper) describing the crime or loss, affixing the paper to the god's weapon or the leg of one of his horses. A young man in the village of Sentirankillai gave the following account of such a story:

> Firstly, someone's things were missing in Periya kumiti, so he came here and put *cīṭṭu*. And this god went and tortured the thief. His friends came and told the man, "You remove the *cīṭṭu*." But he refused. They then went to a sorcerer and he advised them to break off the legs and hands of the god. With that idea, the men came here and broke

everything and threw it all around. But what He did, with His power, He killed them one by one. (Field Notes, January 4, 2007)

Such willingness to exercise power on behalf of their devotees makes these deities excellent *kulateyvam*s (lit. "family/lineage gods"). Whether local resident or far-flung émigré, devotees typically return to the temple of their *kulateyvam* for the god's annual festival and to conduct or announce important life cycle rituals. The groves are thus frequently a backdrop for rituals such as the ear-piercing and head-shaving ceremony for new children and the presentation of wedding invitations, both of which are key opportunities to expresses gratitude to the god (accompanied by sacrifice of a goat or chicken) (figure 3.1).

FIGURE 3.1 The guardian deity Veerabhadran, Puttupattu sacred grove, Villupuram district

Sacred groves here as elsewhere are closely linked to social and property relations at the local level. One of the simplest reasons people do not cut the trees in them is that they belong to the deity, which people everywhere stressed repeatedly. But, because the god cannot speak directly, humans must manage the property. Sacred groves thus represent a vestige of a once prevalent variety of collective property ownership, in which the community as a whole owns and manages property for the common good. Antiromanticist scholars such as J. R. Freeman argue that such commonly owned property is rarely governed in an equitable fashion, but rather its produce is distributed according to local power relations. I would agree that in many cases the influence of village hierarchies are clearly discernable in the management of temple forest. But while the distribution of resources is not as equitable as rosy-tinted stereotypes of "the village" lead one to hope, nor is it as venal as some might fear. Indeed, as formerly oppressed groups in Tamil society gain greater power through education and politics, they are challenging some of the most egregious forms of unfairness that shape the management of temple resources.

The following sections describe three sacred groves in two districts: Cuddalore to the south of Pondicherry and Villupuram to the north. Over the course of a week in January of 2007, my field assistant Thavamani and I set forth in a rented Ambassador clutching a hand-drawn map, sketched for us by M. P. Ramanujam, a botanist at the Centre for Post-Graduate Studies in Pondicherry who has conducted extensive research on sacred groves in the region. On the road from Pondicherry to Cuddalore district, one sees everywhere the result of the extensive resource extraction that has been integral to the history of this area for centuries. Yet one also gains a strong sense of the remoteness of these villages. For several days, we were among the few cars we saw anywhere. In the absence of cars, tractors, bullock carts, trucks, and motorbikes plied the road, along with many pedestrians. On the main road between the industrial city of Cuddalore and Mutloor, we passed several factories in the scrubby "waste-land" areas unsuitable for cultivation: Their signs read Pioneer, Cipcot Ltd., Tancot, Chemplast Saman Ltd., Arkemo Peroxides, India Ltd., Bayer Medicals, and Hemalaya Hi-Tech Solutions. The sign for the latter, a small hi-tech company, indicates that some of the "new" India has made inroads here, as do the signs advertising "Internet cafes" (tea shops with computers for rent) in many villages. But after seeing dozens and dozens of men and women stooped over in fields or bearing heavy head loads along the roadside, the main impression one gets is of the back-breaking work involved in rice cultivation, in which workers labor all day for a daily wage of just 25 rupees (US$0.56 cents in January 2007) for women and 50 rupees (US$1.12) for men.

Kuzhandaikkuppam Sri Ayyanar

Ramanujam's hand-drawn map led us first to Kuzhandaikkuppam, a village of about 200 Vanniyar families 41 kilometers south of Pondicherry in Cuddalore district. Here, just outside the village, a 1.5-hectare (3.7-acre) grove encircles a tiny open-air shrine to Ayyanar.[21] No elaborate structure shelters the deity or his two wives from the rain and the sun; rather, a simple brick-and-mortar arch frames the aniconic stones that represent the deities. The dramatic effect is enhanced by the way one advances toward the shrine via a narrow path through the trees, flanked on one side by a dozen brightly painted votive terracotta horses. Ayyanar and his wives appear enthroned like a sovereign and his queens at the end of a natural "great hall" or *mantapam* (figure 3.2). To get to this from the main tar road into the village, one must pass by Ayyanar's ferocious bodyguard, Kadavadi Veeran (*Katavaṭi Vīraṇ,* lit. "door-servant Hero"). With armed

FIGURE 3.2 Lord Ayyanar in state, at the end of a row of votive terracotta horses, Kuzhandaikkuppam sacred grove, Cuddalore district

soldiers standing on either side of him, the veeran faces yet another figure, the *Tōṭṭiparaiyaṇ*, a village servant from a long-past age of Dalit servi-
tude, whose duty was to carry messages from village to village and herald
the arrival of important visitors (figure 3.3). The whole tableau evokes the
Poligar era, an impression confirmed by devotees' vivid stories of Ayyanar's
nightly patrols on horseback with his entourage of warriors and servants.

   From a botanical point of view, the small grove surrounding this
Ayyanar shrine is in relatively intact condition. In 1996, Pondicherry
University–based botanists N. Parthasarathy and R. Kartikeyan counted
1,367 individual species of plants whose girth at breast height was at least 10
centimeters, representing forty-two different species of woody plants. The
total basal area was 15.44 m²ha⁻¹ (in other words, 15.44 square centimeters

FIGURE 3.3 Kadavadi Veeran, Kuzhandaikkuppam sacred
grove, Cuddalore district

per square meter consisted of the woody trunks of trees, averaged over the forest plot, where the basal area for relatively intact dry tropical forests ranges between 17 and 40 $m^2 ha^{-1}$).[22] Today one can see that in places where human traffic is greatest, the forest canopy is open, but mostly one observes the two-layered canopy typical of TDEFs. There is also a small tank (artificial pond) adjacent to the grove. When I visited the grove with Thavamani that late afternoon in January, we saw a mongoose scurrying along the edge of the tank and disturbed innumerable birds and butterflies during our walk in the forest. Later, gathering with a half-dozen residents in one of the simple, mud-walled houses in the town, we learned that the only permitted use of forest produce is the collection of dead wood for cooking *ponkal* (a type of rice porridge typically offered to deities), although we had seen some evidence that herders brought their goats here to graze as well. Nonetheless, such is the community's dedication to the deity that, rather than convert some of the god's forest to productive use, residents of the four villages connected to this shrine contributed 500 rupees a year per household to finance their annual festival.

We were told that each village has its own festival in honor of the village goddess (usually Mariyamman) who resides at its center and watches over the internal affairs of the hamlet. Before the festival can start, a party comes to perform *ponkal* at the forested Ayyanar shrine, thus formally inviting him to take part in the celebration. At this time, villagers also decorate a clay pot filled with water, flowers, and red kumkum powder; they place a coconut ringed with green leaves in the pot's neck to seal it. This is the *karakam*, an essential element of Tamil ritual life. It is the vessel into which the deity descends before it is carried on the head of the entranced person who embodies, or "dances," Lord Ayyanar during the procession from the shrine to the village. Worshipped as a movable icon of the deity (like the *cāmiyāti* god-dancer himself), the *karakam* is present during all the intensely emotional moments of ritual possession that punctuate the village's annual celebration of itself and the vital forces that help it to thrive.

The groves' relatively intact condition can be linked to several factors, including its distance from any main highway. But another factor is surely the coordination among the four villages guarded by this Ayyanar. While the segmentary structure of the villages is suggested by the fact that each village performs its own annual festival, the villages also cooperate by, for instance, collectively sponsoring a new statue for Kadavadi Veeran, complete with cement platform and corrugated tin roof. Residents in Kuzhandaikkuppam told us that a ranger visits about once every six months, but otherwise the protection of the forest is entirely in the hands of locals. When I suggested that perhaps, because their lives were so hard, they might simply take some land from the forest for cultivation, the group I was speaking to responded with such vehemence I had to take back what I said, which was interpreted as a direct exhortation. "That's it, our whole family will die!" exclaimed one woman. "That belongs only to the temple," said the man next to her. "We shouldn't take even a dry stick out of the forest."

One division within the community is, however, very clearly marked: the division between Dalits and non-Dalits. While three of the four villages are dominated by Vanniyars, one is a "colony" (an English word used to refer to the Dalit hamlet located at some distance from a village of non-Dalits, which is linked to the latter by traditional ties of service and ritual obligation). Some years back the colony residents sponsored the construction of their own Kadavadi Veeran, who is almost indistinguishable from the main Kadavadi Veeran except for the fact that he sits in the open air, not sheltered by a corrugated tin shed, and does not have a Tōṭṭiparaiyaṉ drummer standing in front of him (figure 3.4). Though informants were clear that all four villages maintained the forested Ayyanar shrine, it was not clear to me if there were occasions when all four, Dalit and non-Dalit, worshipped together. If they did, it would be a rarity indeed. Discrimination against Dalits is legally prohibited in present-day India, but it is alive and well at the local level. At most sacred groves, as at most lineage or village temples not regulated by the state's Hindu Religious and Charitable Endowments Administration Department (HRCE), Dalits are flatly prohibited from entering. The exclusion of Dalits is one of the ramifications of the purity/pollution ideology that accounts for Ayyanar's presence outside the village. As an excitable, quick-to-punish god, he cannot be exposed to tīṭṭu, whether from women (whose pounding of the ural-ulukkai enrages him) or from Dalits (whose traditional occupations as leather-workers, barbers, and midwives put them in touch with ritually polluting substances on a regular basis).

Sentirankillai Sri Muniyappan

At Kuzhandaikkuppam, annual festivals to the village deities were funded entirely by contributions from each house. However, sometimes gods are in possession of lands beyond those demarcated by the grove, income from which may be used to meet the deity's requirements for worship. Whatever property belongs to the deity is then legally held in the name

FIGURE 3.4 Kadavadi Veeran built by Dalit "colony" dwellers, Kuzhandaikkuppam sacred grove, Cuddalore district

of the god him or herself and managed by a committee of trustees. This is the case in Sentirankillai, also in Cuddalore district, a village of 500 Gaunder (Vanniyar) families about 40 kilometers south of Pondicherry. Here, a clan of twelve families, descendants of a shared ancestor, manages a temple to Sri Muniyappan with the help of village representatives, each family leading the management by annual rotation. Asking directions from tea-shop denizens in the village's center, we bumped along a dirt road in our car for a short distance past the village school and cricket field until the road stopped at a couple of thatched huts. Here, a woman cooking in the open air ceased her labors to lead us along a winding path through the forest and across a stream, where we left our sandals, to the main shrine. Located perhaps a 10-minute walk from the village center, the temple is encompassed by approximately 15 hectares of relatively intact forest, which is bordered on all sides by fields and orchards of cashew trees and bisected by a stream.[23]

In villages where Ayyanar is the resident guardian deity, people typically do not tell stories about how he arrived, suggesting he is a truly autochthonous village deity. In this village, however, while Thavamani and I sat in the concrete verandah of the temple, waiting for the heavy wooden doors of the sanctum to open at the auspicious hour so that we could observe the *pūjā*, the elderly priest of this temple was happy to tell the story of how the lineage deity, Sri Muniyappan, arrived in Sentirankillai. Three or four generations ago, Muniyappan came from Utthankarai (Ūttāṅkarai, west of Neyveli) on a hunting expedition. A horse-riding deity like Ayyanar, Muniyappan was compelled to stay when his horse died upon reaching the village. The priest described him as a very angry god, who requires food without salt (presumably to keep him calm) and jealously guards both the village and his own perquisites of power. Residents have to walk to a nearby town to grind their rice because every time they install a new belt (*vār*) in their own mill, it breaks. After consulting a medium, the people discovered that Sri Muniyappan himself was breaking the belt, which bore too close a resemblance to his own belt-like whip. This ferocity extends to the deity's entourage. The destructive power of Muniyappan's *kāvalteyvam* Agni Veeran is so intense that its gaze alone burned down the village's "colony" of Dalit laborers, requiring them to erect a statue of another *veeran*, Uthandi (Uttaṇṭi, lit. "one who stands opposite"), to intercept Agni Veeran's inflammatory glance. In the wake of this calamity, or perhaps as a part of the underlying ideology that shapes the need to keep the deity away from ritual pollution, Dalits are categorically excluded from the deity's temple but not the grove itself. "If they come at all," said the pujari, "they stand outside [the temple's concrete verandah] and light camphor, and then go away."

The temple appears to have undergone a fair amount of Sanskritization, although not without resistance, as indicated by a number of features. First, the deity is enclosed in a large concrete temple, the walls of which are painted with scenes from Puranic mythology. We were told that the building was hundreds of years old, but the paintings and verandah were built at the time of the most recent *abhishekham* (reconsecration ceremony) in 1975. On one side of the inner sanctum's wooden door, a painting depicts a sage performing a *yajña* (Vedic fire sacrifice) while Agni, the Vedic god of fire, arises out of the flames. On the other side, Daksha, Shiva, and Parvati (with green skin, like Shiva's consort Meenakshi, in Madurai) appear together in a rare moment of relative harmony. One young man identified the figure of Lord Shiva holding a trident as Sri Muniyappan, indicating that at least some people regarded the horse-riding hunter deity as a local form of the pan-Indian Sanskritic deity. Second, the priest and devotees at the temple described the key event of the ritual calendar as the Lakshadeepam (lit. "one hundred thousand lamps") festival that takes place in the Tamil month of Tai (mid-January to mid-February). At this time, the paths through the forest are all swept, cleared of overgrown plants, and illuminated with oil lamps. The community produces a poster advertising the unique affair, attracting hundreds of devotees and curiosity seekers. Third, at one time, the community, or some faction within it, had hired "Aiyars," Brahman priests, to conduct worship. The deity, however, seemed to have other ideas and drove them away. The non-Brahman pujari at work the day Thavamani and I visited described how Sri Muniyappan first sent his tigers to menace the priests, obstructing their entrance to the temple, and eventually chased them off. As the priest's story suggests, in the midst of these efforts to incorporate Brahmanical mythology and ritual, the temple remains incompletely Sanskritized.

The coexistence of Brahmanical and non-Brahmanical elements of worship is evident in many ways. In addition to the Tai Lakshadeepam, the village conducts an annual festival in Āṭi (mid-July to mid-August, when most village festivals occur) that attracts people connected by ancestral ties to the village from virtually all the major population centers in Tamil Nadu (Chennai, Salem, Putukottai, Aruppukottai, Tanjore, Trichy, Karur, etc.). It lasts fifteen days and includes the more usual events: processions, group offerings of *poṅkal*, and sacrifices of goats and chickens. However, neither festival requires the community to contribute funds, because much of the temple's 19 acres of cultivable land is leased and the revenue is used to support the festivities. Rental income is kept in a "dum" box whose five separate keys are kept by five Nāṭṭāṉmaikkārars (traditional village leaders) to ensure its safe management.

The stories that people told about Lord Muniyappaṉ and his fiery guardian deity suggest that fear of divine wrath is a key factor in protecting the forest. As Sentirankillai resident G. Pillaisami said, "Nobody will come and even break even a twig. That's because of the fear of God. If you cut a tree, that same night you will die." However, how people say they behave and how they actually behave can vary. In addition to fear, community solidarity also enhances people's ability and willingness to enforce the ban on using the forest. "They can cut," said Pillaisami when pressed, "but the whole village will oppose them." There is a complex but direct relationship between the solidarity of the community, its ability to act in unison, and its commitment to the deity who protects them. It seems that to the extent that the community is unified, it can confidently sustain the idea that the forest is the god's property (*contam*); however, as people start to view the forest as belonging not to the god but to powerful village factions or an outside entity, the incentive to poach increases.

Urani Sri Seliyamman

Such is the situation behind the less strictly enforced taboos protecting one of the most extensively studied sacred groves in Tamil Nadu, the Urani Sri Seliyamman (*Celiyamman*) temple (figure 3.5). I was first taken here on the back of a motorbike owned by the Siddha doctor and botanist Dr. Loganathan in July of 2004. On that hot day, we walked through the deserted grove and all around its periphery, where it adjoins rain-fed fields cultivating peanuts, without meeting a soul. Two and a half years later, in the winter of 2006–2007, Thavamani and I returned by bus and

FIGURE 3.5 Sri Seliyamman's temple, Urani sacred grove, Villupuram district

auto-rickshaw to visit Urani and its neighboring Dalit "colony" of Bharati Nagar half a dozen times over the course of a month. Urani is a small village of about forty houses of Naidus and Vanniyars in Villupuram district, located 35 kilometers north of Pondicherry directly off the East Coast Road that connects Chennai and Pondicherry. The village has experienced considerable population loss over the past twenty years, as residents have migrated to nearby cities. Much of the open land around the village, once used for rain-fed crops like peanuts, has been converted into prawn hatcheries and commercial tree plantations. The elderly traditional village leaders, the *Nāṭṭāṇmaikkārars*, have long managed the temple's considerable property. But, as I describe below, the widows of a rival lineage to the current village leaders seem to take the greatest initiative in organizing worship at the Seliyamman temple.

As we sat on the threshold of the house of one Nāṭṭāṇmaikkārar, Saktivel, its tile roof sheltering us from the sun's hot glare, he told us how around 1966 the village replaced the goddess's wooden hut with a cement building, after the old one had burned down repeatedly. Today, they annually auction off the use-value of palmyra trees growing on temple land, and they have recently sold some land to a prawn rancher from outside the village to raise money for the construction of a new Pillaiyar (Ganesh) temple in the village center. Some time back, the Dalit residents of the Urani "colony," a neighboring hamlet called Bharati Nagar, demanded and won a share of the Seliyamman temple property after bringing their case before the panchayat. They now separately auction the use-value of 50 percent of the temple's palmyra trees to support their own ritual needs. Residents of Bharati Nagar collect dry wood for fuel from Sri Seliyamman's forest, but the practice is somewhat controversial. In Urani, the fact that colony dwellers collected wood was taken for granted, though the Nāṭṭāṇmaikkārar feared that it was causing the "thinning" of the forest. Thavamani and I visited Bharati Nagar the last Sunday in December, locating the thatched palmyra-roof hut of one its young leaders, G. Rubadarshan, at the far end of a shady coconut grove. As we sat in his courtyard waiting for him to return from an errand, residents gathered around and answered our questions about Sri Seliyamman and her forest. One man observed that the forest was growing over time and that the taboos limiting use of the forest stipulated that one should not cut green trees with a knife but could collect the dry wood. "If you cut the trees," he said, "the forest will be destroyed. There are lots of creatures inside. Birds and animals are there. As it is cleared [lit. "lets more light in"], the birds will not stay." When we asked further about collecting fuel wood, it seemed some families could do so without fear of the goddess, while others could not. As the young up-and-coming Dalit politician we had come to see, Rubadarshan, reported,

> If someone goes and collects firewood, nothing will happen. If my family collects [wood] and puts in the fire, that same night the Amma [Mother goddess] will come in our dream. Otherwise she will do something bad. That is for our family. For others, even from olden days, they break and nothing happens. One night, me and that man [pointing to a man standing nearby] we could not carry a log that was too heavy. So we used a knife to cut it, came home and shared the firewood. My work is climbing [coconut] trees. The next morning, when I went to collect the coconuts, a coconut fell [from a great height] on my hand. It broke into two pieces. Then I went to the hospital and was cured. Like this, I've experienced lots of punishments [tantanai].

The goddess's sanctioning of some families but not others for breaking taboos in the village seems to suggest a kind of intimacy or connection with the goddess that only some possess.

The rituals and myths surrounding the annual *tiruvila* (or village deity festival) convey key information about both the sociology of the village and the nature of the deity who occupies the grove. The festival in Urani had been cancelled a few times over the years, victim to both internal squabbling and the increasing poverty of the village residents. Lately the festival has been performed in a suitably grand style, but the expenses are borne largely by wealthy migrants to Chennai with ancestral ties to the village. Four deities are actually honored in Urani's annual festival: three sisters—Seliyamman, Gangaiyamman, Muttalamman (another name for Māriyamman, the Tamil small pox goddess)—and a male guardian deity for Seliyamman, Kattuvaraiyan (Kaṭṭuvaraiyaṉ, also known as Potturājā). At the annual festival, three *karakam*s are prepared for the deities and are carried in procession by the designated *cāmiyāṭi*s ("god-dancer," an inherited position, often reserved for the most elite male members of the village), while an enormous knife (*katti*) is wielded by the *cāmiyāṭi* for Kattuvaraiyan. At the start of the festival, Seliyamman must be summoned from a small forested area at the outskirts of the village. This tiny patch of trees with its unadorned stone, now surrounded by a eucalyptus plantation, is Seliyamman's natal home, from which she is borne into the village accompanied by a line of devotees holding her *varicai*, plates of feminine offerings like a comb, mirror, and sari, along with flowers, fruit, and incense. The drama enacted is that Seliyamman is a bride brought to the village by her family, who bear the traditional gifts given by a bride's family to the groom's at several junctures in a woman's life (puberty, marriage, and even after the wife's death). Although she is ritually treated like a beloved bride, the stories told about Seliyamman reveal her fierce nature. During our numerous visits to Urani, Thavamani and I heard two stories, which, though different, contain similar motifs evoking both the goddess's seemingly vulnerable femininity and her sensitivity to boundary transgression.

Gayatri, a widow belonging to the lineage currently out of power in the village, told of Seliyamman becoming the object of affection of a roaming low-caste bangle seller. After a series of increasingly impertinent advances, he "had a bad thought" and entered her house. When he crossed the threshold, "What She did," said Gayatri, "She tore him into two parts. One part She stamped upon, the other part She threw all the way to the lakeshore." Saktivel, the seventy-one-year-old current Nattanmaikkarar, who belonged to a different lineage, told the story slightly differently, with an even more hostile edge toward lower castes. The lustful male intruder in his version was a young man named Ayyanar, "from the SC community" (i.e., from the Scheduled Castes, a Dalit). He won a boon from the goddess but then immediately turned the boon against her and made her his slave. Each day she was made to plant 60 acres of paddy in the morning and thresh 60 acres at night. After some time, Mutthalamman came to see her older sister (*akka*) and, after enduring Seliyamman's reproaches for not coming sooner, concocted a rescue plan. When the SC slave-master came to the door calling (in disrespectful terms), "Come here! *Vā ṭi!*", Seliyamman stayed quietly inside. He called again, "*Vā ṭi!*", but still she didn't open her mouth. When he crossed the threshold to come in, Mutthalamman tore him apart. The theme of harsh punishment meted out on a desirous male intruder who inappropriately crosses a threshold is an apt one for the village guardian. As the guardian of the village and the forest, Seliyamman's role is to repel threatening outsiders, whether ghosts, disease, famine, or thieves (just like Ayyanar or Muniyappan in other villages). Told from the point of view of village elites, these stories represent the goddess in opposition to low-caste figures, and thus in a way validate their social dominance. Yet she is also revered by the Dalit residents of Bharati Nagar, who claim that their right to consider her their lineage deity (*kulateyvam*) was wrongfully stolen when they were made "slaves" (*aṭimai*) generations ago. As such, Sri Seliyamman has become a focal point around whom power relations are being negotiated between the traditional elites of the village and upwardly mobile Dalits, newly empowered by education and local electoral politics.

As mentioned previously, the exclusion of Dalits from sacred groves is regarded as part of the complex practices that prevent the forest gods' exposure to ritual pollution, which also includes the ban on wearing chappals, on women who are menstruating or postparturition, and on postcoital men and women. In some groves, Dalits do worship, but, as at Kuzhandaikkuppam and Urani, they do so separately and with some restrictions. Thavamani and I were witness to a fascinating moment that captured the dynamism of religious practices surrounding sacred groves in contemporary India, where supposedly age-old and inviolable customs are undergoing modification. We were present one night for a *pūjā* at the Sri Seliyamman temple in Urani sponsored by Rubadarshan (the ambitious Dalit polician from Bharati Nagar who had recently won an election), where both the continued salience and the persistent contestation of social boundaries based on caste were made clear.

We arrived in the early evening on December 26, 2007, to observe the preparation of the goddess for worship and watched as a stream of bats flew out of the deity's concrete sanctuary for a full five minutes. While Sarojammal, the widow of one of the village traditional leaders, took charge of bathing and decorating the temple's main image to Sri Seliyamman, the non-Brahman pujari she had hired to conduct daily worship during the Tamil month of Margazhi (mid-December to mid-January) prepared the pillar and trident just outside the temple. Called "The One Who Stands Opposite," the pillar bore a figure of a seated woman on the side facing the temple, and this was the goddess's "guardian" or "vehicle," whose role it was to catch and moderate the goddess's potentially destructive gaze. Working separately and with exquisite care, they first bathed the images in multiple layers of liquids—water, milk, yogurt, turmeric, and coconut water (rose water was, unfortunately, not available)—then covered them lightly with bright yellow turmeric paste and adorned them with red dots of *kumkum*. Watching the two work illuminated by a single electric bulb, I felt keenly the care given to these deities through this kind of Brahmanical worship. That it was being delivered with more affection than fear suggests the "softening," at least by some village factions, of this *tuṣṭateyvam*, "fierce" or "angry" goddess. Maybe it was the dim light or the quiet, given the fact that there was no amplified music as at most urban *pūjās*, but it was one of the most beautiful *abhisekhams* I have ever attended—calm, purposeful, with a definite measured pace. Over time, people from the village of Urani began to trickle in, taking their seats on the verandah of the concrete sanctuary. Then, the sponsoring Dalit politician from Bharati Nagar arrived in white shirt and dhoti, accompanied by a crowd of ten to fifteen relatives and supporters carrying baskets with camphor and a huge flower garland for the goddess.

At first, in the casual movement of the crowd, it was easy to miss the fact that none of the Dalit devotees from Bharati Nagar entered the temple, not even stepping onto the verandah to catch a glimpse (*darśan*) of the goddess within. Then, as the high point of the *pūjā* approached, the Urani residents called me and Thavamani inside to join the two rows of worshippers flanking the goddess, standing with palms together. Outside, the devotees from Bharati Nagar stood holding their palms together in two rows on either side of the temple's verandah, just beyond the goddess's line of vision. It was very strange to me that I, a foreign woman with no caste at all, was asked inside while the others stayed outside. Yet the boundary between touchable and untouchable seemed clear to everyone. Even the sponsor himself gestured for me to go in. Meanwhile, the Dalit *parai* drummers had lit a fire with dried palmyra leaves and heated up their drums. As the three of them drummed loudly to warm things up, the pounding rhythms suffused the temple (figure 3.6). During the offering of the camphor flame that marked the *pūjā*'s final climax, the caste people inside the temple vigorously rang two handbells and struck the bell that hangs from the ceiling of the temple, while outside the drummers' crescendo rose and rose. At last, I had a powerful sensation of the divisions dropping away, at least at the level of sound, as the music merged into a single vibration of praise going up to the goddess.

The very real social boundaries within the community are, however, clearly reflected in the ecological state of the grove. At the core lies 1.8 hectares (4.4 acres) of well-preserved forest. But around this core are 3.2 hectares (almost 8 acres) of relatively degraded forest, where a thinning canopy has allows the growth of thickets (probably caused by extensive lopping).[24] Still, in the intact core the two-layered forest canopy is dense and tall with trees averaging 8 meters in height.[25] The canopy in the core has few openings aside from a 3- to 4-meter-wide path that runs straight through the length of the grove, which the temple committee recently paved with tar. In about 2000, Ramanujam and Kadamban found thirty

FIGURE 3.6 *Parai* drummers outside Sri Seliyamman's Temple, Urani sacred grove, Villupuram district

different kinds of woody species, a stand density of 1,070 individuals per hectare with a girth at breast height of at least 20 centimeters and a basal area of 25.55 m^2 ha^{-1}.[26] Local residents are aware that the goddess's grove harbors species of plants not found anywhere else, as well as plants with great medicinal value, which is not surprising given the number of botanists who have conducted field studies at Urani. But no one I spoke with said they themselves used the plants for medicine. Changes to the grove have taken many forms, from the partial paving of the dirt path through the forest to the appearance of vans bearing students from Pondicherry University and motorbikes carrying entrepreneurial gatherers of medicinal herbs. As the pūjā in which Thavamani and I participated suggests, changes are also taking place at the level of worship, as internal conflict among the village leaders and the emigration of males has created a power vacuum that women and others traditionally marginalized or excluded from sacred groves seem eager to fill.

Given all these changes and the pervasive atmosphere of conflict within the village, not to mention the temptations to sell land to enterprising outsiders, I can perhaps be excused for doubting whether the forest would survive for the course of my fieldwork. When I first visited Urani in the summer of 2004 with Dr. Loganathan, the only person we could find to speak with on an unbearably hot afternoon was a woman who did not really want to talk to us. Citing numerous reasons why she had to go (to prepare the evening meal, to send a message to a neighbor, etc.), she finally spoke with bitterness about a team of men who came in a yellow van, investigated the forest, took plants or seeds away in bags, and sprayed yellow paint on the trees. These marks had been obvious to me too when I walked through the forest earlier with Dr. Loganathan. I assumed, with a sense of dread, that they were left by foresters selecting trees for harvest. Yet when I returned to Urani two and a half years later, the temple and its surrounding grove were still there. The village was still riven with conflict but members had, once again, successfully pulled off a grand annual festival. It seems the people I had assumed were forest contractors were actually students and professors from Pondicherry University, engaged in their work of studying the forest with perhaps a little more sense of ownership over Sri Seliyamman's forest than was warranted.

One important conclusion to draw from these three groves is that Sanskritization can coexist with relatively intact forests. The botanical observations taken from the sacred groves of Urani and Sentirankillai, where village guardian and lineage deities have been partially Sanskritized, suggests that the construction of temples and the introduction of Brahmanical rituals does not necessarily entail complete clearing of the forest. In addition, Sanskritization did not introduce Brahmanical ideas of purity and pollution into previously harmonious, integrated villages. Indeed, as the example of Urani indicates, the social hierarchies legitimated by purity/pollution discourse were well entrenched by the time village elites started their campaign to endow the goddess with more *vacatikaḷ* (lit. "facilities," "conveniences") and a higher style of worship. Moreover, as the rising self-assertion of Dalit groups in Urani, and less directly Kuzhandaikkuppam, indicates, purity/pollution discourse does not stop low castes from making claims on the deities and the deities' property, seeking to tap sources of income and divine power to support their own aspirations. Such

developments make the arrangements governing the use of forest produce more complicated, but they are opening up new possibilities for worship and perhaps alliances with outsiders.

Puttupattu: From Sacred Termite Mound to Regional Pilgrimage Temple

About 19 kilometers south of Urani on the East Coast Road one finds the
best-known sacred grove in the region, Puttupattu, which is presided over
by a form of Ayyanar known as Sri Manjaneswarar Ayyanarappan (Śri
Mañcaṉīśvarar Ayyaṉārappaṉ). Though I had driven past the rusted sign
for it many times on my way from Chennai to Pondicherry, I had never
really noticed it. I entered the sanctum for the first time with Dr. Loganathan
in July of 2001. Though I was used to open-air shrines, Puttupattu was
remarkable in its extent, 18 hectares in area. I had gone many times before
I finally found someone to walk me around its full perimeter, which took
a good 30 minutes. Recognized for its ecological value as early as 1986 by
V. M. Meher-Homji, today Puttupattu is celebrated by devotees as the place
where Ayyanarappan was conceived from the miraculous coupling of Shiva
and Mohini (Vishnu in his female form).[27] Here Ayyanar, the prototypical
village protector, has been thoroughly assimilated with Ayyappan, another
son of Vishnu and Shiva with close ties to the pan-Indian Sanskritic tradition.[28] Though Ayyappan's ascetic bachelorhood and penchant for meditation make him an unlikely candidate for a merger with the twice-married
martial god Ayyanar, it appears their shared birth-story makes this possible. The process of converting a village deity to a Sanskritic pan-Indian
deity has been facilitated by the transfer of temple management from
Kizhputtupattu village to the Tamil Nadu government's HRCE.

While botanists measure forests in terms of forest canopy, basal area,
and stems per meter, nonspecialist village residents spoke more often
about the forest's "thickness." Residents of the area with whom I spoke
reported that the forest used to be very thick. A forty-nine-year-old gardener at a guesthouse I stayed in recalled that when he was a boy the deity
enshrined in the Puttupattu forest served only as a lineage and guardian
deity for residents of Kizhputtupattu, the adjacent Vanniyar-dominated
village. People did not even enter the forest to worship, it was so dense
and forbidding and the deity so frightening. If one happened to cross Lord
Ayyanar's path while he was out hunting at night, one would be struck
down by a mysterious illness known as *canti pātai* (literally "cross roads

path") characterized by severe vomiting, diarrhea, stomach pain, and fatigue in legs and hands. Residents of the area testify that for many years there was no built structure indicating a main shrine, although a termite mound associated with the deity may have served as a locus of devotional attention, along with a nearby pond considered sacred.[29] There was no road leading through the shrine either but simply a path, which another local resident said was so narrow and thickly lined with trees that one had to walk along it in a crouch. But as the fame of the temple grew, more and more people came to regard this Ayyanar as their own. Several visitors I interviewed in the winter of 2006–2007 said that even though they were not from the village of Kizhputtupattu, this Ayyanar was their lineage deity. One man recalled that in his youth he and his relatives would come on bullock cart in large groups of families, spending three days in the forest cooking, camping, and conducting worship for the deity. The men would carry stout staves to defend themselves against thieves and wild animals. In a manner typical of lineage and guardian deity worship, people would bring terracotta horses to dedicate to Lord Ayyanar in fulfillment of vows made to obtain the boon of children.

The deity's reputation for ensuring fertility seems to have attracted devotees from an ever-larger catchment area, so that around 1974 it came under the administration of the HRCE.[30] This government branch regulates public temples through an appointed governing board that is responsible for supervising construction projects, hiring priests to conduct *pūjās*, and collecting revenue, a portion of which the HRCE then redistributes among all the temples under its supervision. When I first visited the temple in July of 2001, it had already grown to encompass numerous structures. The priests were actively promoting the site as the birthplace of Baby Ayyappan in an open bid to capitalize on the massive growth of the annual pilgrimage to Ayyappan's main shrine in Sabari Malai, Kerala. A dirt road led from the main road, 200 yards from the East Coast Road, into the forest. One passed several subsidiary shrines along the way, including a substantial but open-air shrine to Lord Ayyanarappan's principle guardian deity, Sri Veerabhadran (Śri Vīrabhadran, also known as "Malayattar," lit. "the one from Mayalayam [Kerala]"; see figure 3.1) and the seven Kannimar (virgin goddesses very popular in non-Brahman temples) (figure 3.7). The road through the forest led to a medium-sized stone temple, which constituted the main shrine to Lord Ayyanarappan, an imposing structure complete with compound wall, temple tower, (*kopuram*) and stone-lined inner sanctum (*garbha gṛha*) (figure 3.8). The dirt path around the temple

FIGURE 3.7 Seven Kannimar and Veerans, Puttupattu sacred grove, Villupuram district

FIGURE 3.8 Main entrance to Lord Ayyanarappan temple at Puttupattu sacred grove

wall led to four enormous terracotta horses and what appeared to be the original termite mound, now sheltered from the elements by a corrugated tin roof and festooned with votive cradles hung by grateful devotees in fulfillment of vows made for children. People had tied hundreds of written requests (*cīṭṭu*) around the horses' legs, for example, to find lost objects, to shut the mouth of an enemy, or for the boon of children (figure 3.9).

Since 2001, four new sites have been added to the "must visit" list of subsidiary shrines provided by priests at the main shrine: another termite mound shrine, which is dedicated to an up-and-coming female deity also associated with fertility; Nagattamman (lit. "the goddess of the Naga," or divine serpent), a small concrete temple dedicated to Vinayakar (Ganesh), the pan-Indian deity of auspicious beginnings; a shrine to a wandering *sadhu* who lived for many years on the shore of the pond; and a neglected concrete goddess temple that may still be connected to Kizhputtupattu village.[31] Each year since 2001, I have seen new improvements made to the main shrine. In the summer of 2001, a *mantapam* (a simple roofed

FIGURE 3.9 Lord Ayyanarappan's votive horses, with petitions tied around legs, Puttupattu sacred grove, Villupuram district

platform raised slightly above the ground) had been newly constructed near the main shrine where pilgrims could cook, sleep, and rest during the day. Between 2004 and 2006, metal barriers were erected on the sheltered verandah outside the main shrine to control and direct crowd traffic on festival days, and the ceiling of the verandah's cool sitting area was adorned with painted concrete statues telling the story of the temple. In spite of considerable evidence suggesting that all this construction has taken place in the last twenty to thirty years, the antiquity of the temple is heavily promoted. When I visited in the summer of 2001, the head priest pointed out the stones in the inner sanctum inscribed with what appeared to be antique Grantha script and said the temple was thousands of years old.

As the above description suggests, by now the temple complex is quite large. Though in his main shrine Lord Ayyanarappan is worshipped with complete Brahmanical honors, the more emotionally intense and embodied forms of worship continue to take place in the subsidiary shrines found intermittently through the forest. During my visits since 2001, for example, I have observed families clustered around the shrine to the guardian deity, Sri Veerabhadran, or one of the legs of the enormous terracotta horses, with one member in trance channeling the voice of a lineage deity as the family seeks advice on some troubling issue (unemployment, fertility problems, unusual illness, etc.). The Veerabhadran shrine is also where families sacrifice a goat or chicken to their lineage deity during life-cycle ceremonies. Each of the subsidiary shrines is serviced by a different group of non-Brahman priests, whereas Brahman priests hired and managed by the temple administrative board run the main shrine. The right to run one of these subsidiary shrines is highly lucrative and is auctioned off to different parties who provide ritual services for devotees in exchange for modest fees. Similar to the auctioning of the right to collect forest produce in family- and village-run temples, the government here auctions off the right to collect revenue from these shrines.[32]

Families blessed by Sri Ayyanarappan or one of the deities ensconced in a subsidiary shrine establish a regular relationship with that deity, returning when their children are older for the first haircut and ear-piercing ritual. During the week, just a few such people visit the forested shrines to conduct ritual business such as bringing wedding invitations to announce the happy event to their *kulateyvam*. However, on festival days, particularly during Mondays in the Tamil month of Aṭi, the crowds can reach into the thousands. As at many forested shrines, people can gather dead wood to cook *poṅkal*, but when thousands of devotees come at once, the result is extensive trampling of the understory. Puttupattu's growing fame has greatly increased the level of human interference in the grove. As mentioned previously, elderly devotees recall making the trip to the temple by bullock cart, when priests and pilgrims had to brush aside branches on the narrow path to get to the shrine in the center of the forest. Now a wide dirt road (tar in some places) connects all the subsidiary shrines in the forest. Devotees can freely drive from the East Coast Road all the way up to the main temple gate. On auspicious days (Mondays) when devotees throng the temple complex, many people park their vehicles along the road through the forest, inadvertently widening it still further (figure 3.10).

The impact on the grove of increased vehicle ownership among middle-class Tamils was felt quite keenly one Monday in January, when Thavamani and I visited on New Year's Day. We had gone hoping to find more ordinary devotees to interview, reasoning that a Monday would be a big draw for Ayyanarappan whatever month it was. What we had not anticipated was that so many Tamils would take the first of January as a holiday worthy of a temple excursion. As several devotees put off by the crowds grumpily observed, this itself was a sign of the penetration of Tamil culture by cosmopolitan global culture, since Tamils have tended to be staunchly loyal to the specifically Tamil calendar and its new year holiday, Pongal. Perhaps the most striking aspect of the crowds was the number of vehicles. Two-wheelers (motorcycles and motor scooters) and four-wheelers (sedans, trucks, and SUVs) lined the road through the forest all the way from the East Coast Road to the gate of the main shrine. Of the twenty-three people we interviewed, eleven came by private vehicle (either two-wheeler or car). Of the remainder, three gave no answer or an indeterminate one, six came by bus, and two walked (one from neighboring Kizhputtupattu and one in fulfillment of the vow he had taken in preparation for a longer trek to Sabari Malai, the main shrine of Lord Ayyappan). With all these changes, it is understandable that the taboos associated with the temple have also altered. In a textbook instance of the pattern of degradation through Sanskritization identified by Donald Hughes and M. D. Subhash Chandran, only the main temple remains today as a zone of sacrality: Practices once forbidden throughout the grove are now banned only within the physical temple.[33] Whereas at most sacred groves the boundaries indicating the deity's sanctified domain are marked by the command to remove footwear, here one can wear shoes or sandals all the way up to the gates of the temple. Veeradasan, the long-time pujari,

FIGURE 3.10 Conducting a *pūjā* for a new truck outside of main temple, Puttupattu sacred grove

affirms the forest-god qualities of Ayyanarappan mixed in with the newer Sanskritic mythology when he explains that Ayyanarappan lives in the forest because he should not hear the sound of the *ural* and *ulakkai*. Indeed, he is so hot-tempered and averse to domesticity that even the sound of mustard seeds popping in hot oil annoys him. But this is so only within the walls of the temple. Beyond that, says Veeradasan, the priests cannot control what people do. One pilgrim, who had been coming since he was a child, dryly observed that people still say that Lord Ayyanarappan should not hear the sound of the *ural* and *ulakkai*, but somehow he does not seem bothered by the sounds of all these motorized vehicles.

Advocates of sacred groves as examples of traditional community resource management point to diminishing religious sentiments as a

primary cause of forest degradation. Rather than reflecting a diminishment in people's faith, I would argue that the development surrounding
the temple in Puttupattu suggest that the temple has become a significant
center of religious activity. But with the temple's connection to the local
village largely severed and the state in charge, it is not clear whose job it is
to protect the forest.

Were the grove surrounding the temple not so large (18 hectares), the
construction and heavy pilgrim traffic would impact the forest ecology
severely. But while evidence of disturbance is present and growing, the
grove is still fairly well preserved. The forest proper retains its characteristic two layers, but the density of tall trees is low, and medium-sized
trees dominate. Parthasarathy and Sethi recorded fifty-one different species of woody plant in 1997, with a mean stand density of 1,338 stems
per hectare and a mean basal area of 32.8 m^2 ha^{-1}.[34] By 2003, however,
Venkateswaran and Parthasarathy reported a startling diminishment in
species diversity, counting only twenty-four species, although the stand
density (1,329 stems) and basal area (37.6 m^2 ha^{-1}) was largely unchanged.[35]
This may be due to different sampling methods, but if confirmed such
species loss is quite worrisome. Equally disturbing is evidence that the
margins of the forest are also shrinking: Complete clearings can be seen
on both the eastern and the western sides of the forest, and the temple
committee cut several trees recently in order to build the pilgrim's shelter
near the main temple.

Conclusion

What these four case studies indicate is that, far from being simply a matter of the presence or absence of strong religious sentiments, a variety of
sociocultural factors affect the ecological condition of sacred groves. The
notion that diminishing "fear and faith," as Amrithalingam puts it, alone
is responsible for forest degradation in these groves is too simplistic, as
is the Sanskritization = degradation formula that Chandran and Hughes
advance. Certainly people's convictions surrounding taboos on forest
produce play an important role in limiting human use of the shrines.
Moreover, one does see a relationship between Sanskritization and an
increase in built structures within a shrine at the expense of the flora, but
Sanskritization does not spark an immediate or irreversible decline in forest health, in my view. Rather, my research suggests that conservation or
degradation comes about as a result of the *interactions between* belief and

other fundamental factors. Three factors are particularly significant: community solidarity, nature of ownership, and the physical size of the groves. Community solidarity plays a significant role in supporting the community's ability and willingness to supplement the god's sanctions with their own. Conversely, lack of unity can lead to the erosion of a grove's margins over time or the thinning of the understory due to unrestricted fuel gathering and lopping for animal fodder (as at Urani). As we have seen, the nature of ownership of a shrine can also support or undermine a grove's physical integrity. Groves managed by temple associations or traditional village leaders in coherent villages (or a group of relatively amicable villages, as in Kuzhandaikkuppam) can effectively police infractions of the taboos against poaching, but when a forested shrine slips out of the control of a local community and instead becomes the center of a more diffuse and far-flung network of devotees, people's commitment to protecting the flora surrounding a temple appears to wane, as is happening at Puttupattu. This may be due to the heightened anonymity at a large, "public" temple where individuals, even the priests, do not feel empowered to reprimand let alone sanction those who mistreat the forest. But community solidarity and local ownership are not guarantees against degradation of the forest, especially in smaller groves. A small grove has less canopy cover to begin with, such that even moderate construction or poaching can have a deleterious effect on the ecological health of the forest. On the other hand, a large sacred grove, such as Puttupattu, can withstand, to a certain extent, considerably more human impact brought on by a change of ownership or the wide diffusion of the community that originally maintained it.

Community solidarity and the nature of ownership are related in another significant way. Central to the complex of beliefs, narratives, and practices that give force to the taboos restricting the use of forest produce is the idea that the trees constitute the property of the god, the god's *contam*—what is his or hers. Relatively cohesive villages or groups of villages—such as Sentirankillai and Kuzhandaikkuppam (and, we could add, the Ambalakkarar villages in the Madurai region) are able to maintain broad adherence to the belief that the groves belong to the god and not to any human group. But this is a fragile fiction, sustained by the collective interpretation of calamities as acts of divine vengeance meted out against transgressors of the god's property.[36] However, when people start to view the management of temple property (including forests) as a monopoly held by a particular fraction of the village, the temptation to poach waxes and the fiction of divine ownership wanes.

Yet to call these beliefs "fictions" is probably too strong a statement. Tamil village deities and lineage deities function as powerful metaphors for the community itself, metonymically standing in as a symbol for the whole.[37] Therefore, saying that a grove "is the god's *csontam*" is tantamount to saying it belongs to the whole community. The ecological health of the grove (whether measured by its "thickness," as residents describe it, or in terms of species richness and basal index, as botanists measure it) thus functions as an index of the community's ability to enforce its own rules, including rules governing who is and who is not fully part of the community and what they do with collectively owned resources. With education and rising political influence, Dalits are starting to assert their rights to membership more aggressively. Whereas once they were categorically forbidden entrance to the groves, now they are gaining access not only to the goddess's temple (if not its interior, yet) but also to her property (i.e., the productive land often held in the deity's name). Whereas once Dalits might have muttered about dominant groups monopolizing the deity's temple, now they are empowered to challenge that monopoly in public and in the courts.

Along these lines, we should mention that the physical developments in these groves such as road-building and temple construction also have an impact on Dalits. The takeover of the Kizhputtupattu's village Ayyanar temple by the HRCE surely advanced the pace of construction in the grove, leading to more traffic, both foot and vehicular, and a corresponding degradation of the forest ecology. But making the temple "public" means its doors are now open to members of groups formerly forbidden to enter. Environmentalists concerned about the destruction of sacred groves often decry such changes as harbingers of doom for the forests that distinguish these religious sites. The way the groves in this region have developed over time generally confirms Hughes and Chandran's argument that people do cut down trees in forested shrines as their religious practices and beliefs become more Sanskritized, and yet Sanskritization may be a long process that proceeds in fits and starts. My research suggests that rather than precipitating swift degradation of the surrounding forest, built temples in sacred groves can coexist with abundant and diverse flora for decades, perhaps indefinitely. Such development may also lead to democratization of access to the groves, making them available to groups long excluded or marginalized from worship in them.

Neither sacred groves nor the communities that maintain them are isolated from the new flows of information, money, and people that penetrate virtually all polities and places in the contemporary world. Just as these flows bring entrepreneurs seeking land to start prawn hatcheries to the door of temple managers, they also bring botanists, state foresters, and environmentalists. As we shall see in the coming chapters, these latter agents of change come bearing new ideas about the value of the trees and plants that provide shade and shelter to forested deities, although whether these ideas are changing the way villagers think about them remains an open question.

4

Soteriology and Stakeholders

THE GREENING OF THE AUROVILLE PLATEAU, 1973–2007

Introduction

In the late 1960s, newcomers to the Coromandel Coast were astonished to find in Puttupattu's thick forest a vision of what the rest of the barren coastal plain north of Pondicherry could be like. Drawn to the area by neo-Hindu gurus, Sri Aurobindo, and the Mother, as Mirra Alfassa was known to her disciples, these European, American, and Australian émigrés discovered in this "miracle forest" indigenous plants well suited to the arid climate and sandy soil. They had come to the region to participate in the founding of Auroville, a utopian city of the future free from the war, greed, and strife that characterized human history. Among the first challenges they faced was the need to restore a largely barren, salinated wasteland that was, in places, becoming a desert. Thanks to their efforts, Auroville is well known today among restoration ecologists as the site of a remarkable transformation.

It is not, however, widely known among Tamilians. For one thing, it is not visible from the East Coast Road connecting Chennai, Urani, Puttupattu, and Pondicherry. For another, the values and lifestyles of its Western and cosmopolitan Indian members are a world away from those of most Tamilians. Auroville's center, the Matrimandir ("Mother's Temple"), lies far from the East Coast Road and the travel paths of most Tamilians in the region. A massive geodesic sphere covered with gold-plated reflective discs, the Matrimandir appears as if emerging out of the earth, bursting through twelve concrete pedals around its base (figure 4.1). Spiraling out from this center via a network of paved and unpaved roads are an abundance of schools, guest houses, work units, residential

FIGURE 4.1 Matrimandir at Auroville

communities, Internet cafes, European-style bakeries, post offices, cricket fields, farms, and forests.[1]

When I began visiting Auroville in 2001, the township itself struck me as a massive sacred grove standing out from the surrounding landscape as a site of unusual verdancy. Yet Auroville prides itself on being a place of no religion, and its founders and their followers have tried to prevent the emergence of anything like organized religion, including worship of a deity. Even at the heart of the Matrimandir one finds neither a darkened inner sanctum (*garbha gṛha*, lit. "womb-house"), nor a *murti*, the physical form of a deity used in worship in most Hindu temples; rather, in its capacious, dome-shaped, and immaculately white meditation chamber one finds a large crystal sphere resting on a pedestal. Sunlight projected down from a gap in the Matrimandir's roof falls on this sphere, symbolically evoking a central premise of philosophical Hinduism: that the divine above also dwells within each individual. Nevertheless, as I show in this chapter, despite the founders' refusal of the label "religion," Auroville remains a place where distinctly religious beliefs and practices have motivated people to foster and protect trees.

Auroville's environmental restoration efforts are the outgrowth of the teachings of two spiritual teachers, Aurobindo Ghose (1872–1950) and his collaborator and long-time disciple, Mirra Alfassa Richard (1878–1973), 20th-century cosmopolitan intellectuals whose school of yoga, called Integral Yoga, now attracts thousands of followers worldwide. As such, a very different style of Hinduism informs the conservation and cultivation of trees here than the intensely embodied, visceral, and emotional worship surrounding the lineage and guardian deities typically found in forested shrines. Indeed, many Aurovillians would regard the kind of Hinduism practiced in Tamil sacred groves as gross superstition. For this very reason, it is all the more striking that efforts have been made to reach across this cultural and ideological divide. Over the past fifteen years, Auroville has become a regional center of environmental activism and education, involving Aurovillians in a wide range of projects with Indian nongovernmental organizations (NGOs) and local Tamils. Thus, while Auroville itself provides a fascinating example of forest conservation motivated at least in part by religion, examining the interactions between villagers and Aurovillians around environmental restoration allows one to see how different varieties of Hindus are or are not mutually intelligible when they speak to each other about the spiritual significance of trees and forests.

In the first section of this chapter I discuss the history of Auroville in order to demonstrate how environmental concerns came to occupy center stage in a community founded as a laboratory for cultivating human unity. I then turn my attention to the history and career of one environmentally minded Aurovillian, Joss Brooks, who, in a manner somewhat parallel to Auroville's founders, built a complex environmental education and restoration organization, Pitchandikulam Forest, out of humble beginnings. Seeds gathered from Puttupattu and other forest remnants in the 1970s and germinated in Pitchandikulam's nurseries have now grown into towering trees that, though interspersed with a fair number of exogenous species, constitute a significant patch of restored forest. Thirty years after the establishment of Pitchandikulam, Joss Brooks and others sought to conserve and protect the tropical dry evergreen forest (TDEF) in Puttupattu. My investigation into this endeavor illustrates the challenges and the stakes involved when Hindus of such different kinds work together under the banner of sacred grove restoration. Though in many ways Aurovillians seek to apply a relatively light touch in their interactions with local communities and not impose their cosmologies or values, cultural differences and varying expectations surrounding forested shrines have made enduring partnerships difficult.

Auroville: An Experimental City

Auroville's founding, conceptually and practically, took place over several years, so it is not surprising that one finds numerous origin narratives for the site. One of them is as follows. In 1968, as experimental movements were bursting through the seams of convention around the world, the Mother drove north from Pondicherry through parched land dotted with palmrya trees, stopped the car, and pointed in the direction in which her followers would find two banyan trees. These would be the site of a new city, a center for the realization of human unity.[2] With Sri Aurobindo's ashram in Pondicherry well established, the idea of a whole city dedicated to the practical working out of Sri Aurobindo's grand vision for humanity was a logical next step. The idea for such a place had been surfacing in the Mother's mind for several years as she sought practical outlets for Aurobindo's conviction that human beings were at a crucial turning point in their evolution, just on the brink of a powerful breakthrough to a fuller realization of their inner divine potential.

The school of thought within which Sri Aurobindo located himself was Advaita Vedanta, which, with its emphasis on the idea that all reality is *māyā* (illusory or only real in a provisional way compared to Ultimate Reality), is often characterized as an other-worldly philosophical persective. But from the beginning, Auroville was animated by a profoundly this-worldly application of Advaitin nondualism in at least two ways. The first was through the aspiration to rise above national divisions by emphasizing the unity of humanity. Having lived through two world wars, the Mother conceived of Auroville during the long decades of the Cold War, with its seemingly interminable skirmishes and proxy wars. As early as 1954, she wrote,

> There should be somewhere on earth a place which no nation could claim as its own, where all human beings of goodwill who have a sincere aspiration could live freely as citizens of the world and obey one single authority, that of the supreme Truth; a place of peace, concord and harmony where all the fighting instincts of man would be used exclusively to conquer the causes of his sufferings and miseries, to surmount his weaknesses and ignorance, to triumph over his limitations and incapacities; a place where the needs of the spirit and concern for progress would take precedence over the satisfaction of desires and passions, the search for pleasure and material enjoyment.[3]

The second application of Advaitin thought came through the conceptualization of Auroville as a place to transform and spiritualize the very material basis of existence. One of the distinctive features of Aurobindo's cosmology was the idea that spiritual perfection lay not merely in *escaping* a flawed material existence characterized by flux, desire, and suffering but in manifesting the in-dwelling divine within the material world. Based on his understanding of Vedic cosmogonies, Aurobindo affirmed that spirit was already present in matter. Thus, spiritual "evolution" does not entail freeing oneself from the shackles of matter so much as "the progressive manifestation by Nature of that which slept or worked in her."[4] Combining Western concepts of evolution with Vedic cosmologies, Aurobindo argued that

> there seems to be no reason why Life should evolve out of material elements or Mind out of living form, unless we accept the Vedantic solution that Life is already involved in Matter and Mind in Life because in essence Matter is a form of veiled Life, Life a form of veiled Consciousness.

According to Aurobindo, in the course of cosmic creation, the vitality of life had been invisibly embedded in matter, and consciousness had been similarly "veiled" in living things. The process of spiritual self-development consists, then, in reversing this process such that one brings life out of matter and consciousness out of living beings. Ultimately, in a further leap toward perfection, human beings would push themselves to become spiritually perfected, immortal supermen.[5] The bidirectional nature of spiritual evolution is captured visually in the mandala that Aurobindo and the Mother designed (figure 4.2).

As Larry Shinn writes, "In Aurobindo's *maṇḍala*, the upward pointing triangle signifies the aspirations of matter (personalized in the novice) seeking true life, light and love. The descending triangle represents the descent of the Divine Shakti as truth, being and bliss."[6] In this philosophical context, physical work carried enormous significance.

According to Sri Aurobindo and the Mother, the goal of labor when undertaken as a conscious *sādhana* (spiritual practice) was to enspirit matter or, in other words, to accelerate the evolution of matter from inert substance to living material, to conscious being, to superconsciousness. Aurobindo, like several Hindu thinkers of his generation, conceived of a radically activist form of Advaita Vedanta, which substituted the old ideal of a yogi as a renouncer retreating from the world in order to pursue spiritual wisdom

FIGURE 4.2 Sri Aurobindo Mandala

with the new ideal of the karmayogin, the yogi of action, who would discover, test, and apply the insights of spiritual knowledge (*jñāna*) in whatever field of activity he found himself. Auroville was conceived as a place where humanity's progress toward this ideal state could be accelerated, as a community of like-minded individuals engaged in both inner spiritual self-cultivation and the transformation of the world around them through work. "Auroville is created to realize the ideal of Sri Aurobindo who taught us the Karma Yoga," declared the Mother. "Auroville is for those who want to do the Yoga of work. So all Aurovillians must take up a work and do it as Yoga."[7]

Emergent Environmentalism in Integral Yoga

Aurobindo's philosophy provided the soteriological framework for the spiritual and physical labors of Aurovillians, but it was the Mother who created the concrete organizational and social contexts in which the growing community of disciples could put these ideas into practice. A gifted organizer and a shrewd businesswoman, the Mother built a network of institutions, from an international school and a publishing center designed to promote the study of Integral Yoga to a sugar mill in Pondicherry whose income would help support the community. With its integration of commercial, cultural, and spiritual enterprises, Auroville represented in many ways the culmination of the Mother's lifework. Moreover, because of the dire ecological condition of the degraded plateau she chose as Auroville's site of physical realization, it became an effective arena for working out in practice the basic Aurobindian concept of producing life out of matter and consciousness out of life.

In order to understand the ways in which Aurobindo's philosophical worldview gives purpose and meaning to Auroville, it is helpful to know something about Sri Aurobindo himself, as well as about his close disciple, Mirra Alfassa (the Mother) who founded the "international township" eighteen years after Aurobindo's passing. A former freedom fighter from an elite Bengali family, Aurobindo Ghose was educated in England from the age of seven. Imprisoned by the British in 1910 for his supposed involvement in an assassination plot, he took shelter after his release in French-controlled Pondicherry, then a sleepy provincial seaside outpost.[8] For decades after his retirement in Pondicherry, Nationalist leaders of diverse camps sought to enlist him in the movement for independence, but Aurobindo remained unmoved.[9] Instead, the activist, revolutionary spirit of Aurobindo's early career took a new shape in his philosophy, worked out over decades and eventually called Integral Yoga, animated as it was by the conviction that all aspects of life—the emotional, spiritual, practical, ethical, aesthetic, and so forth—should be integrated in the pursuit of one's spiritual evolution through a series of levels of consciousness.[10] Aurobindo reworked his political ideas about liberation and India's potential as a seedbed of greatness into a pacifist soteriology aiming at revolutionary spiritual transformation through active engagement with the world. In Pondicherry, Aurobindo gathered around him a half-dozen disciples. The movement behind him, however, did not really take off until the arrival of Mirra Alfassa Richard, a Frenchwoman of Egyptian and Turkish descent.

Aurobindo recognized Mirra Alfassa as a co-creator of his system of thought and eventually came to see her as the avatar of the dynamic principle propelling the evolution of the cosmos.[11] Yet one finds slim recognition of this in scholarship on Aurobindo or Integral Yoga. Indeed, outside of books written by her disciples, the Mother tends to play the role of controlling autocrat at worst and a "born organizer" at best. Because of this persistent bias, the Mother's role in shaping Integral Yoga has generally been under-recognized. As a result, though dozens of scholarly monographs have been written about Aurobindo and his thought, not one exists on the Mother.

From her own autobiographical writings and recorded talks, we know that Mirra Alfassa studied art and married a fellow artist, Henri Morrisset, in 1897. They had one child, André, who lived primarily with Henri's sister and father.[12] Sometime between 1901 and 1903, Mirra Alfassa's brother, Matteo, introduced her to the teachings of Max Théon and his wife, Alma Théon, early theosophists who created a kind of salon in Tlemcen in northern Algiers (like Pondicherry, another seaside colonial French city). In Paris, she joined Théon's organization of like-minded seekers, reading Indian scriptures in translation, helping to publish Théon's journal, *Revue Cosmique*, and living with the Théons in Tlemcen in the summers of 1906 and 1907.[13] Her involvement with the Théons gave direction to spiritual inclinations and experiences she is said to have had since childhood. One can find in the Mother's recollections of the occult experiences she had at this time intimations of her "animistic" sensitivity to nature, which would inspire her followers in the reforestation of the Auroville plateau. In a conversation with disciples recorded on June 23, 1954, she recounted,

> It was at the end of July or the beginning of August. I left Paris, the house I was staying in, and went to the countryside, quite a small place on the seashore, to stay with some friends who had a garden. Now, in that garden was a lawn...[ellipsis in original] where there were flowers and around it some trees. It was a pretty place, very quiet, very silent. I lay on the grass, like this, flat on my stomach, my elbows in the grass, and then suddenly all the life of that Nature, all the life of that region between the subtle physical and the most material vital, which is very living in plants and in Nature, all that region became at once, suddenly, without any transition, absolutely living, intense, conscious, marvelous.[14]

Understood literally, her words exhibit some ambiguity as to whether the living natural world around her became at that moment "absolutely living, intense, conscious, marvelous" (as through a sudden descent of the divine Supramental into the material plane) or whether she, in a flash of heightened consciousness, was able to perceive the natural world as being always already alive and conscious in this way. Though some might interpret this passage as a foreshadowing of the cosmic mission Aurobindo attributed to her, I'm inclined to read it as an indication of the animistic elements of her cosmology. In her later practice as a guru, she emphasized in many ways how an attuned observer can perceive plants as not only alive but "intense, conscious, marvelous." Indeed, her description of this early spiritual experience anticipates a key aspect of Integral Yoga, which is to overcome the nature–spirit dualism engrained in both Western and

Indic philosophical thought by cultivating one's awareness of the many interpenetrating levels of the cosmos from grossly material and "vital" to the purely spiritual.

In 1908 Mirra left her first husband for the more spiritually minded French lawyer Paul Richard.[15] It was Richard who first met Aurobindo in Pondicherry in 1910. In 1914, Mirra traveled to India with Richard, and together they spent many afternoons with the charismatic and erudite Bengali thinker. The two founded a philosophical journal, *The Arya*, as a vehicle for disseminating Aurobindo's distinctive rereading of Advaita Vedanta through the lens of modernism, evolution, and Indian nationalism. Many of Aurobindo's most significant works were published in serialized form in this journal (e.g., *The Life Divine, The Synthesis of Yoga, The Human Cycle*, etc.). Only six months into their joint venture, however, the Richards were compelled to return to France when Richard was called to serve in the conflict that would become World War I. In 1920 they returned to Pondicherry, where Mirra would stay even after Paul left. As Robert Minor writes, "Her relationship with Paul Richard had basically ended. She had turned her attention completely to Aurobindo."[16]

The collaborative relationship between Sri Aurobindo and Mirra Alfassa deepened over the next six years. Though she managed affairs for the growing number of disciples in Pondicherry, Mirra mostly stayed in the background. In November of 1926, however, Sri Aurobindo had what he believed to be a significant spiritual experience interpreted as the descent of the Overmind consciousness, which in Integral Yoga terminology is a level between Mind (ordinary human consciousness) and Supermind (the innate divine principle undergirding the cosmos). Entrusting complete control of the ashram to Mirra, Aurobindo went into seclusion for the next twelve years to concentrate on his own *sādhana* (spiritual practice). Though he communicated regularly with his disciplines in letters and through his writings, he removed himself almost entirely from direct contact with them.[17]

In his history of Auroville, historian of religion Robert Minor argues that Aurobindo's efforts to bolster Mirra Alfassa's authority at this juncture laid the foundation for the successful transfer of charisma to her, ensuring that the community would remain on a stable footing even after his death.[18] For Aurobindo, Mirra Alfassa was nothing less than the embodied form of the Supermind on earth. He regarded and referred to her as the Mother, the *shakti* or energy behind the evolution of the cosmos itself. "Her embodiment," he wrote, "is a chance for the earth-consciousness to receive the Supramental into it and to undergo first the transformation necessary for that to be possible."[19] Though his followers, and much of India, grieved deeply when Aurobindo passed away on December 5, 1950, the ashram was spared any succession disputes. As befits a *sādhu* according to Hindu funeral practices, his body was interred in a concrete *samādhi* (vault) installed in the courtyard of the main building of the ashram, where it is even now visited by hundreds of devotees every day.

The Mother's followers believed she possessed supernatural powers (*siddhis*) acquired through both her natural gifts and her intense spiritual practice. In a manner parallel to Sri Aurobindo's dramatic "descent of the overmind consciousness" in November of 1926, she was said to have experienced the descent of the "Supramental consciousness" on February 29, 1956. During a meeting of disciplines, she announced the historic breakthrough:

> This evening the Divine Presence, concrete and material, was present amongst you. I had the form of living gold, bigger than the universe, and I was facing a huge and massive golden door, which separated the world from the Divine. As I looked at the door, I knew and willed in a single movement of consciousness, that "the time has come," and lifting with both hands a mighty golden hammer I struck one blow on the door and the door was shattered to pieces. And then the Supramental Light and Force and Consciousness rushed down upon earth in an uninterrupted flow.[20]

The anniversary of this event is celebrated every year at the Ashram and in Auroville as the Supramental Manifestation Day. Comparable to the advent of a messiah, the event represented the fruition of Sri Aurobindo and the Mother's efforts to bring down the force of the Divine into the material plane. It was a turning point from which there was no turning back—from here on out the promise was assured that a race of supermen would soon come into existence. Indeed, Auroville, whose existence the Mother had already begun to conceptualize, was meant to be a "cradle of the superman."[21]

Records that shed light on the Mother's role as a guru suggest that she crafted her own distinctive style of religious leadership, never fully assimilating the pattern of an Indian female ascetic (as did, for example, Gandhi's famous English disciple Meera Behn [Madeleine Slade]). Rather, stating that she was born French with an Indian soul, she maintained her French style and identity throughout her life. Particularly after Sri Aurobindo's death in 1950, she became the focal point of devotion for a growing body of devotees. Robert Minor writes, "Her personal interests, her personality, and even her hobbies, such as tennis, gardening and stamp collecting, were viewed by her followers as profound statements about the nature of the universe. They began to speak of her appearances to them in visions and dreams and cherished her words, her touch, and her methods."[22] But perhaps what Minor interprets as the hyperbolic adulation solicited by and given to a charismatic (and potentially manipulative) guru may have been for her followers signs of her distinctive talent. As they saw, her great gift as a spiritual teacher lay in making Aurobindo's abstruse philosophy accessible and finding ways to apply his thought to everyday life.[23]

For instance, the Mother was passionate about gardening. Flowers were to her a profound symbol of a key concept of Integral Yoga—aspiration. Flowers were a vivid example of what she and Aurobindo saw as the germ of consciousness present in matter and the aspiration of that latent consciousness to find expression. "The psychic, when it manifests in a plant, in the form of a flower, is in the form of a wordless prayer; it is the élan of the plant toward the Divine."[24] One of the areas in which the Mother is said to have applied her extraordinary powers was in discovering the true names of flowers.[25] "When one is in conscious contact with one's own psychic," she said, "one becomes aware of an impersonal psychic behind the whole creation and then, through this, one can enter into contact with flowers and know the psychic prayer they represent."[26] The red lotus represented Sri Aurobindo, while lotuses of any kind signified the Divine Wisdom. The hibiscus was the "Supramental beauty in the physical," the sweet-smelling night jasmine (*Nyctanthes arbor-tristis*, or Parijata) carried the name Aspiration, and the coconut tree, every part of which is put to use in Tamil Nadu, was called Multitude. This kind of animism, attributing a form of consciousness to plants, can seem quaint or even laughable, and yet in the years since environmental restoration of the region has become one of the central organizing features of Auroville, it has taken on new importance. These ideas gave broader meaning to the hard labor required for the restoration of the soil and watershed that the first generation of Aurovillians had to undertake for their own survival.

The Reforestation of Auroville

[Q:] *It seems to me that the very land of Auroville aspires. Is it true, Sweet Mother?* Yes, the land itself has a consciousness even though this consciousness is not intellectualized and cannot express itself. (March 21, 1968)[27]

On February 28, 1968, the long-germinating plans for Auroville took form at the inaugural ceremony, held at a spiral concrete amphitheatre built beside a spreading banyan tree. Its internationalist ambitions were symbolized by the placing of soil from 124 nations into a marble urn. The French architect Roger Anger was hired to plan Auroville as "an ideal city," similar to what Le Corbusier had done (badly, in the Mother's opinion) in Chandigarh, the new capital of the Indian state of Punjab, after Partition.[28] Well-connected members of the Sri Aurobindo Ashram, supported by members of Integral Yoga centers all over the world, successfully lobbied for support from UNESCO and the Indian government. At the center of the township was planned a spiritual "cathedral," the Matrimandir (lit. "the Mother's Temple"), a futuristic temple that would be built in the form of a massive geodesic dome, adorned with gold-plated discs. In a trembling voice (she was ninety when the inaugural ceremony took place) broadcast via radio hookup from her room in Pondicherry, the Mother read aloud the Charter that would govern the development of the idealistic, futuristic, spiritual, and international township:

1. Auroville belongs to nobody in particular. Auroville belongs to humanity as a whole. But to live in Auroville one must be the willing servitor of the Divine Consciousness.
2. Auroville will be the place of unending education, of constant progress, and a youth that never ages.
3. Auroville wants to be the bridge between the past and the future. Taking advantage of all discoveries from without and within, Auroville will boldly spring toward future realizations.
4. Auroville will be a site of material and spiritual researches for a living embodiment of an actual human unity.[29]

Inspired by the promise of a new age, young people came as homesteaders from all over the world but mostly France, Germany, and Italy. After being initiated into the practice of karma yoga as envisioned by the Mother and Sri Aurobindo, they began to settle in the arid Auroville plateau.

In a manner not clearly anticipated by the Mother, the first requirement was the hard physical labor necessary to make the land livable. Planting trees was critical for basic survival in a region beaten by the tropical sun for ten months out of the year; it was also necessary to stabilize the soil enough to allow for agricultural cultivation. But to keep the saplings alive, one needed to carefully protect and nurture them. By means of painstaking labor, Aurovillians set to work on an intensive program of soil and water conservation—building bunds and check dams to prevent the runoff of rainwater and planting hundreds of thousands of saplings.[30] Most of the money received by the Indian government and UNESCO to support the fledgling city was used for land reclamation.[31] Among the most successful species was an exogenous one, *Acacia auriculiformis*, from Australia, which the Mother dubbed "Work Tree." It grew to maturity within fifteen to twenty years and provided shade in which indigenous species could gain a foothold. The community began to make trips to surrounding Reserve Forests (Marakkanam) and sacred groves (Puttupattu, Urani) to collect seeds.[32]

Joss Brooks: Accidental Environmentalist

Longtime residents describe the hardships and pleasures of the early homesteader years, exemplified for many by the memory of bullock carts transporting water great distances across the parched region. One sometimes finds in their reminiscences indications of how the teachings of Sri Aurobindo and the Mother influenced their efforts and how they saw them. The career and leadership style of one such "old-timer," Joss Brooks, mirrors that of Sri Aurobindo and the Mother and illustrates how the process of environmental restoration was made meaningful within the cosmological and soteriological framework of Integral Yoga, at least by some Aurovillians. One thing scholars and Aurovillians agree on is that the decentered and highly autonomous nature of organization in Auroville has resulted in a wide range of views about its history, significance, and purpose. It should be noted that though a highly articulate, dedicated, and long-time member of the township, Brooks's views are not necessarily representative of the majority of Aurovillians. Nonetheless, Brooks's personal narrative, as told to a group of "Newcomers" to Auroville (individuals who committed to a one-year trial period of living and working in one of the township's many projects), offers a vivid glimpse of the early years in Auroville and of the motivating factors behind people's involvement with the community.[33]

Brooks was among the first Aurovillians, having settled in the township in early 1970. Like many of the first settlers in Auroville, he was a refugee of the 1960s. Raised a Quaker, Brooks left Australia in about 1966 to avoid being conscripted into the Vietnam War. Following routes established by countercultural tourists since the early 20th century, he traveled in Turkey and Ethiopia. He also explored Central America, before finally settling briefly in France. He was in Paris during the labor strikes of 1968, throwing stones from the barricades alongside student leaders of the uprising. He explicitly connects his own withdrawal from political activism to that of Sri Aurobindo, describing May of 1968 as a moment similar to 1908, when a whole group of people were "thinking like Aurobindo," faced as he was with the decision "Shall I go on fighting or shall I go inside?" Brooks's restless traveling and his desire to take the work "inside" took him to India, where he lived in ashrams and studied Vedanta. Yet after a year he grew tired of the inefficiency of post-independence India, in which he felt that a general lack of "care for matter" led to poor design and planning. He made plans to study Zen in a Japanese monastery. He was about to leave India when in a dream a woman's voice told him to stop in Pondicherry. A chance encounter with friends on the street led to an evening spent over coffee talking with a group of Aurovillians. They were "insane" people, recalls Brooks, their feet stained red from the Auroville mud, yet they were inspired by "these dreams and talking about this Lady…who just had a vision of something absolutely new and remarkable." He was hooked.

As the description above suggests, what appealed to Brooks was the Aurovillians' combination of practicality and idealism—their heads were full of dreams but their feet were set firmly in the red mud of the Auroville plateau. Also clear is the settlers' sense of the Mother's benevolent guiding presence, which both authorized and supported the creative spontaneity of those early years, although she rarely left Pondicherry. "It was playful at that time," recalls Brooks, "and I think from the beginning that's what we understood. She said, 'Look here's an empty place, it happens to be an empty plateau, it's your playground. Will you play? Please use your imagination, your intuition.'" Synthesizing diverse countercultural streams, the new settlers drew on European traditions of craftsmanship, American hippie "back-to-the-land" self-sufficiency, and futuristic visions of unrealized human potential.[34] They experimented with new technology by, for example, building geodesic dome dwellings in the style of Buckminster Fuller (figure 4.3). In an anecdote that evokes both the inventive freedom of those early days in Auroville and its barren landscape, Brooks describes how an aluminum geodesic dome structure blew away in a storm and rolled all the way from Pitchandikulam to the beach, a distance of 3 kilometers, unimpeded by any bushes or trees.[35] Brooks's account underscores the

FIGURE 4.3 Geodesic dome in Auroville made from casuarina poles circa 1972.
© Dominique Darr. Reprinted with permission.

amount of physical labor it took to build the infrastructure and reclaim the land. Such sacrifices are embodied for him, even today, in the scarred legs and feet of "greenbelters," those who choose to live in the more remote parts of Auroville, where the project of environmental restoration is ongoing. Hard manual labor under difficult conditions at times led to accidents and illness. Yet there was also much personal care given to the Mother's "children" in Auroville by both the Mother and senior Ashramites, like Shyamsunder Jhunjhunwala, a lawyer and businessman entrusted with much of the day-to-day administration of the Ashram.

After living in several communities within Auroville, Brooks started his own enterprise, Pitchandikulam (lit. "Lake of the Begging, or Healing, Sadhu"), in early 1973. Brooks included local Tamils in his enterprise, noting that "a group of Harijan boys from Edeyanchavadi...and a few from Kuyilapalayam [two Tamil villages encompassed by the Auroville township]" joined with him in the work of fencing the area to protect their plantings. Many groups at this time were engaged in reforestation, and Brooks's team specialized in building a nursery (figure 4.4). Experimenting with different methods of plant propagation, they created an informal botanical garden. They learned about the flora of the region

FIGURE 4.4 Joss Brooks, Shanti, Amudha, and Anita Brooks, Auroville. ©
Ireno Guerci. Reprinted with permission.

from their Tamil neighbors, walking and bicycling to nearby villages and
forests to gather seeds from indigenous plants. Over the years, by learning from and collaborating with local scientists and foresters, they came
to understand the botanical significance of the unique forest type found
in this region, TDEF.

At the time, however, Brooks and his collaborators did not see themselves as restoring the TDEF; rather, they envisioned their work more as
planting a garden for the Mother. Understood within the framework of
Aurobindian cosmology, one could interpret their labor as a form of physical preparation of themselves and the earth for the descent of the spirit, as
they coaxed the indwelling divine within both to manifest and gain richer
and fuller expression. They saw themselves as seeding the landscape with
plants whose intrinsic energies would enrich the landscape, nurturing its
inner tendencies toward aspiration, its own nascent consciousness. As
Brooks recalled, "From the beginning, we knew the plants through the
Mother's names.... Those first years, we were planting Transformation,
or Psychological Perfection, or Realization, or Miracle. And it was very
very sweet, really sweet." Aurovillians also took flowers they found in the
area to the Mother for her to bestow them with names. As mentioned
previously, the Mother's occult or psychic powers with respect to plants

are the stuff of legend, both personal and collective. Here Brooks reports one such example:

> I remember the last time I met the Mother, it was my birthday. And you know Mother in those darshans, 71–72,... sometimes a messenger would come out and they would say, "You stay in Auroville. Much better to stay in Auroville to do work. You need not come to darshan." This birthday I remember I was working here, and my God, I was late. I cycled into Pondy—sweaty, stinky probably, and covered with mud.... And I had taken the flower of the Kathamani; [it] is our fencing plant.... It's one of the commonist plants. It will grow anywhere. The goats don't eat it. Nothing like that. It's a *really* strong plant, and we'd been planting it on the fences to keep it as a protection for our plantation.... So I took this to the Mother, and every body else... the room was full of these huge hibiscus and roses and all this sort of thing. Here I'd turned up with this tiny little flower and she said, "*Les chevres n'aimez pas ça.*" "The goats don't like that one."

The story captures simultaneously many dimensions of the guru–disciple relationship as it played out between the refined French Mother of Pondicherry and her (at times) unkempt followers among the Aurovillians. One sees Brooks's self-presentation as an inadequate but earnest follower, bearing the humble fruits of early Auroville: a small, tough, unassuming flower that even the goats don't eat. While the story clearly conveys the Mother's uncanny perceptiveness, what is less clear is if her laconic statements ("you need not come to darshan today"; "the goats don't like that one") are meant to suggest her emotional distance from Auroville and the rank-and-file Aurovillians or her spiritual authority. Or perhaps, in this instance, the Mother was just intuiting the inner truth of the flower and stating something that traditional healers in this area have known about plants for centuries, namely, that each one of them, however thorny or visually uninteresting, has its uses.

Not all Aurovillians regard the Mother as a spiritual leader central to the founding and ongoing creation of Auroville, but among those (like Brooks) who do, one finds a fascinating dialectic between *work* and *play* in the Mother's teachings. As noted earlier, Brooks recalls the Mother giving her "children" the "empty" Auroville plateau as their playground. Interestingly, the open patio where devotees at the Pondicherry Ashram gathered to listen to the Mother was also known as "the Playground." Yet recorded conversations with close disciples suggest that the Mother was at times discouraged by what she perceived as the "laziness" of at least some disciples.[36] She could express great dismay at both those would-be Ashramites who felt yoga entailed a withdrawal from action in the world and from her "children" in Auroville, who saw the utopian community emerging there as a site for hedonistic self-expression, interpreting her refusal to institute clear rules for governance as an endorsement of uninhibited individualism.[37] In particular, she feared that Auroville would gain a reputation for drug use, sexual promiscuity, and general loose morality, endangering not only its support from the Indian government but also negatively influencing the conservative Tamil culture that surrounded the fledging community. Though she recognized these emerging issues, the Mother did not seek to remedy them through codified rules. Rather, she consistently articulated her faith that the Supramental Divine was guiding the development of Auroville and that selfless karma yoga would positively transform whatever counterproductive aspects arose from the anarchism she promoted.

The Hosts of the Experiment: Relations between Tamil Villagers and Aurovillians

In November of 1973, the Mother passed away at ninety-five, only five years after Auroville's formal founding. Her physical frailty combined with her staunch belief that powerful divine forces were guiding the direction of developments in Auroville limited her ability, or willingness, to actively manage the increasingly complicated project. It also may be that she was moving into the more indirect mode of guru-ship modeled by Sri Aurobindo in his later years. Two problems that were never fully resolved by the Mother had to do with the lack of a formal organizational structure to govern Auroville after her death and the absence of clear guidelines for managing relationships with local Tamils. The former has been well analyzed by several scholars, including Larry Shinn, Robert Minor, and David Lorenzo, who explain the circumstances that led to significant discord between Aurovillians and the senior Ashramites deputed by the Mother to manage the affairs of the international township.[38] The conflict largely emerged over financial irregularities and with time erupted into feuds, intimidation, lawsuits, and, on occasion, physical violence. It led the Indian government not only to intervene on multiple occasions but ultimately to assume control of the township in 1988 as its titular "owner" and head.

The conflicted relations between Aurovillians and local Tamils, on the other hand, have rarely been explored in depth by scholars, even though such relations are, like the reforestation efforts that receive much more attention, a defining element of present-day Auroville. The origin stories of Auroville almost always suggest or imply that the Aurovillians landed in a largely uninhabited area, but in 1968 the residents of several Tamil villagers used the 2,000 acres encompassed by the future township.[39] The internationalist ethos that inspired so many early Aurovillians seems to have been applied with difficulty to relations between themselves and local Tamils. Strategies for dealing with the inevitable tensions have included erecting fences; social development projects in areas such as education, medicine, and women's empowerment; direct employment in the many work units in Auroville; and integrating Tamils as full members of the community.

In 1969 the Mother exhorted her followers to treat the neighboring villagers with respect, suggesting that some needed this stern reminder. She wrote, "Those who are in contact with the villagers should not forget that these people are worth as much as they are, that they know as much, that they think and feel as well as they do. They should never therefore have an attitude of ridiculous superiority. They are at home and you are the visitors."[40] Accompanying the land-reclamation efforts were competition over scarce water and conflicts with local herders whose goats could no longer roam where Aurovillians were attempting to cultivate young saplings.[41] As Aurovillians attempted to expand the boundaries of their utopian settlement by purchasing land, they encountered some stiff resistance, as indicated in this note written from Auroville to the Mother in Pondicherry:

Mother Divine,

A few points on which Thy divine guidance is required.

There is resistance from the villagers in selling their lands. This may be because we have done nothing to integrate them with Auroville. They feel it is a foreign imposition on them which will do them no good but will drive them from their hearths and homes.

Should we not demonstrate to them our real intentions by providing them with facilities such as a dispensary, a school, clean drinking water, etc.? This would be money well spent if it is done with love and humility and not as charity. (April 1969)[42]

"This is indispensable," was the Mother's terse reply. Some of the earliest work projects initiated at Auroville as forms of karma yoga were focused on this kind of philanthropic or humanitarian outreach to locals. They ranged from the playful (like the traveling circus that brought the broad humor of European performance artists to village children) to the serious, such as the Last School, inaugurated by the Mother on October 6, 1971, at one of the pioneer settlements in Auroville, Aspiration. Meant to educate both Tamilians and Aurovillians through the Mother's theory of progressively more independent education, the Mother endowed it with the motto "The future belongs to those who want to progress."[43]

Similar strategies for creating common ground between Aurovillians and local Tamils are employed today. Outreach efforts such as those envisioned in 1968 have been a continuing element of the work undertaken by Aurovillians. There are six schools for village children, a health center with mobile outreach units, and a village action group with numerous women's development groups, and so on. In fact, few work units in Auroville are *not* involved in humanitarian or educational outreach in one way or another, including sponsoring schools, vocational education workshops, reforestation schemes, and so on. Yet the one-way flow of humanitarian aid creates its own inequities, requiring Aurovillians to constantly devise ways to restore parity in their relationships with villagers. Joss Brooks articulates the difficulty of maintaining a balanced, just, and equitable relationship with local villagers: "How to honour their rights as the original inhabitants of the land, the host to the experiment, as fellow humans in the effort toward human unity, remains as yet insufficiently understood. How to learn the quiet lessons of their traditional culture? How to avoid imposing on them and yet maintain the main thread of our endeavor?"[44]

Another significant context for cooperation between Aurovillians and Tamil neighbors has been through paid work. From the beginning, local villagers were employed as paid laborers to help plant saplings and build bunds and in construction where their skills in using local building materials were invaluable. Many Aurovillians talk about those collaborations with pleasure. Tamilians from the villages in and around the township also helped care for the growing community of Aurovillians through paid service work as cooks and nannies. The difficulty of coping with the climate and the amount of labor needed to cook, clean, and care for children was overwhelming for many, and pioneering residents like Jan Allen gratefully recall the *ammas* (lit. "mothers," "ladies") in their lives, as local women who work for Aurovillians are often known.

Today, the number of local Tamilians employed by Auroville and its numerous work units—from bakeries and textile factories to guest houses and environmental education—greatly exceeds the number of official Aurovillians. In 2001, the Auroville master plan placed the number of

Tamil "day-workers" at 5,000, 48 percent of whom are women, while the number of "resident Aurovillians" was 1,519.[45] As related in a candid article in the community newspaper, *Auroville Today,* the relationships between Aurovillians and the Tamils who come each day to work alongside them, especially service workers, is complex. Based on interviews with eight ammas, Priya Sundaravalli writes,

> There is sometimes a discussion in Auroville about the "correctness" of employing people to do one's housework, something The Mother was opposed to, instead of doing it oneself. Having a househelp is seen by some as "colonial." But the ammas are quick to disagree. "I am not educated," says Shankari. "And it's only because of this job that I am able to live with dignity, provide special things for my children, and have some respect in my village. If we were not allowed to do this job, what would we do?"

Working at Auroville has offered men and women opportunities to earn money and acquire new skills, from artisanal crafts to cooking. The official Auroville position reflects the teaching of the Mother that Tamils should be treated with dignity and respect, but sometimes cultural and class divisions create hardships for Tamils working in the homes and businesses of Aurovillians. Several women interviewed by Sundaravalli describe a "walking-on-eggshells" feeling, a heightened and somewhat fearful sense of self-consciousness when working in the presence of European and North American employers who demand, for example, complete silence while they work. Others regard the relatively secure and well-paying jobs they obtain in Auroville as necessary compensation for the sale of land their families owned years ago.[46] As the value of the land around Auroville has soared in value (from roughly 2,000 rupees an acre in 1973 to 350,000 rupees an acre in 2009), the resentment among those who sold their land decades ago can be understandably intense.

Perhaps the most enduring way of creating common ties and interests between Aurovillians and local Tamils has been the inclusion of Tamils who come forward to become full members of the community. Even during the Mother's lifetime, Tamil individuals and families were accepted as full members.[47] Some Tamil Aurovillians are motivated to join by the promise of freedom from convention and tradition, just as many Western Aurovillians were. Others are attracted by the monthly stipend given to all working Aurovillians in order to maintain the ideal money-free economy envisioned by the Mother. As some argue, in this, Tamilian Aurovillians are not so different from those Western Aurovillians who come here in essence to "retire." But many find that no matter why they joined, once they do, the philosophy of the place starts to work on them. "When people would ask me directly, why did I join, then a spark comes!" recalled Ramadasan, one Tamil Aurovillian, "The question of 'why?' Thinking and thinking on that you begin the process of evolution."[48] Though the census figures taken by Aurovillians do provide a breakdown of membership by nationality, they do not differentiate between Tamils and other Indians. As of the latest census in April 2012, of 2,257 members of Auroville 950 (42%) are of Indian origin.[49]

Conflict between Aurovillians and local Tamils was and remains, in my view, inevitable, at least until the unity of spirit envisioned by the Mother reaches its full realization. In the meanwhile, given the vast cultural gulf that existed between the idealistic young enthusiasts who founded and continue to come to Auroville and the Tamil villagers who for centuries have herded and farmed on this arid plain, it is remarkable that people manage to coexist as well as they do.

Religious Encounters in the Field: Collaborative Efforts in Sacred Grove Restoration

Environmental restoration work undertaken with residents in the villages within and surrounding the Auroville township is one of the many areas in which one sees intensive interaction between Aurovillians and locals. Several work units at Auroville are involved in reforestation, including Aurobrindavan, Palmyra, Sadhana Forest, Auroville Botanical Gardens, and Joss Brooks's Pitchandikulam. Since its beginnings in 1973, Pitchandikulam has grown into a multifaceted enterprise, Pitchandikulam Forest, with numerous interconnected projects related to environmental restoration and education. Examining its growth and its involvement in TDEF restoration at a sacred grove (Puttupattu) allows us to see how difficult it is for environmental NGOs to capitalize on the promise of sacred groves as a form of indigenous ecological conservation, because the discourses surrounding these sites, generated by actors with very different interests in them, are hard to harmonize. While botanists and new advocates of traditional medicine see them as invaluable repositories of germ plasm—a kind of Noah's ark for preserving species threatened by the engulfing tide of development—local people see them, when they pay attention to the forests at all, as backdrops for the play (*līlā*) of gods and goddesses. Furthermore, whatever their ecological value, sacred groves are also temples and thus focal points for local struggles over status, property, and the politics of identity and inclusion.

The reforestation efforts at Pitchandikulam began in 1973 on about thirty acres of land. The regenerated forest coaxed out of the ground by Brooks and his coworkers now covers about seventy acres, and nestled within it lie several carefully designed buildings: guest houses, office and storage space, laboratories, outdoor meeting rooms, and the home of Brooks and his partner Anita. With an almost entirely Tamil "team" of 100, Pitchandkulam Forest is involved in numerous educational and environmental projects. Some entail direct restoration of TDEF—for example, the development of Mugaiyar Eco-Park on eighty-eight acres of degraded coastal land off the East Coast Road, complete with newly created ponds, sand dunes, and patches of forest planted with indigenous species. Other initiatives provide environmental education to groups of all sorts, from schoolchildren to housewives, with an emphasis on learning about the traditional medicinal uses of herbs and plants. Pitchandikulam Forest also supports scholarly studies of biological diversity in the area, local health traditions, and the use of medicinal plants. I have been visiting Pitchandikulam since 2001, and each year I find Brooks initiating more and more ambitious projects. The latest is perhaps the most far-reaching: the creation of an eco-park, the Adyar Poonga, in the southern part of the densely populated and heavily polluted city of Chennai, along fighty-eight acres of the Adyar Creek estuary. While the work of restoring the ecology of a wetland whose water sources flow ever more sluggishly as they pass through the city is difficult enough, what is perhaps more daunting is the diplomacy necessary to navigate the political waters—evicting slum-dwellers who have squatted illegally on land for decades; getting necessary permits to clean, drain, and dredge the area; and coordinating funding and permissions with the ever-changing constituency of city and Tamil Nadu state government.[50] Though they have now expanded well beyond the Auroville area, Pitchandikulam's signature in each place are the distinctive stone slabs painted with exquisitely detailed illustrations of local flora and fauna, produced in Pitchandikulam's outdoor artists studio (figure 4.5). These can be seen, for example, at the toll booths of the East Coast Road between Chennai and Pondicherry. In addition, in almost every Pitchandikulam Forest project site, a 1- to 3-acre garden is planted with indigenous species with medicinal uses, which are often characterized

FIGURE 4.5 Pitchandikulam Forest's signature granite slab signs.

as a miniature TDEF. If there is an echo today in Pitchandikulam of the Integral Yoga goal of enspiriting matter and cultivating one's own higher consciousness through karma yoga, it is a very faint one. Although they may have their own religious commitments, most of the paid staff and volunteer interns who work at Pitchandikulam Forest, whether Indian or Western, are educated young professionals with degrees in social work and/or environmental science with a decidedly pragmatic orientation toward environmental education and restoration.

A crucial turning point in the evolution of Pitchandikulam into one of the region's most active environmental organizations was its designation in 1992 as a Medicinal Plants Conservation Area, part of a network of parks and organizations coordinated by the Bangalore-based NGO the Foundation for the Revitalization of Local Heath Traditions (FRLHT), whose aim is to revitalize India's medical heritage. Pitchandikulam, with its expertise in propagating indigenous plants from seeds, cuttings, and even bird droppings, was designated one of fifteen Medicinal Plants Conservation Parks in India.

The connection between the revitalization of local health traditions and botany lies in the fact that the foundation of both nonsystematized and systematized traditional medicine in India has always been their *materia medica*, which are overwhelmingly drawn from local plants. Sacred groves are crucial to the preservation of some of these plants insofar as they pro-vide habitat for species that would otherwise be destroyed to make room for more economically useful plants. The desire to revitalize Indians' tra-ditional knowledge about the medicinal uses of plants gained urgency in the 1990s in part as a response to controversies around the world sur-rounding "biopiracy," the unremunerated exploitation by multinational corporations of indigenous knowledge about plants. In India, these fears were sparked by the case of the W. R. Grace pharmaceutical company, which was granted a patent by the European Patent Office in 1994 over the use of neem (*Azadirachta indica*) for a variety of purposes, including as a fungicide, even though it had been used as such by Indians for genera-tions. After six years of lobbying by a worldwide coalition of Indian and European activists, the patent was revoked. W. R. Grace appealed, but in 2005 it lost the appeal. Among the most vociferous critics of W. R. Grace's actions, and of the neocolonial aspects of the widespread practice of inter-national "bioprospecting," was the Indian environmentalist and scientist Vandana Shiva, whose Research Foundation for Science, Technology and Ecology was involved in the litigation.[51] The W. R. Grace controversy stim-ulated awareness in many sectors of Indian society regarding the value of traditional ecological knowledge and the need to document it in order to prevent similar instances of biopiracy.

Darshan Shankar, a former social worker among tribal communi-ties, founded FRLHT as a loose network of local healers designed to share knowledge and revitalize local, orally transmitted health traditions as a means of supporting rural health development. In 1993 he added medicinal plant conservation to the organization's mission. With fund-ing from the Danish International Development Agency and the Indian Ministry of Environment and Forests, he began compiling a massive database of the therapeutic uses of plant remedies by practitioners all over the country. Fundamental to this work were in-depth surveys of rural communities to discover what remedies they employed for com-mon, nonfatal ailments. Much of this knowledge, Shankar discovered, was being lost as the authority of local health traditions declined in the face of competition from Western biomedicine and modernized forms of Ayurveda. FRLHT associate P. M. Unnikrishnan argued that at one time people so took for granted the knowledge of traditional plant-based remedies and other healing practices that to question them revealed one's fundamental alienation from that place. As he stated in an inter-view, "Like if there is a plant that soothes itching, and you ask, 'does it really soothe the itching?' They ask, 'are you such a stranger from this place that you don't even know that?'"[52] The purpose of the surveys conducted by FRLHT was thus not only to discover and document local health traditions so as to prevent the theft of intellectual property by multinational pharmaceutical companies but also to restore the confidence once placed in local healers and remedies based on locally available herbs. Once FRLHT staff established which plants were used in a particular area to treat various common ailments, they created and distributed packages of seeds for the cultivation of "kitchen gardens" so people would have the resources to start using those rediscovered herbal therapies themselves.[53] One of the primary values of the organization is its commitment to pluralism. Consistent with efforts to secure a place for traditional Indian medicine in the face of the growing hegemony of Western biomedicine, the FRLHT sought to give as much authority and legitimacy to unsystematized forms of local medicine (such as snake-bite healers and bone-setters) as to systematized forms like Ayurveda and Siddha.

Though the primary concerns of these two organizations varied somewhat—while Pitchandikulam was concerned about the loss of TDEF habitat, FRLHT was concerned about dwindling support for traditional health practices—the partnership between them rested on the fact that they found themselves facing a similar predicament: The things they cared about were threatened by a population that had largely lost familiarity with local flora. They feared that even in rural areas people did not see any pragmatic, let alone spiritual, value in plants that did not bear edible fruit, produce hard wood, or otherwise have obvious utilitarian value. Together, these two NGOs hit on a solution that promised to raise people's awareness of the actual and potential value of these plants. In 1993 FRLHT, with Pitchandikulam as its local partner, entered into a loose agreement with the temple board at Sri Manjaneswarar Ayyanarappan Koyil, the site of the forested temple in Puttupattu that I described in the previous chapter. Their goal was to study and restore the indigenous species of the grove, using land in the interior of the forest as a nursery for new medicinal plants, and to use the temple itself as a base for spreading awareness of the environmental value of the forest and the medicinal value of the plants in it. As mentioned previously, Puttupattu had been known to Aurovillians for decades. It was the "miracle forest" and one of the places that Aurovillians went in the 1970s to collect seeds from indigenous plants.[54]

At the grove's main entrance, where a dirt road led people and vehicles from the East Coast Road to the main path through the forest, FRLHT-Pitchandikulam staff erected a signboard in Tamil (which still stands) that reads:

Puttupattu Temple Forest Protection Scheme: The ancient forest that has spread approximately twenty-five acres around the Holy Temple of Manjaneswarar is a treasure that needs to be protected. The evergreen dry-hot region forest [TDEF] is a very important type of forest the resources of which are being destroyed. Puttupattu forest is one of that type.

In the area where we [inclusive] live there remain today several thousand acres of forest. [But] now this forest which was protected for many centuries is diminishing and becoming polluted because of the increasing numbers of devotees and the lack of sufficient awareness among the public about forest protection.

Now, with the help of the Foundation for the Revitalisation of Local Health Traditions, this temple forest is being protected by the Auroville Center for the Protection of Medicinal Plants with the cooperation of the temple trustees and the other village people. The distinctive qualities of more than 140 plants along with 80 different medicinal herbs are being investigated in this forest. Through the unanimous support and awareness of devotees the distinctive qualities of the many medicinal plants living here can be protected.

During festival days when the temple thronged with devotees, Pitchandikulam staff gave departing devotees seedlings, or sometimes a mini herb garden of nursery-grown plants with medicinal uses as *prasād* after having visited the deity. They thus sought to raise awareness of both the plants in groves and the riches of traditional medicinal knowledge, in the process making a broad argument for the preservation of the grove. Pitchandikulam staff also distributed a printed Tamil version of the temple's *sthalapuranam* (sacred history or mythology connected with a holy place) written by N. Loganathan, the botanist and Siddha medical doctor described in the previous chapter, who has worked on several Pitchandikulam–FRLHT projects. Based on his own medical and botanical expertise and extensive interviews with temple priests knowledgeable about the deity's official mythology, Loganathan's pamphlet was just one facet of the overall project, but a close examination of it sheds light on the difficulty of synthesizing the environmental, medical, and mythological discourses that different parties involved in the collaboration wished to bring to the fore.

A *sthalapurana* for a sacred grove

Titled *Puttuppaṭṭu enum aivēlaṅkāṭu: tala purāṇamum kāṭṭin makimaiyum* (lit. "Puttupattu Known as Aivelan Forest: The Story of Its Place and the Forest's Greatness"), the cover shows a diminutive, leopard-skin-clad Shiva taking the shape of a seed from the Aivelan vine and diving head-long into its flower (figure 4.6). The opening lines of the pamphlet locate the tradition of sacred groves in the context of broader Hindu ideas often cited as evidence of the ancient ecological wisdom inherent in the tradition:

> In countries throughout the world, sacred groves (*kōyil kāṭukaḷ*) have been protected for many years because of their great importance. It is necessary to make known that in countries like India and Sri Lanka the distinctive custom (*pārampariyac cirappu*) of maintaining sacred groves as important places of worship flourishes. A distinctive custom among our ancestors is that they saw the gods they worshipped in many forms: trees, plants, vines, mammals, birds, insects. Nature's many forms such as the five elements (water, earth, wind, fire and sky/atmosphere) were also famously forms that were suitable for worship.

Like the sign at the entrance to the forest, this introduction, along with the cover and the pen-and-ink drawings interspersed through the pamphlet's pages, seek to highlight the environmental elements of the "story" of Puttupattu. The goal is to shape devotees' experience of the temple, drawing their attention to the surrounding forest.

The pamphlet can be divided roughly into two parts. The first part meets all the conventions of a modern *sthalapurana* (Tamil *talapurāṇam*), which is meant to elevate a sacred site by locating it within the broader pan-Indian mythological context while celebrating the local specificity of a particular place that divine beings once graced with their presence.[55] The second part comprises a survey of the various plants found in the forest, along with information about their uses and the religious lore associated with them. While the treatment of the temple's mythology takes thirteen pages, the description of the "abundance of plants" found in the forest

FIGURE 4.6 Cover for "Puttupattu Known as Aivelan Forest: The Story of Its Place and the Forest's Greatness." Drawing by N. Loganathan. Reprinted with permission.

takes eight pages and contains a three-page "miscellanea" section that consists of a compilation of mostly mythological information related to the Puttupattu *sthalapurana.*

In the first part, the story of Shiva and Vishnu's miraculous escape from the villainous Padmasuran is told several times, embedding it firmly in the narrative world of Hindu *puranas* by framing the adventures of Shiva and Vishnu in Puttupattu as a story told by the Vedic "king of the gods," Indra, to his wife Indrani to quell her fears at a time when they too were being hunted by Asuras (the demonic antigods of Vedic mythology). In general, after the pamphlet's opening page, environmental themes take a back seat to various retellings of the temple's mythology in verse and prose, in short and long form, complete with commentary revealing the story's ethical significance, discussion of the histories of the story's minor characters, and etymologies of the names of people and places. The pen-and-ink drawings illustrating the story do depict the floral backdrop of the temple, but the forest itself recedes to the background of the narrative, significant more as the setting for the adventures of Shiva, Vishnu, Padmasuran, and later Ayyanarappan and his wives and associates rather than in its own right. The pamphlet's purpose as a pedagogical tool to raise awareness of the value of the forest and its plants is conveyed more directly in the second half. Loganathan observes that religious beliefs, specifically the devotion and awe directed toward the gods, have led to the conservation of forests such as Puttupattu. He then enumerates the varieties of plants found in Puttupattu forest, sometimes providing a brief description of the religious lore associated with the plant (e.g., under the heading for "Tumbai" [Leucas aspera, or White Dead Nettle], one learns that "its flowers are used in Murugan worship").

Mirroring its overall organization, the discussion of plants and gods in the pamphlet generally takes place side by side, with almost no connections made between them. This parallelism may be a "safer" approach in the sense of not presuming to dictate what the forest backdrop really means. As such, it can accommodate a plurality of meanings or no meaning at all. One exception is found in a section located in the middle of the pamphlet between the extensive history of Aiyannar and a discussion of the temple's festival days and customs. Here a short paragraph elaborates on a small detail of Puttupattu's mythology, which also serves as the illustration for the cover. This is the episode when Shiva, having given Padmasuran the boon of being able to burn to ash anyone he touched, found himself pursued by the latter. He took form as a bee and found shelter in the seedpod of the Aivelan vine. One learns that this vine grows abundantly in the area, including in the Puttupattu forest, and its seeds bear a striking resemblance to a Shiva lingam. Loganathan writes, "Noticing all the parts of Shiva's lingam in the clearly visible lines of this seed makes known the importance of the background of the story!" Loganathan does not specify what importance this correspondence has, but behind the exclamation point one can surmise the glorious interconnectedness of everything associated with the shrine: its plants, their seeds, and the gods who graced the forest with their adventures.

Though written in a rather scholarly form of Tamil, the pamphlet is an absorbing if occasionally dry read, which provides a wealth of individual facts—mythological and botanical—related to the temple. As I interpret it, the central purpose of the pamphlet as a piece of the FRLHT–Pitchandikulam environmental education program is precisely to bring what is normally in the background, the verdant setting of the temple, into the foreground. Although the text does not link the forest and gods who inhabit it in a substantial or sustained way (the above section constituting an exception), the work of bringing the forest and its plants to the fore depends largely on the illustrations. It is also notable how much the pamphlet is invested in the Sanskritization of the temple's mythological traditions. The author repeatedly underscores the connections between the local story and important motifs, themes, and figures from Brahmanical religious literature. As a result, Ayyannar—the fierce boundary guardian, lineage god, and shrine's principle deity—seems to play a decidedly minor role compared to Vishnu and Shiva, whose love play results in his birth. A critical reading of the pamphlet reveals how working closely with temple officials, a necessity for an NGO initiative such as this, may have limited a fuller representation of people's religiosity, slanting it toward the Brahmanical elements of the complex traditions at Puttupattu, which have been promoted by priests and trustees since the temple came under the management of the Hindu Religious and Charitable Endowments Administration Department (HRCE). The emphasis on the Brahmanical elements may also be due to Loganathan's own personal predisposition. Walking with him through the Puttupattu forest past the subsidiary shrines, I struggled to interest him in the men and women swaying in trance at those shrines, surrounded by crowds of family members eager for a word of prophecy (*kuṟi*) from their temporarily embodied *kulateyvam*. It may be that Loganathan wanted to respect the privacy of devotees who had come to the temple to discuss intimate personal problems and shield them from the curiosity of a white anthropologist. But he also seemed in a hurry to get to the priests and the main Brahmanical temple at the center of the grove, whom he regarded as the most authoritative repositories of knowledge about the deity, the temple, and its sacred history. My interviews with and observations of ordinary temple goers suggest their experiences are not entirely shaped by the views of temple officials (see chapter 3). They control their own experience of the temple by visiting different sites within it, interpreting those experiences according to their own, sometimes non-Brahmanical frameworks. However, the temple management is now securely under the control of the HRCE and thus very likely set on a trajectory of further development and Sanskritization. Whether the HRCE will manage the temple in such a way as to slow or hasten the destruction of the surrounding forest remains to be seen.

Effectiveness of the Campaign

Did the Pitchandikulam–FRLHT campaign to raise awareness of the medicinal value of the forest's flora have an impact on local people? In my conversations with visitors to the site in 2001, 2004, and the winter of 2006–2007, environmental issues did not surface, except when some long-time residents of the area noted a reduction in the forest's perceived density as it gained fame (as discussed in the previous chapter). However, conversations with priests at the main temple and its subsidiary shrines suggest that environmental education efforts did have an effect on those whose livelihood is bound up with the site and who spend the most time in the temple. As Kelly Alley shows in her study of the environmental campaign to clean up the Ganges River in north India, the priests at a pilgrimage site can play a role in promoting or obstructing restoration efforts.[56] So it is not insignificant that all the temple workers I spoke with—from the main temple's Brahman priests and its accountant to the non-Brahman priests or attendants at the subsidiary shrines—recognized that scientists, at least, saw value in the grove and knew that some of the plants in it are rare and have medicinal value. For example, Veeradasan, a non-English-speaking Brahman assistant priest at the main temple at Puttupattu, readily volunteered information about the forest's distinctive qualities: "It is [ever]green forest (*pacumaiyāṉa kāṭu*). This is one of two places with evergreen forest in the world. No matter how hot it gets, it is always green. In these forty acres of land, [you can find] 108 evergreen herbs not found any other place."[57] Veeradasan has clearly absorbed some of the environmental education provided by Pitchandikulam, but it is filtered through his own interpretive lens, as when he enumerates the species of evergreen flora as 108, an auspicious number in Hinduism, rather than 140, which is the number given on the signboard erected at the entrance to the forest. It is also striking how his discussion of the special floristic qualities of the shrine passes seamlessly into a celebration of the power and benevolence of the god who guards over it. Immediately after citing the number of evergreen flora found in the grove, he went on to describe the rituals undertaken by pilgrims (milk offerings, taking of vows, giving votive clay horses in gratitude for vows fulfilled, etc.).

At times, the priestly predilection for exaggerating the glories of the place they tend is applied to the unique flora of the forested shrine. During my visit to Puttupattu in July of 2004, Ramesh, a Brahman with openly Tantric leanings, was the head priest. He made an impressive sight with his bushy grey beard and chest laden with strings of *rudraksha* beads, amulets of tiger's claws, and a large shell "om" symbol. A fluent English speaker, who had held a salaried job for many years before becoming a priest, Ramesh was eloquent about the multifaceted value of the forest, citing studies done at Pondicherry University that documented the decreasing density of the forest (in fact, it appears to be species diversity that is diminishing).[58] This density was essential to generating rain, he said, and the rain was essential to not only people's happiness but also government welfare and ultimately peace.[59] However, people were ignorant of the forests' real value, and so they treated it carelessly. What was needed, Ramesh insisted, was firm intervention by outside forces to first protect the forest through proper fencing or other means and also to raise people's awareness about the value of the forest and the ecological balances that sustained it. He spoke admiringly of the ban on plastic bags enforced by the government in Jammu-Kashmir, far to the north of India. He saw physical cleanliness too as connected to the ecological health of the forest: "If you come to this forest area and throw even a small paper, the ecological balances will go."[60]

As an educated individual with a voracious appetite for knowledge and a drive to see inner connections among all things, Ramesh offered a fascinating, if idiosyncratic, explanation for the taboos against cutting trees at temples like this. In answer to the question of why people do not cut down trees in sacred groves, Ramesh referred to the presence of the god. He continued, drawing on theories of plant sentience pioneered by 19th-century Indian writer Jagdish Chandra Bose, popularized by writers such as Peter Tompkins and Christopher Bird and advanced by the Mother of Pondicherry:[61]

> The tree has vibrations.... It's also having a sense. If you want to make a tree grow, if you daily watch the tree it will grow.... So when you watch that tree daily it will automatically grow. [This shows that] it is having a sense. So when you take an ax to cut the tree, the tree will say, "don't cut me." [But] because we don't know that language, we are not able to understand it... we keep trying to cut that tree.

Given our inability to fully appreciate or understand trees, we need the intervention of governmental or social organizations to keep from harming them, argued Ramesh. Only agencies with such authority had the ability to make people understand the value of the forest. "Only the forest department or government or social organization should take efforts and make them to understand the value of the forest: When you bring the thickness of the density, then thickness is there, then only rain comes, when the rains come, people are happy, when people are happy, government is happy, when the government is happy, the world is happy." Ramesh's description of the cascading positive effects of forest restoration suggests that the Puttupattu initiative did equip some people with the words to describe the benefits provided by forests. His explanations convey exactly the premise behind a great deal of intervention in sacred groves in the 1990s, including at Puttupattu, which is that because people had forgotten or were ignorant of the value of the trees, they were neglecting or destroying them. Environmental education, thus, sought to make known to people the importance of forests in the water cycle and their significance as repositories of medicinally useful plants.

After about five years of collaboration between the temple, Pitchandikulam, and FRLHT, the relationship broke down. In conversations about this, all parties were somewhat circumspect about the reasons. Veeradasan put it most succinctly: "They were here for five years. And then they said, 'For us it is over. We are going to some other village.'"[62] From Joss Brooks's side, it seems the Auroville NGO found it difficult to work with a government-run temple because issues could become so easily politicized. With each election or each nomination of a new District Officer, the whole temple board changed and one had to build relationships with the new leaders.[63]

Another explanation for Pitchandikulam's decision not to continue the collaboration is possible if one considers the collaboration in light of the complex sociology of a Hindu temple, though this hypothesis was not offered or confirmed by any of the participants. The most ambitious hope behind the Pitchandikulam–FRLHT initiative at Puttupattu was that the collaborations would "spark" some kind of initiative on the part of the temple organization to take up these ideas in new ways on their own. But a Hindu temple does not function like a Christian congregation or even like the circle of devotees that surround a Hindu guru figure in modern sectarian Hinduism. In a Hindu temple, devotees of various social strata, from the principal sponsor to the diverse social groups that make up a community, offer to the deity the fruit of their labor (as money, garlands, silk garments, flowers, or fruit) and sometimes their labor itself (as *seva*, "service" to the temple), and then these goods are pooled and redistributed by the deity (or his human representative, whether priest or secular sovereign).[64] I wonder if the NGO's efforts to catalyze environmental awareness at the grove were ultimately incorporated into the temple's own discursive and sociological structure, such that, to put it plainly, the initiative devolved merely into Pitchandikulam's "sponsorship" of paid workers to clean and guard the temple's forest, in the manner of a traditional temple donor, without changing the mentality of devotees, who continued to destroy the flora and foul the forest with litter? The temple's need for a "man to guard" the temple's flora and a team of women to clean up the garbage after festival days was still deeply felt. Even I, the visiting scholar, was asked to help support such service to the temple.

Given the complexities of working with collectively managed sites such as sacred groves, compounded by the legacy of tension between Aurovillians and villages in the immediate region, it is perhaps not surprising that in 2000, Joss Brooks and the Pitchandikulam staff took the work of environmental education beyond Auroville's borders and established a new partnership with a whole village, Nadukuppam, located some twenty-five miles away (figure 4.7). In Nadukuppam, their organizational

FIGURE 4.7 Children's march for the environment in Nadukkuppam, December 2006

center was not a temple but a school, and their emphasis was on education and women's empowerment rather than religion and medicine.[65] It seems they found it easier to create restored landscapes from scratch, or collaborate with a whole village, than to work in partnership with temple associations with their internal power struggles and multiple stakeholders. In any case, both the difficulties of continuing the collaboration at Puttupattu and the fact that it ended without obvious bitterness are conveyed in Brooks's tactful summary of his organization's relationship with Puttupattu: "We've backed away for now."[66]

The trend of supporting sacred grove restoration preservation by advocating traditional health traditions needs to be seen in light of the perception among many scientists and environmentalists that religious beliefs of awe and devotion (*bayam-bhakti*) surrounding sacred groves throughout India are diminishing and no longer provide the protection for groves once had. To prevent the wholesale destruction of sacred groves, it seemed to many, religious beliefs need to be complemented by a new understanding of the practical value of forests, for example, in their relationship to the water cycle or the conservation of medically valuable plant species.

As we saw in the previous chapter, the religious beliefs and practices surrounding sacred groves are changing. Such changes are manifested in Puttupattu as an obvious trend toward increasing Sanskritization. What is interesting is that the FRLHT–Pitchandikulam campaign at Puttupattu did not try to mitigate against Sanskritization in spite of arguments that such trends could have a deleterious effect on the ecological dimension of forested groves, particularly as the concentration of sacrality in the deity's icon or temple desacralized the shrine's surrounding forest. Rather, the pamphlet produced by Loganathan reinforced the Brahmanical elements of the complex religious system at Puttupattu, even while it sought to foster interest in the forest itself.

Conclusion

What broader conclusions can we draw about the kind of religious environmentalism at work in the restoration of Puttupattu's sacred grove? Historians of environmentalism have generated a host of classification systems for sorting different kinds of environmentalism. In their jointly authored book, *Varieties of Environmentalism: Essays North and South,* Juan Martinez-Alier and Ramachandra Guha contrast the "full-belly environmentalism" of the developed global North with the "empty-belly environmentalism" of the global South.[67] Given India's population density and relative poverty, and the fact that many people directly depend on access to natural resources (land, forests, water) for their basic livelihoods, one rarely encounters postmaterialist forms of environmentalism that, for example, advocate a return to "simplicity." Rather, what one finds are varieties of environmentalism that typically share a pragmatic concern for people's immediate needs, each one of which draws on a number of different ideological positions. Separately, Guha has advanced a three-fold typology of Indian environmentalism: (a) "the crusading Gandhian" approach that regards the self-sufficient, preindustrial village, with its ethic of prudent self-restraint, as the prototype of environmental sustainability; (b) the "appropriate technology" approach that embraces technology as a means of enhancing efficiency and solving environmental problems; and (c) the "ecological Marxism" approach that regards both prudence and technology as inadequate to address the problem of how to raise standards of living for India's huge population without spoiling the environment beyond repair. Ecological Marxists argue that only large-scale changes to prevailing economic and political systems will bring environmental justice, the equitable distribution of resources and sustainable development.[68] Amita Baviskar has added two more varieties of Indian environmentalism to Guha's three: (d) the conservationist, exemplified by campaigns by former hunters-turned-wildlife-enthusiasts of the aristocratic class; and (e) the indigenous.[69] The variety of environmentalism that one finds in the FRLHT–Pitchandikulam initiative at Puttupattu corresponds most closely to Baviskar's indigenous type, which is rooted in the assertion that "the cultural beliefs and practices of 'indigenous communities' constitute a critique of ecologically destructive relationship and provide an alternative vision of sustainable human-nature relationship."[70] Subir Sinha, Shubhra Gururani, and Brian Greenberg refer to this type as the "new traditionalist" variety of Indian environmental discourse and note its enormous appeal within the global environmental movement, perhaps because of its connections to "deep ecology" and ecofeminism.[71] Since the 1990s, this variety of environmentalism has proliferated within India, much of it drawing explicitly on religious discourse to motivate people (as I discuss more thoroughly in the next chapter).

Emma Tomalin further distinguishes among types of religious environmentalism in her comparative study of religious environmentalism in India and England, *Biodivinity and Biodiversity*, making a distinction between "weak" and "strong" religious environmentalism. Where weak environmentalism does not subscribe to the religious beliefs surrounding the sacredness of nature but rather seeks to use local sentiments to motivate environmental action such as forest conservation or river restoration, strong religious environmentalism, by contrast, "strongly affiliates with the discourse and values it highly in itself."[72] Compared to weak religious environmentalism's emphasis on guiding local, pragmatic initiatives, strong religious environmentalism often upholds "saving the world" as the long-term goal of praxis, a goal requiring fundamental transformations in human consciousness, human–nature interaction, and the structuring of society.

Advocates of sacred grove restoration tend to display the weak type of religious environmentalism, as exemplified in the statement of Jawaharlal Nehru University professor of environmental science, K. G. Saxena, that "the fundamental objective or challenge these days is in what way you promote sustainable resource management.... Instead of commanding and controlling the people, you build on religion, culture. So that is one way of mobilizing people's participation."[73] In many ways, the FRLHT–Pitchandikulam campaign at Puttupattu followed this pattern. Those involved at Puttupattu were not noted Ayyanarappan devotees, nor were any of the gods associated with the shrine their *kulateyvam*; rather, they wanted to steer the devotion manifested at the forested shrine toward awareness of the forest's value and thus foster concern for its conservation.[74] In my conversations with activists and priests, I never encountered anything like the confident affirmations of the centrality of religion to environmental activism, such as those espoused by the strong religious environmentalists whom David Haberman interviewed in his study of the restoration of the Yamuna and Ganges Rivers, who testified that "'religion is the key' to an effective environmental movement in India that will work to save her sacred rivers."[75]

Yet the participants in the Puttupattu initiative are themselves religious Hindus, so one finds in it a dimension of strong religious environmentalism.[76] Tomalin herself is quick to say that these categories are not hard-and-fast descriptors but heuristic devices meant to clarify observable patterns among different varieties of religious environmentalism. In practice, any particular environmental initiative that takes up religious discourse will exhibit varieties of both. But what Tomalin's classification system does not capture is the hybridic qualities of discourse surrounding religion and nature among religious environmentalists, especially ones with strong personal religious commitments that may not necessarily conform to those of the local people with whom they work. In spending time with several of the men involved in the Puttupattu initiative, I observed a fascinating blend of "scientific" and "religious" worldviews that sought holistic understandings of complex phenomena such as sacred groves.

Although Joss Brooks of Pitchandikulam keeps a low profile about his own religious commitments, his long involvement with Integral Yoga suggests some investment in the soteriological aim of bringing forth life from matter and consciousness from life, which finds a broad field of application in Pitchandikulam's many environmental restoration projects. In conversation, Brooks displays an openness to the possibility of convergence between traditional religious cosmologies and scientific ones, traceable to the teachings of Sri Aurobindo and the Mother, so that, for example, customs that appear mysterious or even nonsensical from a strictly rational point of view are seen as not yet (but potentially) explicable by modern science. One afternoon, Thavamani and I visited him at a Pitchandikulam project in Otteri, one of Chennai's poorest urban neighborhoods. Here he had taken the site of a former landfill, capped it with soil, and planted a park of mostly indigenous species, creating a miniature TDEF over what had been a reeking dump. Walking through the park, Thavamani pointed out a thorn bush the branches of which villagers would throw on their roofs to prevent them from being harmed by thunder and lightening. Though it is hard to imagine how this folk belief could be substantiated by a purely materialistic explanation, Brooks maintained a tactful neutrality, observing that there was considerable wisdom in many local customs and practices.[77]

Similarly, though trained in botany and Siddha medicine, Loganathan's interest in flora was not that of a strictly rational, atheist scientist. He attested to a belief not only in the mysterious and unique energies of plants but also in the invisible forces mapped by Hindu astrologers and mobilized by traditional temple architecture as well. Discussing the importance of fostering greater appreciation for traditional knowledge in general, Loganathan argued for the importance of learning modern ways to condense the energies of plants. "In old temples made according to *vastu* [the Vedic science of architectural design traditionally applied in Hindu temple construction], not these new ones," he continued, gesturing to a plain concrete roadside temple, "there are dynamic forces at work. There are forces too in the images that are used for worship, which are made of special materials, of granite and stones, and these may be activated by the different materials used in worship. In all these things there is a meaning."[78] Like Brooks, and many involved in religious environmentalism, he has a strong interest in convergences between science and religion. In

Loganathan's desire to understand these hidden meanings and energies, as in Brooks's openness to the potential wisdom inherent in traditional practices, one finds a compelling faith in the scientific basis of religious beliefs and practices. Loganathan and Brooks share an expansive epistemology, which affirms not only the compatibility but also ultimately the synergy of religious and scientific understandings of nature.[79]

In addition, both Brooks and Loganathan take a long-term view of environmental work that is informed, I would argue, by a distinctively (though not necessarily uniquely) Hindu perspective that affirms the importance of individual effort while recognizing the impossibility of fully predicting the outcomes of that effort or its final ethical value. Speaking about the variety of ways that people in the area were approaching forest restoration, Loganathan described how, in the old days, wise men could see into things at a very deep level. Nowadays, however, he says, we all approach things in our own way. "Everyone has his own dharma," he said. "It's not easy to say one way is right and the other is wrong. One man gets his living from destroying the forest, another gets his living from restoring the forest. We may think one way is right and another wrong, but we don't know."[80] He concluded with a remark that could describe a number of environmental initiatives around the world, from the assiduous suppression of forest fires in US forests since the 1960s to recently proposed schemes to seed the ocean with iron to mitigate global warming: "We may think we are doing a good thing, but it turns out many years later to be harmful." In a similar fashion, Brooks once ruefully noted the irony, or poetic justice, of the fact that Aurovillians were now planting trees where the first followers of Sri Aurobindo and the Mother went to collect fuelwood.[81]

Such an ethical orientation of tolerance resonates with Lord Krishna's teaching in the Bhagavad Gita, which begins with the observation that people are driven by their own senses of what is right. Arising from their own social locations and often motivated by narrow self-concerns, people's actions always contain a measure of self-delusion and also inevitably come into conflict. In such a world, Krishna counsels not the abandonment of action altogether but rather the adoption of a long-term view that allows for some critical distance from one's own endeavors and an awareness that diverse paths may ultimately lead to the same goal. Loganathan's recognition of the validity of all livelihoods, even those that destroy the very forests he is working to conserve, may appear as a form of fatalism that embraces everything and condemns nothing. It may seem woefully uncritical, especially in a situation where stakes are high, such as when one is facing the near extinction of a unique ecosystem such as the TDEF. But it may be appropriate, even adaptive, in an environment in which success lies not in enforcing a single transcendent moral standard but in harmonizing the interests and motivations, and thus enlisting the cooperation, of the widest cross-section of people.

Some people do long for a strong ruler who could enforce a single, indubitable standard. In conversations with villagers and priests about the challenges of protecting forests amid what can seem like pervasive corruption—where people do whatever they can get away with as long as no one is watching or as long as they can bully others into acquiescing to their breach of rules—I often got a sense of yearning for sovereigns who would rule with a firm hand, compelling people to do the right thing through punitive force if necessary. In such a context, the fierce nature of forest gods may take on additional meaning as an expression of an unrealized wish. But Brooks and Loganathan articulate a more nuanced view of the realities of grassroots environmental work, which entails finding some sort of dynamic equilibrium among diverse stakeholders, suspending harsh judgment against any of them. At highly developed forested shrines such as Puttupattu, one finds pilgrims who want to conduct life-cycle rituals at the temple of their lineage deity (for which they need both shade and fuel wood), non-Brahman priests at subsidiary shrines seeking to increase pilgrim traffic to their small corner of the forest, and Brahman priests and temple trustees eager to spread the fame of their temple (toward which aim they initiate building projects at the expense of trees). More recently, one finds neatly dressed botany students in search of a remnant patch of "climax" forest for their dissertation project, practitioners and promoters of traditional health practices collecting medicinal plants, and conservation biologists concerned about the potential extinction of a unique type of tropical forest. How does one get all of these stakeholders, with their varying cosmologies, levels of education, livelihoods, and interests, to cooperate toward the goal of conserving the forest while also using it in a sustainable way? What the modest success of the FRLHT–Pitchandikulam initiative at Puttupattu suggests is that to accomplish anything over the long haul in a complex social nexus such as one finds in Tamil sacred groves, one must be sensitive to the shifting, dynamic, and decentered nature of power relations within which environmental organizations must work to accomplish their goals. What the project's eventual suspension indicates, however, is that this is not easy to achieve in practice.

5

Sacrifice and Sacrality

SACRED GROVE RESTORATION
PROJECTS NEAR CHENNAI

Introduction

Whereas the previous chapter examined sacred grove restoration projects in which an environmental nongovernmental organization (NGO) sought to partner with villagers to restore extant forest patches, this chapter turns to more radical interventions, where environmentalists have sought to create sacred groves virtually from the ground up. In 1993, the Chennai-based CPR Environmental Education Centre (CPREEC) initiated a project to restore groves in Tamil Nadu, Andhra Pradesh, and Karnataka, seeking to consciously and systematically enlist the beliefs and behaviors surrounding sacred groves in a culturally sensitive reforestation effort. In villages where residents have over the course of time destroyed or degraded the groves of trees that surround local shrines, the CPREEC seeks to help raise trees from bare, rocky ground and educate people about the ecological services provided by even small forests. One measure of the campaign's success reported by the CPREEC staff is that when they restore a site in one village, residents from adjacent villages almost invariably request that the organization start a project with them. Yet the ambitions of the CPREEC sacred grove restoration project go beyond utilitarian goals. Like other environmentalist projects based in some way on the revitalization of traditional community resource conservation practices, the CPREEC project communicates an inspiring utopian model of society, according to which the failures of the recent past can be reversed by developing more culturally sensitive methods that draw on the best elements from the ancient indigenous past, updated for the present. Subir Sinha, Shubhra Gururani, and Brian Greenberg identify this as a common refrain in the "new traditionalist" varieties of Indian environmental discourse. The appeal of this vision for transforming Indian society stems in large part from the failed promises of large-scale mainstream development programs, but it also taps into deeper longings. As the authors write, "As part of the ongoing critique of Indian modernity, the construction of a tradition of unity and ecological sustainability addresses a post-colonial sense of cultural fragmentation, inauthenticity and loss of integrity. The distance from modernity, the quest for authenticity and purity, become the measure of contemporary social-ecological relationships."[1] They contend, however, that the new traditionalist (or "indigenous," as Amita Baviskar terms them) environmental prescriptions are not adequate to meet the complex environmental challenges of today's world, based as they are on simple East–West, modern–traditional dichotomies. How can the reconstitution of tradition be reconciled with, for example, the desire of many rural residents to escape the entrenched hierarchies of "tradition" and attain the pleasures and convenience of modernity enjoyed by middle-class urbanites?[2] Building on the concerns raised by Amita Baviskar, Emma Mawdsley, and Sinha, Gururani, and Greenberg, this chapter focuses on the following question: In the process of the new traditionalists' cultural adaptation of the old or the "traditional" to meet new needs, what exactly is retained as valuable or essential and what is rejected as worthless, harmful, or inessential? What criteria, spoken or unspoken, guide the process of selective adaptation that underlies the revitalization of tradition?

By examining the CRPEEC's sacred grove restoration project, one can see that the manner in which this NGO identifies customary practices and styles of religiosity for revitalization in the service of nature is decidedly selective. This is not surprising, given that the environmentalists at work for CPREEC lie somewhere between "weak" and "strong" environmentalism, to use Emma Tomalin's typology. They are weak religious environmentalists in that they do not wholly share the religious sentiments held by the communities with whom they seek to partner but strong religious environmentalists in that their own religious convictions deeply inform and motivate their activism. Where some religiously motivated environmentalists, however, are content to leave untouched the religious sentiments of the communities with whom they work (even if they do not fully agree with or understand them), Dr. Nanditha Krishna, the dynamic leader of the CPREEC, advocates a more active role of catalyzing religious change. We could add to Tomalin's typology, then, perhaps an "extra-strong," or evangelical variety of religious environmentalism. Like many other scholars and activists interested in

India's sacred groves, Dr. Krishna and others associated with the sacred grove restoration project of the CPREEC enthusiastically celebrate the environmental impact of the sacred groves, but they are ambivalent or openly critical of some of the ritual practices associated with them. In their revitalization efforts they seek to promote expressions of reverence and gratitude for the natural bounty fostered by the presence of the sacred while adopting an evolutionist stance toward some of the other, traditional ritual practices associated with the groves, particularly animal sacrifice, which, for a time, they vigorously discouraged in groves they helped to restore. Sacred groves in Tamil Nadu are generally dedicated to deities worshipped almost exclusively by non-Brahman castes. The CPREEC, on the other hand, is guided by the reform-minded values of its Brahman founder, C. P. Ramaswami Aiyar, the 19th- and early-20th-century Tamil statesmen and industrialist. The implicit selective criteria that guides the CPREEC's revitalization of the sacred grove tradition are heavily influenced by Brahmanical values that privilege vegetarianism over nonvegetarianism and reverence for nature over forceful, even violent, engagement with it. In this way, the CPREEC's opposition to animal sacrifice can be seen as an attempt to encourage non-Brahman groups to adopt Brahmanical values in a kind of internal conversion. This dynamic is not specific to CPREEC. As noted in the previous chapter, the Sanskritization of sacred groves has been widely observed (e.g., by M. A. Kalam; M. D. Chandran and J. D. Hughes). However, the CPREEC's campaign is notable for its self-conscious intentionality and its embeddedness in a broader vision of a unified Hindu society, purified of its "coarser" elements. More gravely, in the context of contemporary trends in Indian society toward the normalization of Hindu chauvinism, it is a reminder that the environmental movement is by no means immune to harmful ideologies.[3]

I begin this chapter by describing the mission and history of the CPREEC and the specific techniques it uses in its sacred grove restoration project. Focusing on the restoration work it has done in one particular village, Nenmeli, I reflect on what elements of the organization's environmental education efforts seem to have had the most impact. In keeping with the overall pragmatism of rural residents, my findings suggest that while villagers do seem to have a heightened awareness of the ecological services provided by forests, they do not necessarily regard the trees planted by the CPREEC as sacred, per se, nor have large numbers of them internalized the organization's message about the need to respect animals by abstaining from animal sacrifice. I then turn to a closer examination of the CPREEC's attempted ban on animal sacrifice by investigating the arguments raised by Dr. Krishna in support of a state law to abolish bird and animal sacrifices in all temples. It is here that we can clearly discern not only the larger moral–religious vision within which the organization's ban is embedded but also its connections to Hindu nationalist thought and political practice.

Catalyzing Conservation: The Methods of the CPREEC

The CPREEC is but one component of the multifaceted social development work undertaken by the C.P. Ramaswami Aiyar Foundation, which also includes a center for indological research, an art center for the promotion of Tamil folk arts and artisanal crafts, and a school for children with learning disabilities. The Foundation was established in 1966 to carry on the work of Dr. C. P. Ramaswami Aiyar (1879–1966), a politician and social reformer active both before and after India's independence. Today, his great-granddaughter, Dr. Nanditha Krishna, is the center's public face and charismatic leader. Trained in art history and archeology, Nanditha Krishna received her Ph.D. from the Department of Ancient Indian Culture of University of Bombay in 1975, writing a dissertation on the "The Iconography of Vishnu Narayana." A prodigious writer, she has edited or authored twelve books on environmental education, art history, and heritage conservation. In a 2004 interview for *The Hindu* newspaper, she cites several sources for her interest in environmentalism. First, her graduate studies in ethno-archeology raised her consciousness about the damage that people could do to their environment over time. Second, travelling with her father, a wildlife enthusiast, led her to see first-hand the devastating effects of deforestation. After marrying and having children, she put aside dreams of becoming an archeologist and moved to Chennai, where she took over the administration of the CPR Foundation in 1981. It was in Chennai that her awareness of the imminent dangers of environmental destruction was consolidated. "The biggest culture shock I experienced was the water shortage," she recalled in the interview. "It set me thinking."[4] Dr. Krishna founded the environmental education center in 1989 as a joint project of the Foundation and India's Ministry of Environment and Forests.

As indicated by its name, the main mission of the CPREEC is environmental education, and, as such, its sacred grove restoration projects are seen as a means of raising "awareness through action." In addition to the sacred grove project, it produces a variety of educational materials for students, host workshops for teachers to integrate environmental issues into the curriculum, and teach women to create kitchen gardens with medicinal plants to promote self-sufficiency and women's empowerment.[5] As with my observations of Joss Brooks's work, following CPREEC since 2001 leads me to marvel at the breadth of its accomplishments. Each year sees the organization, and Dr. Krishna, involved in more and more projects. For example, in 2011–2012 the CPREEC was one of thirty groups entrusted with the responsibility of organizing the Ministry of Environment and Forests' national campaign for environmental awareness on the theme of Forests for Sustainable Livelihood.

Drawing on their own field experience and in conversation with national experts on sacred groves like Madhav Gadgil, activists at the CPREEC have done a great deal to educate people about sacred groves. Their publications and educational outreach campaigns draw attention to the way that the different beliefs and practices surrounding groves—especially the taboos on forest produce and tales of divine punishment for transgression—work together to limit human overuse of the groves' natural resources. The environmental degradation of sacred groves is evidence, they argue, that this ideological system is diminishing. Yet their prescriptions for remedying the situation are strikingly different from those of the Forest Department, which has a history of regarding weakening faith as justification for taking over the management of community-owned natural resources. While advocating for national policies on sacred grove conservation that would meet the needs of all stakeholders, the CPREEC's primary strategy is to support the community's own traditional conservation efforts through the revitalization of those sentiments that granted sacred value to the grove. In addition, the center produces a variety of education programs that supplement what it regards as diminishing religious sentiments with an awareness of the ecological benefits of the groves as seed banks, sites for medicinal plants, and water-table stabilizers.

From Krishna's associates I learned more details about the work necessary to restore the sacred groves of villages where sometimes nothing remained save a small temple, a few tall trees, and memories of the forest that once surrounded it. Between 1993, when the sacred grove restoration project began and the summer of 2001, when I first visited the Foundation headquarters in Chennai, the CPREEC had surveyed 349 villages in Tamil Nadu, Andhra Pradesh, and Karnataka. Thirty-two individual grove restoration projects were underway, of which twenty-three groves had completed the initial restoration process. In general the process for restoring groves consists of several stages: selecting a suitable site, generating interest among the residents in the project, signing an agreement that transfers management of the land to the CPREEC for three years, restoring the soil, planting and maintaining trees, and then returning the site to village management.[6]

When officers of the CPREEC first arrive at a potential restoration site, they begin by asking the older residents to describe conditions in the village. Was there once a forest surrounding the village? What was the water situation like? Were your wells full? In questioning elders about past days in the company of younger residents, they seek to prompt awareness of the connection between forests and water level. Then, they present cultural programs meant to both entertain and educate residents about the environment using traditional folk performance forms (*vilpāṭṭu, terukottai, bomai* [puppet]-show). For example, to highlight the many benefits of their ecological heritage, these productions stage scenes from the well-known Indic epics the Ramayana and Mahabharata with pieces inserted about sacred groves, water, and soil conservation. In the evening, they meet with all the village elders, or the members of the *panchayat,* and ask them to sign an agreement legally transferring management of the land to CPREEC for three years. "What is their number one doubt?" said P. Sudhakar, then co-director of the CPREEC, rhetorically. "That you will take this land."[7] Given the pervasive problem of land-grabbing by powerful interests in India, considerable reassurance is necessary to convince local residents that the CPREEC is not interested in owning their land or even managing it over the long term. In 2001, when I first visited the center, I was told that residents who enter into such a partnership with the CPREEC are asked to agree not to perform any animal sacrifices in the restored groves, for reasons that I discuss in more detail later. Moreover, at this time the CPREEC also sought to appeal to the villagers' pragmatic sense by using bio-fencing that had utilitarian value, such as mango and neem trees. That is, around a core of indigenous plants suitable to the soil and water conditions of the site, they would plant a small margin with trees that bore edible fruit and also functioned as a barrier or boundary marker for the forest. But by 2004 they had stopped this practice (and moderated their ban on animal sacrifice) because of its potential for generating conflict. As Dr. Krishna quipped, "If there were four of us and seven mangoes, how will we decide who gets what?"[8]

After an agreement is reached, the center provides the plant matter, soil testing, and expertise and labor necessary to establish the trees. But the maintenance of the trees remains the villagers' responsibility. Village elders can impose a fine of 1,500 rupees on an individual who cuts wood or grazes animals in the grove, or that person must take care of the grove for two months. Every year the staff from the center returns with their cultural education van and different cultural programs to remind residents of the environmental value of the grove. Such cultural programs also attract the interest of residents from neighboring villages, and when they see the connection between the restored grove and the water table, they too urge the CPREEC to undertake a project in their village.

Nenmeli—A Model Sacred Grove

During the course of my research, I visited two sacred groves restored by the CPREEC. One of them stood on land belonging to the Archeological Survey of India, at the bottom of the hill leading to the famous Jain rock-cut beds at Sittanavasal (fifty-eight kilometers from Trichinopoly). On December 29, 2005, the caretaker paid by the CPREEC enthusiastically showed me around the fenced site where numerous trees with trunks two to three inches in diameter dotted the landscape. Unfortunately, I was not able to talk to any of the local residents. The caretaker claimed they had little regard for the sacrality of these trees; without his presence, the trees would definitely be cut. It is hard to know if this statement reflected an accurate assessment of the situation or his desire to demonstrate his indispensability. A more productive visit to a restored sacred grove took place on July 9, 2004 in Nenmeli, when Mr. Amrithalingam, the botanist and expert on sacred groves whose pioneering book has done so much to raise awareness on the subject, agreed to show me around for the day.

Nenmeli, located about seventy kilometers from Chennai in the Tirukkalakundram taluk of Kanchipuram district, is in many ways typical of villages in northern Tamil Nadu. With a population of about 260 families in 2004, its residents are divided among several castes, including Naicker, Idayar, Mudaliyar, and Iyer, with a few Nadar trading families who immigrated some years ago. Children can study up to the eighth grade in the village school, but there are high schools and colleges within easy travelling distance. A colony of Dalits resides about two kilometers from the village and is connected to the village ritually at the time of the annual festival to the village goddess, Muttumariyamman. At this time,

Dalits play drums and the goddess's procession visits their colony during the last three days of the nine-day festival. In addition to the *amman̠* temple, there is a grand, 600-year-old stone Perumal temple dedicated to Vishnu in his Narasingha (man-lion) avatar, which did not appear to be heavily used but was clearly a village destination shown to visitors.

The restored sacred grove in Nenmeli is a showcase of the CPREEC's work in this area of environmental restoration. It has been profiled in newspaper stories, in CPREEC newsletters, and by a visiting animal rights activist in her blog.[9] According to CPREEC accounts, villagers in Nenmeli approached the organization with an acute water problem in 1995. Adjacent to a temple dedicated to Muttumariyamman, a village "mother" goddess, were four acres owned by the temple, which had been utterly devastated by deforestation and soil loss. A nearby hillock had been stripped of its forests over time, and the heavy rains pouring down from it had washed the topsoil into the temple tanks, which were now filled with silt. Many steps were undertaken in the recovery of the land: Initial baseline data on soil and water quality were collected, then the CPREEC, with help from local residents, created bunds with local rock to slow the movement of water off the hill, mulched deep pits to allow for the absorption of rain water, planted saplings of twenty-six species, and erected bio-fencing around the perimeter of the area to protect the young trees from grazing animals. Other assistance directed at the water scarcity problem was the desilting of the tanks, which serve as a reservoir for the village, and repairs to a well on the temple grove property. One year after the initial planting, the water level in the well remained high even in the hottest months of the summer. An avifauna survey conducted by the CPREEC found thirty-nine species of birds. Encouraged by the initial results, the village agreed to work with the organization to restore another 5.5 acres.

Walking around the restored site, one is struck by how hot it is. We were not asked by the priest of Sri Muttumariyamman's temple or the forest caretaker to take off our chappels, which was fortunate for the ground was not only hot but also covered with sharp rocks. Many species of tree are 9 to 10 feet high, but they are spaced widely apart; the trees have not yet grown into a forest with a closed canopy that can provide cooling shade. The stony ground is hard, and one marvels at the ability of trees to grow in its soil, and yet, with careful nurturing from the gardener hired to tend them, they are thriving.

Conversations with residents during my visit suggest that, as with the environmental education efforts initiated by the Pitchandikulam–FRLHT project in Puttupattu, the residents of Nenmeli absorbed some, but not all, aspects of the environmental education message disseminated by the CPREEC through its extensive work with the village. While the project in Nenmeli has achieved considerable success as a tree plantation and has had a remarkable—and widely acknowledged—effect on the village's water table, it is striking how little the residents actually regard it as a "sacred grove." For example, when I asked the priest to describe the connection between the forest (*kāṭu*) and the amman temple whose land was used for the project, he did not talk about how the forest belonged to the deity, or how the deity arrived in the forest (explanations I had grown accustomed to encountering elsewhere). Rather, he referred to the "forest" in his answer as a garden (*tōṭṭam*).

> Since the garden has been planted...before there was no water at all. Six years ago there was no water even for the *abiṣēkam* [ritual pouring of liquid offerings over the consecrated image] of the goddess. But now, after putting in the trees, water comes [in the well] even in Āṭi mācam [the hottest summer month, July–August] up to eighteen feet. Also, during the *kumbābiṣēkam* [reconsecration ritual for the temple], when we need particular twigs and branches for the *yākam* [fire ritual], we get them from the forest. (Interview, July 4, 2004)

In addition to the idea that the tree plantings performed valuable environmental services, especially raising the water table, and provided materials for ritual worship, several residents commented on the medicinal value of the trees and plants, building on the temple's preexisting reputation as a site for healing. Clients from as far away as Chennai come to Nenmeli, I was told, seeking remedies for personal, professional, familial, or health problems in consultation with the resident *cāmiyāṭis* (lit. "god-dancers"), who serve as vehicles for Sri Muttumariyamman. Such clients will stay in the temple, sleeping there and cooking food without salt for seven, ten, or fifteen nights, according to the *cāmiyāṭi*'s prescription.

Commenting on the presence of many trees with medicinal properties, one educated man said, in English, "If a disease comes, these medicinal plants purify body and mind." Continuing in Tamil he explained, "Compared to going to a hospital, if you come sit here you will feel the *iyaṛkai kāṛṛu* ["the natural wind/breeze"], which will be healing." This led to a discussion of the religious and healing qualities of particular species

of trees, like the miraculous powers of a banyan and a neem tree growing up intertwined together. Such a combination tree had given rise to a
shrine not far from the village where, reportedly, two couples wishing for a
baby had conceived shortly after having worshiped at the shrine. However,
the residents allowed that the restored forest did not have any such powerful trees yet. Mr. Amrithalingam suggested that the trees were still so
small, and the forest so obviously manmade, that such forms of tree worship had not yet emerged.[10]

While residents seemed to have incorporated into their own discourse
concepts linking the forest plantation with the water level and the potential
healing qualities of some of the plants in it, it seemed the CPREEC's message about the cruelty of animal sacrifice had not sunk in. As with most
villages in the northern Tamil Nadu region, the annual festival for the
goddess is marked by rituals in which food or other resources are pooled
and redistributed, symbolically encompassing everyone who counts as a
member of the village in these cycles of reciprocity. For example, villagers
make an offering of *kūḻ* (a porridge made from cooked grains, especially
ragi) to the goddess on the occasion of her annual festival; every household contributes a portion of ragi to be cooked in a giant pot. Residents
I interviewed also freely stated that they sacrificed goats and chickens during the annual festival and distributed the meat to all the households.
Sometimes as many as ten to twenty goats would be sacrificed, depending
on how many people had made a vow to do so that year. In the car on the
way back to Chennai, Mr. Amrithalingam granted that the CPREEC did
not, and practically speaking could not, compel people to abandon this
practice. While the importance of finding alternatives to animal sacrifice
remained a significant part of its environmental education efforts, and
the organization had obtained a written agreement from all the household heads pledging not to sacrifice, he added that "we cannot compel the
people to stop this; they should stop on their own. Some realize and stop
on their own when the cruelty of the practice is pointed out to them; others do not, they keep practicing."[11]

Indeed, by 2004 the organization seemed to have moderated its opposition to animal sacrifice. Whereas in 2001, Dr. Krishna and her staff were
adamant about the importance of this feature of their environmental
awareness through action program, in the summer of 2004, they emphasized that while the organization tried to educate people about the cruelty
of animal sacrifice in every site they worked, their policy banning animal
sacrifice was imposed only when the question of rebuilding a temple

arose. Dr. Krishna explained that government funds were used only for the reforestation efforts (plant material, soil testing, etc.), but when the people saw a grove begin to emerge, they frequently wanted to renovate the temple as well. So if she gave money from her own funds for the restoration of a temple, then she would ask them to agree not to sacrifice.[12] The change in the organization's attitude toward the centrality of the ban to their overall mission may have been a response to the difficulty of enforcing it, or a concession to the firmness of people's resistance to it; however, in the summer of 2004, any talk of animal sacrifice was almost certainly affected by the roiling debate over it that was taking place in tea shops and newspapers.

Animal Sacrifice and the Politics of Dravidian and Hindu Nationalism

Between 2001 and 2004, Tamil Nadu had heard a great deal of talk about the morality of both animal sacrifice and state interventions to condemn it. In the last week of August of 2003, Tamil Nadu Chief Minister J. Jayalalitha issued an order to District Collectors and police officials to once and for all put an end to animal sacrifice in temples by enforcing strictly a law long prohibiting such sacrifice, the Tamil Nadu Animals and Birds Sacrifices Prohibition Act of 1950. Predictably, the move encountered vociferous resistance, from open defiance of the ban at the Pandi Muniswarar temple outside Madurai to the detention of the *cāmiyāṭi* at the Sudalai Andavar temple near Tirunelveli. Nearly one year later, in the wake of a rout at the polls during mid-term elections, Chief Minister Jayalalitha not only retracted her call to enforce the Act from 1950—she took a step further and urged the repeal of the Act altogether. On July 30, 2004, less than two weeks after my July 19 visit to the CPREEC, the Tamil Nadu State Legislature duly repealed the now highly contentious Tamil Nadu Animals and Birds Sacrifices Prohibition Act of 1950. In the swirl of controversy stirred up by the ban, animal rights activists and environmentalists, including Nanditha Krishma, spoke passionately about the cruelty of the practice and its connections to other forms of human cruelty, while Dalit activists and politicians of all stripes condemned the ban as state interference in the free exercise of religion.

It is not entirely clear what motivated Chief Minister Jayalalitha to order District Collectors and police officials to step up enforcement of the fifty-year-old law prohibiting such sacrifice. In the summer of 2003, Jayalalitha was in power again in Tamil Nadu. The object of both passionate support and opposition, the former film actress and leader of the All India Anna Dravida Munnetra Kazhagam (AIADMK) party had held political office for fifteen years. Now, she was enjoying her second term as Chief Minister, succeeding her archrival M. Karunanidhi of the Dravida Munnetra Kazhagam (DMK), a former screenwriter with equally deep roots in Tamil cinema, with whom she has alternated in the position of Chief Minister since 1989. From a pragmatic point of view, the decision to take a bold stand on such a divisive issue in Tamil culture and politics seems an act of remarkable hubris. Yet seen in the context of the maneuvering so necessary to the survival of regional political parties in India's parliamentary democracy, it seemed part of a larger bid to ally with the Hindu nationalist party, the Bharatiya Janata Party (BJP), which had been in power at the center since 1998.

Hindu nationalism is an organizationally complex movement.[13] Its activists are organized through a variety of groups from political parties (the BJP) and global advocacy associations (the Vishwa Hindu Parishad, or VHP) and their youth wings (Bajrang Dal), to social work "volunteer" organizations whose members undergo ideological and paramilitary training (Rashtriya Swayamsevak Sangh). Known collectively as the Sangh Parivar, these diverse organizations share a similar vision of the Indian nation as essentially belonging to Hindus. Their broadly shared ideology, known as *Hindutva* (lit. "Hindu-ness"), has both a centripetal, homogenizing dimension and a centrifugal, antagonizing, or differentiating dimension. On the one hand, Hindutva ideologues seek to encompass a broad range of communities within the Hindu fold, including Sikhs, Jains, Buddhists, tribals, and Dalits—minimizing or effacing their particularities. On the other, they seek to heighten the contrast between Hindus and "foreign others," including Indian Muslims and Christians, who are regarded as outsiders to the nation who may be tolerated only so long as they take a subordinate position. While Hindu nationalist organizations have exercised influence in India since the 1920s, they went into a period of latency after a Hindu nationalist was convicted of assassinating Mohandas Gandhi in 1948. In the 1990s, the Sangh Parivar's main political party, the BJP, rose to power, winning sufficient votes to form the central government in 1998 in part because of the power vacuum left by the Congress Party's collapse under a series of scandals. It also successfully tapped into a sense of righteous indignation among many Hindus that religious minorities were getting "special treatment" from the state while the interests of the majority Hindu population were being neglected.

However, in order to stay in power, the BJP needed to maintain the support of a host of regional political parties, including Jayalalitha's Tamil party, the AIADMK and its arch-rival party, the DMK. Jayalalitha's abrupt departure from the BJP-led coalition in 1999 created an opportunity for Karunanidhi's DMK party to play the role of southern supporter. But in 2003, Jayalalitha was eager to regain that role, and she began heavily courting the favor of the BJP through a variety of measures, both social and economic. Neo-liberals within the BJP, who favored cutbacks to costly, state-run welfare schemes, applauded Jayalalitha's harsh suppression some months earlier of a teacher's strike and her imposition of a 5,000 rupee ceiling on the monthly income for eligibility for an all-important ration card. For their part, Hindutva activists within the party had cause to cheer when she pushed through an anticonversion bill in Tamil Nadu granting the state power to scrutinize religious conversions for evidence of "coercion" and "material inducement." Some media observers interpreted Jayalalitha's decision to enforce the 1950 Act making animal sacrifice illegal, as I have, as one more sign of Jayalalitha's desire to ally herself more closely with the BJP.[14] Yet the move had unexpected consequences. One year later, Jayalalitha was compelled by widespread public outcry to support the repeal of the original Act from 1950, and by 2006 the reins of power had once more shifted to the Karunanidhi's DMK party.

In some ways, one can read Nanditha Krishna's effort to catalyze the consciousness of Tamil Hindus by educating them about the cruelty of animal sacrifice in a similar light. Though operating at a local level and on a much smaller scale, Dr. Krishna's campaign against animal sacrifice in restored sacred groves may be seen as one part of a larger bid to ride the tide of the Hindu right's rise to power in Indian society and politics in the 1990s, similar to Chief Minister Jayalalitha's measures to reform and regulate religious behavior in Tamil Nadu. Interviews with Dr. Krishna at this time as well as a close reading of her newspaper columns in response to the Chief Minister Jayalalitha's order to enforce the Act of 1950 provide insight into the broader moral vision for society that informs her work in sacred grove restoration and reveals the ways it is shaped by themes familiar to the Hindu right.

Dr. Krishna makes a powerful first impression. The morning of July 10, 2001, during one of my first visits to Tamil Nadu to study sacred groves, I sat waiting for my appointment in the grand hall of her organization's headquarters in Chennai, gazing at the antique family photographs that lined its walls. The doors suddenly opened and in came Dr. Krishna. The whole staff, which had been huddled around desks and computers for most of the morning, stood up promptly at attention as she strode across the room and through the doors to her inner office, calling out greetings along the way. In her office, she was warm, gracious, and wonderfully articulate as she described the central mission behind the sacred groves restoration project: The reforestation efforts of the past twenty years had been a failure because they had not gone forward with the consent of the villagers in whose areas they were planted. Forest restoration keyed to the preexisting beliefs surrounding sacred groves was a way to elicit the consent and the active involvement of people on the ground and avoid the mistakes of the past.

That day Dr. Krishna spoke openly and passionately about the organization's controversial, in my view, stance on animal sacrifice. Advancing arguments she would rehearse later in her Sunday column in the *New Indian Express*, Krishna saw their persuasive efforts as a catalyst for evolution. Whereas Vedic religion had incorporated animal sacrifice, Vedic priests changed their practices under the influence of Buddhism. Now that Buddhism had failed to uphold its high moral standards, she argued, in a side reference to the violence perpetrated by Buddhists in Sri Lanka, Hinduism alone carried on the tradition of religious nonviolence. Animal sacrifice was a form of barbarism that Hindus needed to jettison as they evolved morally and intellectually. Indeed, she asserted, villagers had already evolved out of past practices—whereas they used to sacrifice a human, a child, or a hapless traveler who didn't run fast enough, now they slaughtered only a goat or a chicken. Similarly, she took the presence of terracotta images of cows and horses in the grove as evidence of a development of sensibilities away from animal sacrifice, insofar as the terracotta images serve as a substitute for the sacrifice of a real horse or cow. Interestingly, she contrasted this kind of moral and spiritual "evolution" with the radical turning away from inherited customs that she saw in religious conversion to faiths such as Islam and Christianity, which she deplored.[15]

Throughout the year between August 2003 and July 2004, Dr. Krishna, a prominent member of Indian animal rights groups such as the Blue Cross, was a vocal supporter of the Chief Minister's ban on animal sacrifice, using her weekly column in the English-language daily, the *New Indian Express*, as a platform. In a piece she wrote one week after the Chief Minister issued the order to enforce the 1950 Act, titled "Blood on Our Hands," Dr. Krishna laid out a series of linked arguments against animal sacrifice and in support of the ban. These can be grouped in five categories: historical, sociological-economic, feminist, psychological, and civilizational. I briefly describe these before turning to a discussion of the counterarguments offered by those in opposition to the ban.

First, Dr. Krishna argues, animal sacrifice is common to all ancient cultures and religions, but as societies evolve it drops away. Ancient Hindus and Jews alike performed blood sacrifice, but eventually the enlightened sages of the Upanishads, and then Buddha and Mahavira (founders of Buddhism and Jainism, respectively), condemned it. Krishna notes that Muslims continue to do it during Eid, as do villagers in India and Nepal, especially in the context of goddess worship, but this, it is implied, is evidence of their backward nature, their refusal or inability to reform this practice as Jews, Hindus, Buddhists, and Jains have. Krishna offers several explanations for why ancient peoples engaged in sacrifice, some of which further help to position it as a retrograde practice. For example, she asserts that sacrifice was a magical tool used to "control negative forces, particularly disease," but now medicine is more effective.[16] Second, she offers a socioeconomic analysis of animal sacrifice that represents it as part of an underground economy riven by corruption and controlled by organized criminals. Moneylenders, priests, and butchers conspire to send illiterate villagers into debt bondage: Priests first persuade them they need to sacrifice to assuage a deity, then butchers charge exorbitant fees for the animal and its dismemberment, for which moneylenders offer deceptive and unfair loans.

Third, Krishna makes a feminist argument asserting that the female deities who typically require sacrifice are depicted as harsh, cruel, and ugly while male deities are seen as awesome and austere. Recognizing that some male deities also demand sacrifices, she says these *teyvam*s are regarded as the goddess's lieutenants, "who have developed a taste for blood." This gender dichotomy among gods perpetuates myths about women's inherently wicked nature, which legitimizes men's efforts to control and suppress them. Fourth, Krishna's psychological argument asserts that "bloody sacrifices brutalize the viewer, confusing the distinction between right and wrong." She supports this contention by citing studies that have shown a connection between violent criminality and animal abuse in childhood. Emphasizing how empathy can get corroded by witnessing or participating in violence against animals, Krishna underscores its role as a slippery first step on an ethical downward slide. "If one man supports animal sacrifice," she writes, "another will support human sacrifice, the killing of children and *sati* [the immolation of widows]."[17]

All of these arguments together culminate in what I would characterize as a civilizational argument: Given all this, she asserts—its barbarism, its enmeshment in organized crime, its misogyny, and its corrosive effect on morality—animal sacrifice cannot be permitted in a civilized society. We need to evolve in this area, she argues, as we have in others. She writes, "Over the years, we have learned to identify and repudiate negative aspects of Hinduism, such as sati and the caste system. Animal sacrifice is another cruelty that must be rejected and discarded." From her very first column on the subject, Krishna anticipated the counterargument that would have the most force as opponents to the ban gathered momentum—that the ban amounted to the state's unwarranted and abrupt intrusion into people's customary practices. Here she writes, "It is surprising to hear people talk of 'customary practice.' Religion should be value-based and ennobling. Sacrifice is neither."[18]

Reportage from the last week of August into October 2003 covered the range of responses to Chief Minister Jayalalitha's enforcement of the ban. Many defended the practice of animal sacrifice on the basis of history, claiming it as an age-old tradition, one that distinguished particular groups in Tamil society, namely, nonvegetarian, non-Brahman communities who worshipped local deities glossed as "the small gods," "village gods," and "people's gods" in the media coverage of the controversy. Some argued that the feasts surrounding these rituals constituted one of the only times in the year when poor, lower-caste people got to eat meat, often emphasizing that the animals sacrificed were raised by them for this very purpose. A reporter for *The Hindu* went to Tirunelveli district to a Sudalai Andavar temple and cited several sources who said that the festival to this cremation-ground dwelling deity was one of the few occasions when individuals came together across caste lines.[19]

Socioeconomic arguments were often linked to psychological ones in alleging that the ban "hurt the sentiments" of thousands of devotees: first, by depriving them of an integral component of their method of worship, second, by doing so in the name of progress they effectively condemned the act as barbaric and backward. This notion that a community's sentiments can be hurt by public discourse is gaining a great deal of traction in contemporary India and deserves greater attention. Aggrieved parties can demand the censorship of any kind of public discourse, from a scholarly study to a popular movie, to, evidently, a law, if it can be demonstrated that the discourse in question defames or hurts the feelings of a group. Here, Dalit advocates represented the Dalits and lower castes who practiced animal sacrifice as the original Dravidians, whose unique culture was under attack by the forces of Brahmanization.[20]

Dr. Krishna's most revealing arguments were made in a column on October 26, 2003, "Who is an Aryan?" that responded sharply to the claim that the ban on sacrifice was a form of "Brahmanization" of Dravidian culture. Asserting that such a division of Indians into opposed groups is a British creation, Krishna criticized the Aryan invasion hypothesis and its mobilization by Dravidian and Dalit activists in contemporary India.[21] The "theory of a foreign origin for the Aryans," she argued, completely lacks evidence. Second, she contended that Hinduism is united, a complex amalgam of "every tradition to be found in this country." Citing popular regional deities like Lord Balaji of Tirumala and Sri Meenakshi of Madurai, she asks,

> Are they Aryan or Dravidian, or even local tribal gods? Who knows, and more importantly, who cares?...So it is time politicians stop hoodwinking people about Aryan and Dravidian, and cease to blame Brahmanization to score points against each other or cover their own failures. No demarcation is possible in Hinduism. We should ask ourselves whether a law is good or bad, and support or oppose it thereafter. And stop politicians from dividing us over non-existing Aryan or Dravidian differences.[22]

In a similar vein, in an column sparked by the Legislature's repeal of the Tamilnadu Animals and Birds Sacrifice Act, Krishna used the occasion of Panguni Uttiram, when many temples celebrate the wedding of the goddess to Shiva, to compare the incorporation of village religious traditions into "mainstream Hinduism" to a marriage alliance.[23] These ritual wedding celebrations, she argued, are the mythological and ritual residue of actual historical processes, which, far from being a kind of forceful "Sanskrization" or "Aryanisation," was "a natural process, a result of entire communities moving voluntarily into the mainstream." "The ten days of prayer by the goddess," celebrated in these festivals, "reflects the 'transformation' process, when the female deity realizes the inevitability—even superiority—of the alliance, and her cult joins the mainstream." In these festivals, all the different components of society are integrated, whether tribal or caste based, as suggested by the inclusion of all devotees "irrespective of caste and class" in the crowd that pulls the massive *ratha*, or chariot, of the deity around the temple, "making the occasion a massive melting pot of Hindu society." In this sense, she argued, the "Sanskritization" of tribals and lower castes is not a new phenomenon "invented by the BJP to garner votes" but an avenue of upward mobility as "old as Indian civilization." That the BJP is supporting measures to Sanskritize and civilize the lower classes now is merely evidence of the party's deep understanding of Indian society.[24]

In a society where internal differences create fissures and divisions within the social body at every turn, such inclusive rhetoric has its attractions. Much of the appeal of Hindutva discourse, I would argue, lies exactly in this vision of a strong, morally upright, and united Hindu Indian society (and, more cynically, vote bank) that transcends the "petty divisions" of caste, class, language, region, and so on. Yet it is precisely here that we see the combined centripetal and centrifugal forces of Hindutva logic. On the one hand, devotees of a variety of deities with widely varying mythologies and practices are brought under the capacious umbrella of "mainstream Hinduism," provided of course that they assimilate to the culturally "superior" Brahmanical religion, like a docile bride conforming to her husband's family. Such assimilation is mapped onto a trajectory of civilizational progress that is "inevitable," its pinnacle Brahmanical Hinduism as embodied in Shaivism and Vaishnavism. On the other hand, a series of exclusions are quietly being made. What is implied is that outsiders to this project—religious minorities that cannot be amalgamated into the Hindu fold and recalcitrant ideologues who refuse the assimilative project (such as Dravidian nationalists)—are regarded as enemies, even demonized as the cause of India's problems. In this vein, it is troubling to see Dr. Krishna, in a speech before the annual convention of the Indian Science Congress, identifying religious conversion as the single most significant threat to India's network of sacred groves (over and against the pressure caused by demand for arable land, road construction, Sanskritization of temples, militarization of areas controlled by Naxalite insurgencies, and so on).[25]

One could go further and consider Nanditha Krishna's praise for Sanskritization as a straightforward championing of the Hindu chauvanism that helped bring the BJP to power and that has led to policies harmful to India's religious minorities, like the anticonversion laws passed in multiple Indian states in the 1990s and 2000s. But this is probably taking things too far. Ultimately, Dr. Krishna is not a politician but an educator and an environmentalist. She is most interested in catalyzing such changes on a local level, through the projects she sponsors. Indeed, in her column "Winds of Change," she notes the process of Sanskritization happening "very naturally" in connection with the CPREEC's sacred groves restoration project. She writes, "Seeing the emerging forests, gardens and water bodies, the local people in most sites have renovated their temples for the goddess of the grove, choosing to reject primitive cruel rituals such as animal sacrifice and preferring more sophisticated forms of worship." Even the potters who typically serve as priests or *pūjāris* at goddess temples have adopted Brahmanical practices such as vegetarianism and wearing the sacred thread. "I would not be surprised," she writes, " if he were hailed as a Brahmin in a few years." What is surprising is her characterization of these changes as "a natural process," neglecting to mention her organization's concerted education campaign against animal sacrifice in these very villages.[26]

The ethos of reform and civilizational progress articulated in Nanditha Krishna's columns and embodied in the goals of the Nanmeli sacred grove restoration project is consistent with the overall mission of the CPREEC, which, though it resonates clearly with contemporary Hindutva ideology, may also be traced back to the principles of C. P. Ramaswami Aiyar. Ramaswami was a pioneering statesman in the years just before and after independence, known for his rational, improving interventions during his tenure as chief advisor to the King of Travancore. A staunch Hindu with progressive ideals, he was instrumental in the Temple Entry Campaign that forced the grand Hindu temples of Travancore to allow the entry of low-caste and untouchable Hindus. He also introduced the free-lunch scheme in public schools in Travancore, making them accessible to a much broader range of Indian society. Like her famous grandfather, Krishna projects a compelling vision of an inclusive Hindu society where internal divisions will fall away as the nation moves into a modern, enlightened future. However, in the 21st century, as left-wing progressive elements within Indian society emphasize Indian pluralism over unity, such a vision resonates more closely with varieties of Hindu nationalism. Moroever, it seems that the pursuit of this vision at times overrides the CPREEC's overall commitment to cultural pluralism and support of local control over forest resources by those whose livelihood depends on them.

Conclusion

One can sympathize with the sensibilities of those who would ban animal sacrifice. It can be shocking indeed to witness the slaughter of dozens of chickens or goats to the point that the soil grows muddy with blood, which happens regularly at festivals held at many sacred groves. Given the social distance between the urban, educated, and mostly Brahman staff of the CPREEC and the rural, uneducated, mostly non-Brahman residents of the villages they work with, it is not surprising that the former would judge negatively some of the practices found in forested shrines "cruel" and "primitive." Seen in this light, perhaps one can view the reformist project at work within CPREEC's sacred grove restoration program as an effort to bridge religious differences rather than as a form of internal proselytization. In interviews, Krishna conceded that, given her own religious background, the religiosity surrounding the deities enshrined in sacred groves initially intimidated and disturbed her. Moreover, conversations I had throughout my research attest that she is not alone in viewing these deities as "the lesser gods of Hinduism," whose worship is organized around fear, not recognition of the in-dwelling divine in nature. Dr. Krishna commented that it was extremely difficult to raise money from private donors to support this work, whereas money flowed in to support the creation of a garden planted with trees corresponding to astrological birth stars, which the CPREEC undertook in collaboration with the Madurai Meenakshi temple and the Hindu Religious and Charitable Endowment Administration Board.

Yet the discourse of cultural superiority at work within the CPREEC's sacred groves project is also undeniable. It is important to recognize that rituals such as animal sacrifice, which are frequently done to remedy transgressions or to fulfill a vow, are not weird or "primitive" to the people who practice them but are powerful means of communicating with deities and manifesting the bond they have with them. In its understanding of the religious dynamics that foster the preservation of sacred groves, the CPREEC emphasizes the taboos on forest produce and the threatening tales of divine punishment but neglects two other essential elements: possession rituals to ascertain the will of the divine and sacrifices to restore harmony between humans and deities. Above all, it is important to recognize that these so-called "small gods" constitute for the communities who worship them vital links to their mythologized pasts and thus are integral to the community's group identity. The CPREEC's ban on animal sacrifice on the grounds that it will serve as a catalyst for evolution seems to contradict the center's otherwise deep commitment to cultural pluralism and local autonomy.

Some would go so far as to cast Dr. Krishna in the same category as the VHP politicians who latched on to the Tehri Dam issue.[27] However, where the latter have only an opportunistic involvement with whatever hot-button environmental issue, bringing it up as an important platform plank so long as it garners votes but then abandoning the issue when it is no longer compelling, Krishna is much more deeply involved, and for the long haul. She definitely fits the new traditionalist type of Indian environmentalist, and she certainly supported, at least in the 1990s, the BJP and other (but not all) elements of the Hindu nationalist program for Indian society, so it is not a stretch to regard her as a Hindu nationalist sympathizer. But, for the purposes of this study, more important is her role as extra-strong religious environmentalist (to build on Tomalin's typology) whose evangelical fervor motivates her not only to deploy popular religious sentiments in gathering support for environmental schemes (as in weak environmentalism) but also to change their beliefs to conform more to her own.

Afterword

DEPRESSING NEWS ABOUT the environment and erratic weather patterns in our own locales make it hard to be hopeful. Yet experiments in habitat restoration taking place all over the world represent one of today's most promising areas of environmental praxis. Unlike traditional interventions that stave off the destruction of natural resources by curbing pollution and exploitation, restoration projects can apparently reverse the negative effects of years of human impact. From the Florida everglades to the wetlands and prairies of Illinois, from the mangrove forests of Andhra Pradesh to the forests of Tanzania, ecological restoration projects are underway to reintroduce native plant and animal species, dismantle human-made obstructions to water flow, remove invasive species, and replenish groundwater reserves. Their successes demonstrate that natural areas can recover from years of neglect and abuse at a startlingly fast pace.[1] Some restoration projects have sought to capitalize on existing traditions of community resource management, especially those where resources have been set aside for religious reasons. Work in Ghana, Japan, and Ethiopia are especially noteworthy.

In India, restoration projects have sprouted all over the country, funded by federal and state government agencies, as well as by local and international environmental organizations such as the World Wildlife Fund for Nature.[2] As the research for this book suggests, Indian experiments in sacred grove restoration often share the anticolonial ideological orientation of other concurrent projects such as the revitalization of indigenous technology in agriculture, medicine, and artisanal craftsmanship. In mobilizing against the imposition of secular, Western models of development espoused by global institutions such as the World Bank, such experiments uphold the value of cultural pluralism. Also, against the imposition of Western models of conservation that emphasize wilderness preservation, they seek a sustainable balance between preservation and human resource use that is seen as more appropriate for a country as densely populated as India. It bears noting, however, that in the current political climate, with the construction of a Hindu temple on the site of the ruined Babri Masjid looming on the horizon, arguments that appeal to the idea of an authentic Indian past should bear careful scrutiny. The language of indigeneity can carry multiple meanings. Appeals to the local can encode not only the celebration of diversity and defiance of universal norms but also religious or cultural chauvinism and suspicion of the foreign.

Significantly, where restoration ecology projects in the United States have typically involved restoring land devoid of human inhabitants (though adjacent to densely populated areas, in many cases), restoration projects organized around sacred sites, such as those profiled here, involve people. In addition, the restoration of the cultural traditions that support the conservation of landscapes is, perhaps, even more challenging and complex than restoring the ecology alone. This is because it almost inevitably entails an intensification of an issue familiar to environmentalists, namely, stakeholder conflicts. How does one harmonize the interests of ecological conservation or restoration with the interests of a range of individuals and groups with their own stakes in this landscape? One clear conclusion of my research is that it is not enough to label the practices and beliefs that have led to conservation of landscapes as "religion" and then to focus wholly on nonhuman ecology. Rather, successful conservation ecology seems to involve refining one's understanding on all fronts—ecological, botanical, and social. The first generation of scholars of Indian sacred groves, who brought these fascinating sites to national and even global attention, oversimplified the religious dynamics that limit human use of forest resources in sacred groves. I hope this study has helped to illuminate these in greater detail, refining our understanding of what is sacred about these diminutive forests to the people who maintain them.

As previous chapters have established, the deities who reign over forested shrines in Tamil Nadu are typically lineage deities traditionally associated with the protection of boundaries: hero-gods like Karuppaswamy and Muniyandi, village guardian deities like Ayyanar, and fierce versions of village mother goddesses, or *ammans,* who reside at the outskirts of the village. The amman goddesses shield the village from disease, the hero-gods are often enlisted in the service of other gods as guardians, while Ayyanar, mounted on his horse, patrols the boundaries of the settlement, the paddy fields, or the village tank. As befits their use of violence to protect the social order, these deities are, with the exception of Ayyanar, all nonvegetarian deities, whose worship involves the sacrifice of animals, mostly fowls and goats. Even the vegetarian god Ayyanar frequently has a guardian deity such as Veerabhadra or Muniyandi, who receives animal sacrifices in the close proximity of the shrine. As many scholars of religion in India have noted, the protective function of these deities is often combined with moral ambiguity: At the same time that they shield their worshippers from harm, these quixotic gods can also inflict it when offended or neglected. When people suspect a supernatural cause for trouble in their lives, one standard method for uncovering it is a possession ritual, in which a medium, a *kōṭaṅki* or *cāmiyāṭi*, enters a trancelike state enabling a god to speak and act through his or her body. The possessing deity can then tell whether he or she, another deity, or a disturbed ghost sent the affliction and what needs to be done. Often, the remedy to having offended or neglected the deity is sacrifice. The offering of a chicken or goat, or a vegetarian substitute such as a rice packet stained with red kumkum powder, may make up for the moral lapse that led to the god's displeasure, whether a forgotten vow, a taboo unknowingly violated, or regular worship that has gone undone. Similarly, gratitude for boons or services obtained (such as the driving out of ghosts) is often expressed through sacrifice. Forested shrines occupy an important place in this system as the homes and temples of these deities. Forests are their special domain. Residing in forests suits these gods' irritable nature by putting them out of earshot of the *ural* and *ulakkai* (the mortar and pestle) and away from the ordinary domestic life its sound evokes. Mostly neglected during the year, sacred groves typically see the most activity during the annual festival (*tiruviḻā*), when lineages deities speak through their *cāmiyāṭi* vehicles recounting the narrative of how they arrived, thereby connecting communities to themselves and to the mythologized pasts in which the community's identity is anchored. Together, the different beliefs and practices described here constitute the ideological system that limits human exploitation of the natural resources of the groves: the taboos on the use of forest produce, the tales of divine punishment for transgression, the possession rituals to ascertain the will of the divine, and the sacrifices to restore harmony between humans and deities, whose connectedness to a mythologized past cements a community's group identity.

We could go on analyzing these dynamics—and we should—not only because of the ecological significance of sacred groves but also to understand better the varieties of Hinduism of which they are integral part. The

work of Diane Mines, Isabelle Clark-Decés, and Eveline Masilamani-Meyer
is advancing our knowledge of Tamil village Hinduism well beyond that
of the early-20th-century studies by Christian missionaries like Bishop
Whitehead (cheaply reproduced editions of which are abundantly available
in India). Here too I hope this study contributes to our growing understanding of how the religiosity surrounding fierce forest gods of Tamil
Nadu is bound up with other aspects of social life—including very old
traditions of sharing collective property and rituals and myths that rein-
voke for aspiring groups such as the Ambalakkarar-Kallars of the Madurai
area and the Malaivazhmakkal Gaunders of the Tiruvannamalai area their
pasts as warriors and hunters integrally connected to the *kāṭu*.

William R. Jordan, one of the leaders of the restoration ecology movement in the United States, argues that restoration projects offer not only
practical methods of increasing forest cover, preserving endangered species and restoring habitat, but also new insight into human relations with
the natural world. Viewing the natural world as an "environment" leads
to conceptualizing nature as "a collection of objects that surrounds but
does not fully include us."[3] The task of environmentally concerned individuals and groups, then, is to exercise restraint so as not to interfere or
harm those objects (consume less; leave no trace). But restoration ecology, as a form of environmental praxis, requires that one engage directly
and deliberately in the process of species selection. Crews of volunteer
restoration ecologists working in neglected woodlots outside the city of
Chicago take out chainsaws and destroy invasive buckthorn (*Rhamnus
cathartica*) to create space for the thin but tenacious saplings of the native
bur oak (*Quercus macrocarpa*). In this way, they start to heal a piece of
the original oak savanna that was once widely dispersed across the great
Midwestern prarie.[4] Such exercises help us to understand nature not as
objects in space but as a process unfolding in time and across space,
in which human beings are very influential actors indeed. Gardeners
and farmers engage in deliberate forms of selective destruction, as do
adherents of sacrificial religion. Both groups boldly take their place in
the biotic continuum, self-consciously killing one thing so that other
things can thrive—in a repetitive, cyclical, perhaps spiral process leading through infinity. In many religions, symbolic substitutes do the ritual work of actual animal victims, but there is something visceral about
the embodied practice of creative destruction—whether with chainsaw,
weeding hoe, or butchers' knife—that provides a jolting reminder of our

embeddedness in predator–prey relationships, whether we recognize it or not. Heightening our awareness of this is vital, for we are not less vulnerable to ecosystem limits than any other species. Water and fuel-wood crises around the world offer stark reminder of this fact.

Indeed, as if we needed more reminders of the old environmentalist chestnut "nature bats last," as I write this conclusion the western coast of Tamil Nadu, especially around Pondicherry, is reeling from the effects of the cyclone Thane, the worst storm to hit the area in thirty years. In my view, the severity of this storm, in combination with increasing numbers of extreme weather events in many other parts of the world over the past decade, points to the fact that global climate change is already upon us. Thankfully, in this instance, due to well-coordinated advance preparation, fatalities as a result of the storm were limited to forty-nine. But the damage to the local tree cover was extensive. When I visited the area just days after Thane hit landfall on December 30, 2012, the tall trees that graced the boulevards of Pondicherry were in tatters—shattered by the winds, their branches strewn across roofs and choking the streets. Auroville was devastated. Estimates suggest that as much as 70 percent of the tree cover, the culmination of forty years of painstaking labor, was destroyed. Particularly hard hit were the towering Work trees (the name given by the Mother to *Acacia auriculiformis*), a fast-growing Australian import that helped to provide necessary shade and wind protection for plantation of native species. While the destruction of this layer of manmade forest canopy has greatly reduced the lush appearance for which Auroville is justly famous, it has created an opportunity for the smaller indigenous trees to flourish. It will be fascinating to see what the next ten years bring to the forests of Auroville and the other patches of tropical dry evergreen forest in the surrounding area and to see if our resourcefulness and ingenuity can help steer us wisely through the challenges ahead.

Notes

INTRODUCTION

1. For an overview of sacred groves around India see P. S.Ramakrishnan, K. G. Saxena, and U. M. Chandrashekara, eds., *Conserving the Sacred for Biodiversity Management* (Enfield, NH: Science Publishers, 1998). For perceptive analyses of sacred groves in particular regions of India, see M. Amrithalingam, *Sacred Groves of Tamilnadu: A Survey* (Chennai, India: CPR Environmental Education Center, 1998) [Tamil Nadu];Frederique Apffel-Marglin and Pramod Parajuli, "'Sacred Grove' and Ecology: Ritual and Science," in *Hinduism and Ecology: The Intersection of Earth, Sky, and Water*, ed. Christopher Key Chapple and Mary Evelyn Tucker (Cambridge, MA: Harvard University Press, 2000), 291–316 [Orissa]; J. R. Freeman, "Gods, Groves and the Culture of Nature in Kerala," *Modern Asian Studies* 33, no. 2 (1999): 257–302 [Kerala]; Ann Grodzins Gold and Bhoju Ram Gujar, "Of Gods, Trees and Boundaries: Divine Conservation in Rajasthan," *Asian Folklore Studies* 48 (1989): 211–29, and Ann Grodzins Gold and Bhoju Ram Gujar, "Malaji's Hill: Divine Sanction, Community Action," *Indian Folklife* 26 (July 2007): 9–14 [Rajasthan]; and M. A. Kalam, *Sacred Groves in Kodagu District of Karnataka (South India): A Socio-Historical Study*, Pondy Papers in Social Sciences 21 (Pondicherry, India: Institut Français de Pondichéry, 2001) [Karnataka].

2. Dietrich Brandis, *Indian Forestry* (Woking, UK: Oriental University Institute, 1897), 12.

3. Ann Grodzins Gold makes the same observation in "Why Sacred Groves Matter: Post-Romantic Claims." In *Village Matters: Relocating Villages in the Contemporary Anthropology of India*, ed. Diane Mines and Nicolas Yazgi (New York: Oxford University Press, 2010), 112.

4. Madhav Gadgil and V. D. Vartak, "Sacred Groves of India: A Plea for Continued Conservation," *The Journal of the Bombay Natural History Society* 72 (1975): 314–20.

5. Gautam Gajula, "Sacred Grove Lore and Laws: On the Beliefs of Ecologists, Environmentalist-Historians and Others," *Indian Folklife* 26 (2007): 21.

6. Madhav Gadgil and Ramachandra Guha, *This Fissured Land: An Ecological History of India* (New Delhi: Oxford University Press, 1999), 24.

7. Ibid., 24.

8. M. D. Subhash Chandran and J. D. Hughes, "Sacred Groves and Conservation: The Comparative History of Traditional Reserves in the Mediterranean Area and in South India," *Environment and History* 6, no. 2 (May 2000): 182. See also M. D. Subhash Chandran and J. Donald Hughes, "The Sacred Groves of South India: Ecology, Traditional Communities and Religious Change," *Social Compass* 44, no. 3 (1997): 413–27.

9. Chandran and Hughes, "Sacred Groves and Conservation," 172, 176.

10. Chandran and Hughes, "The Sacred Groves of South India," 418.

11. Gajula, "Sacred Grove Lore and Laws," 20.

12. Gadgil and Vartak, "Sacred Groves of India," 320 (emphasis added).

13. See, for example, N. Visalakshi, "Vegetation Analysis of Two Tropical Dry Evergreen Forests in Southern India," *Tropical Ecology* 36, no. 1 (1995): 117–27; M. P. Ramanujam and D. Kadamban, "Plant Biodiversity of Two Tropical Dry Evergreen Forests in the Pondicherry Region of South India and the Role of Belief Systems in their Conservation," *Biodiversity and Conservation* 10 (2001): 1203–17.

14. Emma Mawdsley, "The Abuse of Religion and Ecology: The Vishva Hindu Parishad and Tehri Dam," *Worldviews: Environment, Culture, Religion* 8, no. 2 (2006): 1–24; Meera Nanda, *The Wrongs of the Religious Right: Reflections on Science, Secularism, and Hindutva* (Delhi: Three Essays Collective, 2005); Mukul Sharma, "Saffronising Green," *Seminar* 516 (2002).

15. Maharashtra Act No. XXIX of 1975 (The Maharashtra Private Forests [Acquisition] Act, 1975), 1. Available at bombayhighcourt.nic.in/libweb/acts/1975.29.pdf (accessed July 13, 2011)].

16. J. J. Roy Burman, *Sacred Groves among Communities: The Mahadeo Kolis and the Kunbis of the Western Ghats* (New Delhi: Mittal Publications, 2003), 197–204.

17. "Operational Guidelines for the Centrally Sponsored Scheme: 'Intensification of Forest Management,'" Forest Protection Division, Ministry of Environment and Forests, Government of India (August 2009), p. 7. Available at *moef.nic.in/divisions/forprt/OPERATIONAL.pdf* (accessed August 31, 2012).

18. Ibid., 7.

19. Ibid., 8.

20. Vandana Shiva, *Staying Alive: Women, Ecology and Survival in India* (New Delhi: Zed Press, 1988), 57.

21. See Peter Brosius, "Analyses and Interventions: Anthropological Engagements with Environmentalism," *Current Anthropology* 40, no. 3 (1999): 245–69; also cited in Emma Tomalin, *Biodivinity and Biodiversity: The Limits to Religious Environmentalism* (Burlington, VT: Ashgate, 2009), 7. In India see William Elison, "'Bonafide Tribals': Religion and Recognition among Denizens of

Mumbai's Forest Frontier," *Journal for the Study of Religion, Nature and Culture* 4, no. 2 (2010): 191–212.

22. Amita Baviskar, "Tribal Politics and the Discourses of Environmentalism," *Contributions to Indian Sociology* 31, no. 2 (1997): 195–224.

23. Amrithalingam, *Sacred Groves of Tamilnadu*, 17.

24. First coined by Indian anthropologist M. N. Srinivas in the 1950s to describe changes among non-Brahman communities in the Kodaga (Coorg) region of Karnataka, the concept of "Sanskritization" has had a contested history. However, in my view it retains considerable utility in describing changes in the religiosity of upwardly mobile low-caste groups as they seek to raise their status (or assert claims to having already improved their status) by adopting practices, beliefs, values, and norms associated with high castes or dominant castes.

25. Tomalin, *Biodivinity and Biodiversity*, 1–24.

26. Several articles have offered such culturally nuanced examinations of sacred groves, including Freeman, "Gods, Groves and the Culture of Nature in Kerala"; Frederique Apffel-Marglin and Pramod Parajuli, "'Sacred Grove' and Ecology"; and Ann Grodzins Gold and Ram Bhoju Gujar, "Malaji's Hill."

27. Forests, groves, and trees have long had enormous significance in Indic religious life and literature. See Robert Menzies' useful typology of forests in Sanskrit epics: Robert Menzies, "Forest Paradigms in Vrat Kathas," *Journal for the Study of Religion, Nature and Culture* 4, no. 2 (June 2010): 140–49. Also Philip Lutgendorf, "City, Forest, and Cosmos: Ecological Perspectives from the Sanskrit Epics," in *Hinduism and Ecology: The Intersection of Earth, Sky, and Water*, ed by Christopher Key Chapple and Mary Evelyn Tucker (Cambridge, MA: Center for the Study of World Religions, 2000), 269–89. However, ancient texts record only a few isolated instances of the preservation of sacred groves where such protection is attributed to local deities, as in the modern sacred grove phenomenon. For example, the Sanskrit poet Kālidasā's drama *Śankuntalā* (c. 300–470 CE) describes an ascetics' grove whose trees and animal residents the ascetics protect against the depradations of kings addicted to hunting. The Tamil collection of Sangam-era war poems, *Puṛanāṇūṛu* (c. 100–350 CE) cites the importance of the king's tutelary tree (*kaṭivaram*, or *kāvalvaram*) as a symbol of his power, such that its fruit was tabooed, and the trees and groves of rival kings were destroyed in battle (Puṛanāṇūṛu 23:9, 163:4). See George Hart, *Poems of Ancient Tamil: Their Milieu and their Sanskrit Counterparts* (Berkeley: University of California Press, 1975), 16–17.

28. Chandran and Hughes, "The Sacred Groves of South India," 416, 420.

CHAPTER 1

1. John Muir, "The Forests of the Yosemite Park," in *Nature Writings*, by John Muir (New York: Library Classics, 1997), 767.

2. A hectare is a unit for measuring land equivalent to 10,000 square meters (100 meters by 100 meters). One hectare is equal to 2.471 acres.

3. As I discuss in chapters 3 and 4, sacred groves are important to botanists and environmentalists as sanctuaries for indigenous species not found elsewhere, but people I spoke with freely mentioned eucalyptus, a clear foreign import, among those growing in their groves. Moreover, when I asked if medicinal plants (*mulikai*) were more likely to grow in sacred groves, my informants answered with characteristic pragmatism that it is not necessarily the case that medicinal plants are more plentiful around temples, but that in other places they have cut them down to grow plants with greater or more direct economic value. In that way, the taboos against cutting have allowed medicinal plants to be more abundant in sacred groves. (Interview with residents, Azhagapuri village, December 30, 2004).

4. Émile Durkheim, *Elementary Forms of the Religious Life*, trans. Karen E. Fields (New York: The Free Press, 1995), 227.

5. K. N. Radhakrishnan, *Thirumalinrunjolai: Sri Alagar Koil Stala Purana* (Madurai, India: Sri Kallalagar Devastanam, 1942), 240–41.

6. The villages I focus on in this chapter regard the spring as the domain of the goddess Rakkayi Amman, while in the *Cilapatikaram*, it was called Cilambāṟu (lit. "anklet-river").

7. R. Parthasarathy, ed. and trans., *The Cilapatikaram of Ilanko Atikal: An Epic of South India* (New York: Columbia University Press, 1993), 112–13 (Canto 11, verses 87–130).

8. Sumit Guha, *Ecology and Ethnicity in India, c. 1200–1991* (Cambridge, UK: Cambridge University Press, 1999), 37.

9. Arjun Appadurai and Carol A. Breckenridge, "The South Indian Temple: Authority, Honour and Redistribution," *Contributions to Indian Sociology* (n.s.) 10, no. 2 (1976): 187–211.

10. Radhakrishnan, *Thirumalinrunjolai*, 59.

11. Ibid., 60.

12. Ibid., 71.

13. W. Francis, *Madras District Gazetteers: Madura*, Vol. 1 (Madras: Superintendent, Government Press, 1914), 137.

14. For the first, see E. Valentine Daniel, *Fluid Signs: Being a Person the Tamil Way* (Berkeley: University of California Press, 1984), 79–95; Francis Zimmerman, *The Jungle and the Aroma of Meats: An Ecological Theme in Hindu Medicine*, Comparative Studies of Health Systems and Medical Care 20 (Berkeley: University of California Press, 1988). For the second, see Anand Pandian's *Crooked Stalks: Cultivating Virtue in South India* (Durham, NC: Duke University Press, 2009), which examines how British constructions of the nobility of agrarian toil (and the ignominy of those who "preyed" on such hard-working groups) were synthesized with premodern Tamil constructions to consolidate a view of Kallars, an important caste community in the area whom I discuss in more detail shortly, as "inveterate criminals."

15. For the most innovative and comprehensive presentation of this argument, see Nicholas B. Dirks, *Castes of Mind: Colonialism and the Making of Modern India* (Princeton, NJ: Princeton University Press, 2001).

16. Pamela G. Price, *Kingship and Political Practice in Colonial India*, University of Cambridge Oriental Publications 51 (Cambridge, UK: Cambridge University Press, 1996).

17. Like any history attributed to a community's name, the etymology of Kallar can be debated. Many scholars affirm, though, that these usages can be traced to early Tamil when *kaḷvar* meant "thief" and *kaḷḷan* was synonymous with *oṟṟan* for "spy". Personal communication, D. Samuel Sudanandha.

18. Anand Pandian, "Securing the Rural Citizen: The Anti-Kallar Movement of 1896," *Indian Economic and Social History Review* 42, no. 1 (2005): 4–10.

19. Edgar Thurston and K. Rangachari, *Castes and Tribes of Southern India* (Madras, India: Government of Madras, 1909), Vol. 1, 25; Vol. 3, 63.

20. David Ludden, *Peasant History in South India* (Princeton, NJ: Princeton University Press, 1985); Nicholas B. Dirks, "The Pasts of a Palaiyakkarar: The Ethnohistory of a South Indian Little King," *The Journal of Asian Studies* 41, no. 4 (1982): 655–683; Nicholas B. Dirks, *The Hollow Crown: Ethnohistory of a Little Kingdom in South India* (Cambridge, UK: Cambridge University Press, 1987).

21. The poligar system was probably initiated during the Vijayanagara Empire, when local chieftains were entrusted with the responsibility to maintain law and order, collect revenue, and muster troops for the king. In return, they kept one-quarter to one-third of the state's share of the harvest. When the Vijayanagar Empire weakened, their governors in Madurai, the Telegu-speaking Nayakas, gained control over large tracts of territory in southern Tamil Nadu. They too allocated these same responsibilities to local chieftains, even formalizing the *pāḷaiyakkārar* system by dividing the country into seventy-two *pāḷaiyams* ("fortified domain, camp"), each of which was effectively ruled by a *pāḷaiyakkārar* (Dirks, "The Pasts of a Palaiyakkarar," 49–50; see also Sanjay Subramanyam, *Penumbral Visions: Making Polities in Early Modern South India* [Ann Arbor: University of Michigan Press, 2001], 170–71).

22. Thurston and Rangachari, *Castes and Tribes of Southern India*, Vol. 1, 58–59.

23. Stuart H. Blackburn, "The Kallars: A Tamil 'Criminal Tribe' Reconsidered." *South Asia* (n.s.) 1 (1978): 38–51; Pandian, "Securing the Rural Citizen, " 4–10; Pandian, *Crooked Stalks,* 65–99.

24. A. Mohanakrishnan, *A History of the Periyar Dam with Century Long Performance* (New Delhi: Central Board of Irrigation & Power, 1997).

25. Pandian, *Crooked Stalks,* 187–92. Like many Indian communities of foragers, herders, warriors, mountain-dwelling people, etc., this "settling" has been an ongoing process for centuries; see Sumit Guha, *Ecology and Ethnicity in India.*

26. D. Samuel Sudanandha, "The Making of a Muttaraiyar Cati," Ph.D. diss. (Seattle: University of Washington, 1996), 33, 86.

27. Nicholas B. Dirks, *The Hollow Crown: Ethnohistory of a Little Kingdom in South India* (Cambridge: Cambridge University Press, 1987), 270.

28. Dirks, *The Hollow Crown,* 270–71.

29. See, for example, Robert L. Hardgrave, *The Nadars of Tamilnad: The Political Culture of a Community in Change* (Berkeley: University of California Press, 1969).

30. Sudanandha, "The Making of a Muttaraiyar Cati," 132–68.

31. Ibid., 130, 134.

32. David Dean Shulman, *The King and the Clown in South Indian Myth and Poetry* (Princeton, NJ: Princeton University Press, 1985), 355–65.

33. For a Rajasthani example of community policing of a sacred grove, see Ann Grodzins Gold and Bhoju Ram Gujar, "Malaji's Hill: Divine Sanction, Community Action," *Indian Folklife* 26 (2007): 9–14.

34. Physical inaccessibility is, Kalam argues, the principal reason that sacred groves are not destroyed, above and beyond any other factors including strength of religious belief or property relations. M. A. Kalam, *Sacred Groves in Kodagu District of Karnataka (South India): A Socio-Historical Study,* Pondy Papers in Social Sciences 21 (Pondicherry, India: Institut Français de Pondichéry, 2001).

35. Chandran and Hughes, "The Sacred Groves of South India" 420–22.

36. Brenda Beck, "Colour and Heat in South Indian Ritual," *Man* (n.s.) 4, no. 4 (1969): 553–72.

37. Ann Grodzins Gold and Bhoju Ram Gujar, "Of Gods, Trees and Boundaries: Divine Conservation in Rajasthan," *Asian Folklore Studies* 48 (1989): 211–29; Albertina Nugteren, *Belief, Beauty, and Bounty: Rituals around Sacred Trees in India* (Leiden: Brill, 2005).

38. As I have argued elsewhere, the complex nature of ownership of temple forests probably acts as a break on development, since so many individuals (including the deity, speaking through an oracle) must agree before any large-scale changes can take place. Eliza F. Kent and M. P. Ramanujam, "Fierce Gods and Dense Forest: Sacred Groves in Coromandel," *Indian Folklife* 26 (July 2007): 14–19.

39. George L. Hart, "Introduction," in *The Four Hundred Songs of War and Wisdom: An Anthology of Poems from Classical Tamil: The Purunanuru,* ed. and trans. George L. Hart and Hank Heifetz (New York: Columbia University Press, 1999), xvii–xiv; Joanne Punzo Waghorne, *The Raja's Magic Clothes: Re-Visioning Kingship and Divinity in England's India* (University Park: Pennsylvania State University Press, 1994).

40. Eveline Masilamani-Meyer, *Guardians of Tamilnadu: Folk Deities, Folk Religion, Hindu Themes,* Neue Hallesche Berichte 5 (Halle, Germany: Franckesche Stiftungen zu Halle, 2004), 55–63.

41. The following interpretation of the symbolism of fierce gods and their role in village religiosity takes the point of view of dominant castes in the village, in part because almost all the people I encountered in my visits to villages were from such groups. In her marvelously detailed ethnography on the role of religion in village life, *Fierce Gods: Inequality, Ritual and the Politics of Dignity in a South*

Indian Village (Bloomington: Indiana University Press, 2005), Diane Mines investigates the way the pantheon of gods is related to social structure, especially in terms of caste relations. Her long residence in a village in Tirunelveli allowed her the opportunity to discern the subtle but highly significant differences between how low-caste and marginal groups and high-caste and dominant groups viewed these gods. Untouchables and very low castes who are traditionally compelled to live outside the physical boundary of the *ūr* in the *kāṭu* itself feel connected to, and supported by, the *kāṭṭu sāmikaḷ* in distinctive ways. See especially chapters 6 and 8.

42. Richard L. Brubaker, "The Ambivalent Mistress: A Study of South Indian Village Goddess and their Religious Meaning," Ph.D. diss., University of Chicago, 1978; David R. Kinsley, *Hindu Goddesses: Visions of the Divine Feminine in the Hindu Religious Tradition* (Berkeley: University of California Press, 1988); Masilamani-Meyer, *Guardians of Tamilnadu.* But see also Lynn Foulston for an argument that the alleged "malevolence" and "unpredictability" of Hindu village goddesses is overstated and distorting: Lynn Foulston, *At the Feet of the Goddess: The Divine Feminine in Local Hindu Religion* (Portland, OR: Sussex Academic Press, 2002).

43. Masilamani-Meyer, *Guardians of Tamilnadu,* 57.

44. Dirks, "The Pasts of a Palaiyakkarar," 221; Mines, *Fierce Gods,* 130–35.

45. See also Masilamani-Meyer, *Guardians of Tamilnadu,* 63–65; Sudanandha, "The Making of a Muttaraiyar Cati," 57.

46. On a more prosaic level, the phrase may refer to a traditional way of measuring or indicating distance—the gods need to be placed far enough away that they cannot hear this very loud sound.

47. C. J. Fuller, *The Camphor Flame: Popular Hinduism and Society in India* (Princeton, NJ: Princeton University Press, 1992); Alf Hiltebeitel, ed. *Criminal Gods and Demon Devotees: Essays on the Guardians of Popular Hinduism* (Albany: State University of New York Press, 1989).

48. Lawrence A. Babb, *The Divine Hierarchy: Popular Hinduism in Central India* (New York: Columbia University Press, 1975).

49. For a vivid rendering of the relations between the presiding deities of the Madurai region and their complex internal relations, see the classic documentary film, *Wedding of the Goddess,* dir. Mira Reym Binford and Michael Camerini (Madison: University of Wisconsin at Madison South Asia Center, 1976), DVD.

50. Appadurai and Breckenridge, "The South Indian Temple," 190–95.

51. See also Radhakrishnan, *Thirumalinrunjolai,* 210–15; Henry Whitehead, *The Village Gods of South India* (Calcutta: Association Press, 1921), 113–15.

52. Radhakrishnan, *Thirumalinrunjolai,* 212.

53. David Dean Shulman, *Tamil Temple Myths: Sacrifice and Divine Marriage in the South Indian Saiva Tradition* (Princeton, NJ: Princeton University Press, 1980), 348 n24.

54. Ibid.

55. The association of kings with rain has many sources in Indic thought. Certainly, the Vedic god Indra, king of the gods whose weapon is the thunderbolt,

establishes a pattern found in many parts of India. But Tamil literature composed prior to extensive contact with the Indo-European civilization contains
its own version of this association. See George L. Hart's highly suggestive discussion of the ancient Tamil vision of the king as commander of rain: Hart,
"Introduction," xvii–xx.

56. Shulman, *The King and the Clown in South Indian Myth and Poetry*, 355–64.
57. Dirks, "The Pasts of a Palaiyakkarar," 655–83.
58. Cf. Karin Kapadia, *Siva and Her Sisters: Gender, Caste, and Class in Rural South India* (Boulder, CO: Westview Press, 1995), and Mines, *Fierce Gods*.
59. Whitehead, *The Village Gods of South India*.
60. Fuller, *The Camphor Flame*.
61. Shulman, *The King and the Clown in South Indian Myth and Poetry*, 359.
62. In his ethnography of religion among the Pramalai Kallars, Louis Dumont does recognize how Karuppasamy's role of watchman "corresponds with great exact-ness to the traditional social role of the Kallar as watchman," but his obsession with purity and pollution leads him in other directions, and he does not explore this observation in greater depth. Louis Dumont, *A South Indian Subcaste: Social Organization and Religion of the Pramalai Kallar*, trans. Michael Moffatt (Delhi: Oxford University Press, 1986), 408.
63. Laurie L. Patton, "Nature Romanticism and Sacrifice in Rigvedic Interpretation," in *Hinduism and Ecology: The Intersection of Earth, Sky and Water*, ed. by Christopher Key Chapple and Mary Evelyn Tucker (Cambridge, MA: Harvard University Press, 2000), 39–58.

CHAPTER 2

1. Derek Wall, *Earth First! And the Anti-Roads Movement* (London: Routledge, 1999).
2. Robert E. Frykenberg, "On Roads and Riots in Tinnevelly: Radical Change and Ideology in Madras Presidency during the 19th Century," *South Asia* 2 (1982): 34–52.
3. Aravind Adiga, *The White Tiger: A Novel* (New York: The Free Press, 2008).
4. M. Amrithalingam, *Sacred Groves of Tamilnadu: A Survey* (Chennai, India: CPR Environmental Education Center, 1998).
5. Jo Lawbuary, "Eucalyptus Planting in 'Social Forestry' in India: Boon or Curse?" *Ganesha*, http://www.ganesha.co.uk/articles.htm (accessed August 9, 2010).
6. See, for example, Cathy Nesmith, "Gender, Trees, and Fuel: Social Forestry in West Bengal," *Human Organisation*, 50, no. 4 (1991): 337–48; Bina Agarwal, "Participatory Exclusions, Community Forestry and Gender: An Analysis for South Asia and Conceptual Framework," *World Development* 29, no. 10 (2001): 1623–48; V. K. Prabhakar, *Social and Community Forestry* (New Delhi: Satish Garg, 1998).

7. J. J. Roy Burman, *Sacred Groves among Communities: The Mahadeo Kolis and the Kunbis of the Western Ghats* (New Delhi: Mittal Publications, 2003), 197–204.

8. In the absence of detailed historical evidence, the actual origins of the Malaiyali Gounders are uncertain. Historian Velayutham Saravanan describes at least two other theories, based on ancient Tamil Sangam literature composed roughly between 100 BCE to 300 CE. One posits that the Malaiyalis were Aryan migrants from the north who settled in the formerly uninhabited mountains of present-day Tamil Nadu, while the other claims that they were indigenous to the hills areas from the ancient Sangam period. Velayutham Saravanan, "Colonialism and Coffee Plantations: Decline of Environment and Tribals in Madras Presidency during the Nineteenth Century," *The Indian Economic and Social History Review* 41, no. 4 (2004): 469–70. What seems clear is that currently the most salient origin narrative in their rituals and self-presentation is the one retold by Mr. Velu (pseudonym). Based on similarities between it and the narratives related in British manuals, gazetteers, and government reports, it seems likely that this "oral history" has been influenced by written colonial histories, in a manner not atypical in India.

9. W. Francis, *Madras District Gazetteers: South Arcot*, Vol. 1 (Madras: Superintendent, Government Press, 1906), 4.

10. According to Saravanan, in the neighboring Shevaroy range, the percentage of tribals who were working as wage laborers increased from 28 percent in 1871 to 45 percent in 1901. See Velayutham Saravanan, "Colonialism and Coffee Plantations," 477. Elsewhere he shows that the nonsalubrious climate and lack of irrigation facilities of the Kalrayan hills prevented the rapid development of the region for coffee cultivation that one sees in other hilly tribal areas. See Velayutham Saravanan, "Colonial Agrarian Policies in the Tribal Areas of Madras Presidency: 1872–1947," *South Asia Research* 26.1 (2006): 69.

11. S. Thirunavukkarasu, *Land Reforms and Tribal Development: A Case Study of Kalrayan Hills Tamil Nadu* (Delhi: Kalpaz Publications, 2006).

12. This is consistent with the changes measured by the decennial census. According to the 2001 census, the literacy rates for the scheduled tribe population in Tamil Nadu over the age of seven was 41.5 percent, a significant increase from 27.9 percent recorded in the 1991 census. Office of the Register General and Census Commissioner, "Data Highlights: The Scheduled Tribes," *Census of India 2001* (Delhi, India: Office of the Register General, 2001), 2. Available at http://census-india.gov.in/default.aspx (accessed September 6, 2012).

13. Cf. Elizabeth Finnis, "Why Grow Cash Crops? Subsistence Farming and Crop Commercialization in the Kolli Hills, South India," *American Anthropologist* 108, no. 2 (June 2006): 363–69.

14. This response resonates with M. A. Kalam's findings from his historical analysis of sacred groves in Karnataka. He makes the case that people's capacity to rationalize destruction of the groves in order to satisfy material needs is almost limitless, which is why he believes the only sure protection against the exploitation

of sacred groves over time is their remoteness from human settlements and roads. M. A. Kalam, *Sacred Groves in Kodagu District of Karnataka (South India): A Socio-Historical Study*, Pondy Papers in Social Sciences 21 (Pondicherry, India: Institut Français de Pondichéry, 2001).

15. Karin Kapadia, *Siva and Her Sisters: Gender, Caste, and Class in Rural South India* (Boulder, CO: Westview Press, 1995), 66–67.

16. At one time, *adivāsi* people's relative nonchalance about purity/pollution issues was taken as a distinguishing feature proving that they were not Hindus. But here we see comparable beliefs and behaviors about pollution, caste, and gender at work among a tribal community, demonstrating either the extent to which these Malaiyalis have been influenced by Brahmanical Hinduism or the artificiality of these bureaucratic distinctions in the first place.

17. Sumit Guha, *Ecology and Ethnicity in India, c. 1200–1991* (Cambridge, UK: Cambridge University Press, 1999).

18. For an evocative fictional description of the strong emotions surrounding tigers in the Sundarbans, see Amitav Ghosh's *The Hungry Tide* (Boston: Houghton Mifflin, 2005). For a journalistic account of intensifying and multiplying human–elephant conflicts in Africa, India, and southeast Asia see Charles Siebert, "Elephant Crackup," *The New York Times Magazine* (October 8, 2006), [http://www.nytimes.com/2006/10/08/magazine/08elephant.html (accessed August 10, 2010).

19. Cf. Ajay Skaria, *Hybrid Histories: Forests, Frontiers, and Wildness in Western India* (New Delhi: Oxford University Press, 1999); and Sumit Guha, *Ecology and Ethnicity in India*. But see also Jana Fortier's engrossing ethnography of the Rautes, a tribal community in Nepal that has resourcefully managed to maintain an independent nomadic existence, *Kings of the Forest: Cultural Resilience of Himalayan Hunter-Gatherers* (Honolulu: University of Hawaii Press, 2009).

20. One finds a significant exception to this trend in the forests that shelter armed guerrillas like the Maoist Naxalites in Chhattisgarh and other eastern states. For everyday peasants, the guerrillas' presence as fugitives from police makes them as dangerous and unpredictable as the wild forest predators of decades past.

21. Rich [J. R.] Freeman, "Gods, Groves and the Culture of Nature in Kerala," *Modern Asian Studies* 33.2 (1999): 257–302; Rich [J. R.] Freeman, *Forests and the Folk: Perceptions of Nature in the Swidden Regimes of Highland Malabar*, Pondy Papers in Social Sciences 15 (Pondicherry, India: Institut Français de Pondichéry, 1994).

CHAPTER 3

1. *Dalit* (lit. "ground down," "oppressed") is a Marathi word that has been used for about thirty years by politicized members of India's lowest castes. Economically exploited and politically marginalized in Indian society for a long time, people have referred to these groups collectively through a host of labels. They are

often referred to in scholarly discourse as "former untouchables," in Gandhian discourse as *harijans* (lit. "children of God, born of God"), in Ambedkarian discourse as "Depressed Classes," and in present-day Indian governmental discourses as "Scheduled Castes" (or SCs), in reference to bureaucratic lists or schedules that enumerate such communities. In this book, I use the term *Dalit* for consistency and in solidarity with those seeking full inclusion in Indian society.

2. Madhav Gadgil and V. D. Vartak. "Groves Dedicated to the Gods," *The Illustrated Weekly of India*, September 2, 1973, 19.

3. Ibid., 21.

4. Donald Worster, *Nature's Economy: A History of Ecological Ideas*, 2d ed. (New York: Cambridge University Press, 1984), 211. See also Eugene P. Odum's classic article "The Strategy of Ecosystem Development," *Science* (n.s.) 164, no. 3877 (April 18, 1969): 262–70.

5. See, for example, S. M. Nair, "Enchanted Gardens: Rich Pockets of Green," Sunday Magazine, *The Hindu* (Chennai), June 4, 2000; "Groves that Conserve Ecology," *The Hindu*, May 1, 2003; Paromita Pain, "Sacred Wealth," *The Hindu: Young World* [Saturday Feature] May 24, 2003; Mohamed Nazeer, "Vanishing Sacred Groves," *The Hindu*, September 25, 2004; Rachna Singh, "Forest dept. launches initiative to conserve sacred groves," *The Times of India* (Mumbai), September 5, 2008; Patricia Mukhim, "Grappling with Tradition," *The Statesman* (Calcutta and New Delhi), October 14, 2008.

6. Ann Grodzins Gold, "Why Sacred Groves Matter: Post-Romantic Claims," in *Village Matters: Relocating Villages in the Contemporary Anthropology of India,* ed. Diane Mines and Nicolas Yazgi (New York: Oxford University Press, 2010), 115.

7. For scientists like P. S. Ramakrishnan, editor of a massive UNESCO-sponsored volume titled *Conserving the Sacred for Biodiversity Management* (Enfield, NH: Science Publishers, 1998), the linkage between ecology and cultural practices works both ways. The customs surrounding sacred groves can lead scientists to better questions regarding the ecological systems at work in a particular region (e.g., the role of particular keystone species that provide crucial ecological services for the ecosystem), and greater understanding of those systems obtained through scientific methods can lead to more effective interventions for restoring or rehabilitating degraded landscapes.

8. Gold, 107–10. For a broad overview of the positions taken in these debates, see Ronald Herring and Subir Sinha's report on a contentious international conference held in 1993 at the Indian Institute for Science in Bangalore on the topic of "Common Property, Collective Action, and Ecology," *Economic and Political Weekly* 28, no. 27/28 (July 1993): 1425–32.

9. M. A. Kalam, *Sacred Groves in Kodagu District of Karnataka (South India): A Socio-Historical Study,* Pondy Papers in Social Sciences 21 (Pondicherry, India: Institut Français de Pondichéry, 2001).

10. J. R. Freeman, "Gods, Groves and the Culture of Nature in Kerala." *Modern Asian Studies* 33, no. 2 (1999): 257–302.
11. Kay Milton, *Environmentalism and Cultural Theory: The Role of Anthropology in Environmental Discourse* (New York: Routledge, 1996), 109–13.
12. In order to understand the debate among forest biologists as to whether sacred groves actually preserve intact forests, it is helpful to understand several of the parameters that biologists studying these forests use to measure intactness, or lack of disturbance: closed or open canopy, density, basal area, floristic composition, and species richness. Forest ecology is shaped crucially by the availability of light. In forests with a closed canopy, plants growing on the forest floor (such as grasses, saplings, etc.) or on the trunks of trees (vines and lianas) have to make do with little light. Natural disturbances like lightening or wind, as well as human interventions like clear-cutting, create openings for light in the forest canopy allowing young saplings on the forest floor to mature. For this reason, the integrity of the canopy is closely related to floristic composition: Species not found in intact forests can compete for the light in disturbed ones, changing the number and variety of species found. Like the condition of the canopy, density and basal area are also aspects of the forest structure. While density measures the numbers of plants (often over a specified girth) in a given area, basal area measures the area of the forest occupied by woody species over a given girth at breast-height (i.e., trees with thicker trunks). Older forests that have not experienced much disturbance may be dominated by thick-trunked trees while the forest floor is relatively bare. Species richness or species diversity is another determinant of intactness and can be measured through straightforward counting of the number of different species found in given area. Forest biologists also seek to determine which species are dominant (most numerous) because the qualities of those species affect both the forest's overall structure and its floristic composition (e.g., when dominant species exude chemicals into the soil that make it uninhabitable by other species). Finally, while high species richness is greatly valued, *conservation* biologists are especially interested in the number and variety of endemics (plant species whose area of distribution is limited to the area under study), because these species are more likely to become globally extinct if their habitat is irreparably disturbed. All of these measurements need to be considered together to assess how "intact" or "disturbed" a particular forest or patch of forest is. For example, high stand density alone is not necessarily an indicator of intactness because it can also result when strong competitors establish dominance in a disturbed area. In dry tropical forests, such as those found in Tamil Nadu, species richness correlates more clearly with total basal area.
13. Claude Garcia and J.-P. Pascal, "Sacred Forests of Kodagu: Ecological Value and Social Role," in *Ecological Nationalisms: Nature, Livelihoods and Identities in*

South Asia, ed. Gunnel Cederlof and K. Sivaramakrishna (Seattle: University of Washington, 2006), 214.

14. According to the State of the Forest Report for 2009, forests cover 12 percent of the total area of Cuddalore district, but of these, none are very dense forests; 6 percent are open forests and 5 percent are moderately dense forests. The forest cover in Villupuram is similar: 14 percent total forest cover, with less than 1 percent very dense forest cover, 5 percent moderately dense forest cover, and 8 percent open forest. *Forest Survey of India,* "India: State of Forest 2009" (Dehradun, India: Ministry of Environment and Forests, Govt. of India, 2009), 149.

15. W. Francis, *Madras District Gazetteers: South Arcot,* Vol. 1 (Madras, India: Superintendent, Government Press, 1906), 147. As one of the great boondoggles of British colonial rule, the mismanagement of the Porto Novo Iron Works received attention long after its demise. P. P. Pillai discusses it in his report, "Iron and Steel Production in India," *Economica* 7 (January 1923): 55–66, as does the first Inspector-General of Forests, Sir Dietrich Brandeis, in his magnum opus, *Indian Forestry,* 57–58.

16. Pillai, 56.

17. Francis, 49.

18. See the Tamil Nadu Road Sector website: http://www.tnrsp.com/concept.htm (accessed April 20, 2010). See also a United Nations Development Programme's case study on the origins and outcomes of the East Coast Road project as a public–private development partnership: http://ncppp.org/undp/eastcoastroad. html (accessed April 20, 2010).

19. *Imperial Gazetteer of India: Provincial Series. Madras II: The Southern and West Coast Districts, Native States and French Possessions* (Calcutta: Superintendent of Government Printing, 1908), 98.

20. Basal area values for two out of four of the sacred groves examined here are within the range of 17 and 40 m²ha⁻¹ found for dry tropical forests around the world (that is, seventeen to forty square centimeters of each square meter of the forest stand was made up of woody trunks of trees). The basal area of Marakkanam Reserve Forest, by contrast, is just 11.1 m²ha⁻¹. N. Visalakshi, "Vegetation Analysis of Two Tropical Dry Evergreen Forests in Southern India," *Tropical Ecology* 36, no. 1 (1995): 117–27; M. P. Ramanujam and D. Kadamban, "Plant Biodiversity of Two Tropical Dry Evergreen Forests in the Pondicherry Region of South India and the Role of Belief Systems in their Conservation," *Biodiversity and Conservation* 10 (2001): 1203–17.

21. Vanniyars are a large agricultural caste spread throughout Tamil Nadu and Andhra Pradesh. In the late 19th century, they petitioned the British state to be classified as Kshatriyas, or a former warrior caste, but they are now entered as a "most backward caste" and thus entitled to some positive discrimination in regards to access to government employment and public higher education.

22. N. Parthasarathy and R. Karthikeyan, "Plant Biodiversity Inventory and Conservation of Two Tropical Dry Evergreen Forests on the Coromandel Coast, South India," *Biodiversity and Conservation* 6, no. 8 (1996): 1063.

23. To the best of my knowledge, no systematic floristic study of this grove has been conducted yet, but it is regarded as possibly one of the most intact tropical dry evergreen forests in Cuddalore district. (Personal communication. M. P. Ramanujam, Centre for Post-Graduate Studies in Pondicherry.)

24. Ramanujam and Kadamban, "Plant Biodiversity of Two Tropical Dry Evergreen Forests."

25. R. Venkateswaran and N. Parthasarathy, "Tropical Dry Evergreen Forests on the Coromandel Coast of India: Structure, Composition and Human Disturbance," *Ecotropica* 9 (2003): 47.

26. Ramanujam and Kadamban, "Plant Biodiversity of Two Tropical Dry Evergreen Forests," 1208–9.

27. V. M. Meher-Homji, "Puttupet: A Sacred Termit-Mound Protects a Forest," *Blackbuck* 2, no. 4 (1986): 1–4.

28. Louis Dumont, "A Structural Definition of a Folk Deity of Tamilnad: Aiyanar the Lord," *Contributions to Indian Sociology* 3 (1959): 75–87; Lars Kjaerholm, "Aiyanar and Aiyappan in Tamil Nadu: Change and Continuity in South Indian Hinduism," *Folk. Dansk Ethnografisk Tidsskrift Kobenhavn* 26 (1984): 67–92; available at Online Exhibit on Hinduism, Moesgaard Museum, Denmark, http://www.hindu.dk/1d/ar/Ai-Ai1200.pdf (accessed August 10, 2010).

29. Meher-Homji, "A Sacred Termit-Mound Protects a Forest," 1–4.

30. Though none of the people I spoke with mentioned this specifically, this transition may have entailed the displacement of non-Brahman priests of the Velar caste (potters, traditionally the priests at Ayyanar temples) with the Brahman priests who preside over worship in Ayyanarappan's temple today. The date of transition to Hindu Religious and Charitable Endowments Administration Department (HRCE) management comes from an interview with Ramesh, then the head priest, in July 2004.

31. See Amy L. Allocco's Ph.D. dissertation on the rising popularity of Nagattamman: "Snakes, Goddesses, and Anthills: Modern Challenges and Women's Ritual Responses in Contemporary South India," Emory University, Atlanta, 2009.

32. In December of 2006, the temple accountant said that the rights to run the Nāgattamma temple were sold for 20,000 rupees per annum, while the Baby Ayyanarappan anthill went for 15,000 rupees, and the Vīrabhadra/Malayatta shrine went for 75,000 rupees. The Vīrabhadra shrine commanded a higher price because of the more remunerative ritual services associated with goat and cock sacrifice.

33. As I discussed in chapter 1, Chandran and Hughes have identified Sanskritization as one of the major factors leading to the degradation of forested shrines. As

local forest gods become identified with deities from the pan-Indian Sanskritic tradition (Vishnu, Shiva, Parvati, etc.), communities build physical temples for them in the groves. But over time, the sacrality once associated with the forest is transferred to the icon of the deity, and neglect or destruction of the surrounding forest ensues. M. D. Subhash Chandran and J. Donald Hughes, "The Sacred Groves of South India: Ecology, Traditional Communities and Religious Change," *Social Compass* 44, no. 3 (1997): 413–27.

34. N. Parthasarathy and Pia Sethi, "Trees and Liana Species Diversity and Population Structure in a Tropical Dry Evergreen Forest in South India," *Tropical Ecology* 38, no. 1 (1997): 19.

35. R. Venkateswaran and N. Parthasarathy. "Tropical Dry Evergreen Forests on the Coromandel Coast of India," 55.

36. In some villages, people recognize that divine protection of groves is supported by human effort, as when a resident of Sentirankillai said that "you can cut [the trees in the forest], but the whole village will oppose you." Ann Gold has described similar measures to collectively protect a sacred grove in Rajasthan, where village residents organized a committee of volunteers to act as forest guards in rotation. "Miraculous punishments reinforce the rules here," writes Gold. "However, the Motis Minas who accept Malaji as their revered lineage deity have not left the protection of his trees to divine protection." Gold, "Why Sacred Groves Matter," 124.

37. Mines, *Fierce Gods*, 32. See also E. Valentine Daniel, *Fluid Signs: Being a Person the Tamil Way* (Berkeley: University of California Press, 1984), 103–4.

CHAPTER 4

1. Auroville Foundation, Auroville Universal Township Master Plan: Perspective 2025 (2001), http://www.auroville.info/ACUR/masterplan/index.htm (accessed May 25, 2010). According to figures from 2001, of the 1,963 hectares that encompassed the projected township, only 778 were owned by the Auroville Foundation. The AF hopes to purchase the remaining 980 hectares from private owners over the coming decades.

2. Interview with retired General Krishna Tiwari, resident of Auroville since 1976 and head of Auroville Archives, Auroville, December 27, 2006.

3. Sri Aurobindo Ashram, *Bulletin*, cited in Robert N. Minor, *The Religious, the Spiritual and the Secular: Auroville and Secular India* (Albany: State University of New York Press, 1999), 46.

4. Aurobindo Ghose, *The Life Divine*, Vol. XXXIII of the Sri Aurobindo Birth Centenary Library (Auroville, India: Sri Aurobindo Ashram, 1972), 1–5, cited in Robert McDermott, *The Essential Aurobindo: The Writings of Sri Aurobindo* (Great Barrington, MA: Lindisfarne Books, 2001), 53.

5. Ibid., 52.

6. Larry D. Shinn, "Religious Vision and Social Consequences in a South Indian Utopian Community," *Religious Studies* 20, no. 2 (June 1984): 242.

7. The Mother (aka Mirra Alfassa Richards), *Words of the Mother—I*, ed. Sri Aurobindo Trust, Vol. 13 of *Collected Works of the Mother* (Pondicherry, India: Sri Aurobindo Ashram Press, 2004), 227, 228, cited in Minor, *Auroville and Secular India*, 52.

8. Peter Heehs, *Sri Aurobindo: A Brief Biography* (New Delhi: Oxford University Press, 1989).

9. Ibid., 70.

10. In his early writings, Aurobindo often referred to his methods as "synthetic yoga" which he saw as a fusion of the varieties of yoga described in Brahmanical texts: jnana yoga, bhakti yoga, karma yoga, and raja yoga. See McDermott, *The Essential Aurobindo*, 160, citing from *The Synthesis of Yoga*.

11. For example, Aurobindo wrote that the distinctive form of yoga practiced at the ashram was a "joint creation of Sri Aurobindo and the Mother." Volume XXVI of the Sri Aurobindo Birth Centenary Library, 458, cited in Minor, *Auroville and Secular India*, 39.

12. Anonymous, "The Mother as an Artist: Some Biographical Details," in *Mirra Alfassa, Paintings and Drawings* (Pondicherry, India: Sri Aurobindo Press, 1992), 159, 161.

13. Among the other participants in Théon's salon was Alexandra David-Neel, the great promoter of Tibet. The story of women's involvement in early spiritualism is analyzed in Joy Dixon's *Divine Feminine: Theosophy and Feminism in England* (Baltimore: Johns Hopkins University Press, 2001).

14. Anonymous, "The Mother as an Artist," 166–67.

15. Minor, *Auroville and Secular India*, 38.

16. Ibid., 38.

17. Although his retreat into silence often depicted as a nearly complete withdrawal from engagement with the world, Aurobindo maintained close contact with several devotees through written correspondence that could consume eight to ten hours a day. As Peter Heehs writes, "He was willing to offer advice on almost any topic, whether spiritual (the right way to meditate, the central process of yoga), practical (the right way to treat piles, how to deal with a family problem), or trivial (how to clean bathroom tiles, how to cook a half-boiled egg)." Peter Heehs, *The Lives of Sri Aurobindo* (New York: Columbia University Press, 2008), 367.

18. Minor, *Auroville and Secular India*, 39–42.

19. Minor, *Auroville and Secular India*, 40, citing Vol. XXV of the Sri Aurobindo Birth Centenary Library, 49. Aurobindo's references to the honor and submission due to Alfassa as "the Mother" were highly ambiguous because of the broad semantic range of this phrase, which can refer to either the Great Goddess of Hindu mythology, a human woman considered to be the avatar of the goddess, or the personification of the primal energy of the cosmos (*shakti*). It is sometimes unclear

if by "the Mother" he means Alfassa herself or the more abstract active cosmic principle, as when he enjoined disciples to open themselves to the influence of "the force of the Mother" by surrendering wholly to it/Her and seeking to "reject everything that acted against it." Heehs, *Sri Aurobindo: A Brief Biography*, 137.

20. Anonymous, *References to Auroville in Mother's Agenda* (Auroville, India: Auroville Press, n.d.), 7.

21. Ibid., 107.

22. Minor, *Auroville and Secular India*, 42.

23. Such a gendered division of labor seemed to be what Aurobindo had in mind when he positioned the Mother as leader of the ashram in 1926. Peter Heehs describes a letter written in March of 1926 in which Aurobindo wrote that his "personal force" represented "the 'Purusha element,' [and] acted principally in the realm of spiritual knowledge, while Mirra's, 'representing the Shakti element' was 'predominately practical in its nature.' ... Without the Mother, he said, his conception of a divine life on earth could never have been embodied." Heehs, *Sri Aurobindo*, 133.

24. The Mother (aka Mirra Alfassa Richards), ed. Vijay. *Flowers—Their Spiritual Significance* (Pondicherry, India: Sri Aurobindo Society, 1988), 9.

25. Ibid., 11.

26. Ibid., 8.

27. The Mother, *Words of the Mother—I*, 229.

28. Anonymous, *References to Auroville in Mother's Agenda*, 14–15. Interestingly, in addition to being an accomplished, prize-winning architect, Roger Anger was Mirra Alfassa's grandson-in-law, the husband of Françoise Morriset, the daughter of Mirra Alfassa's only son, André. Anupama Kundoo, *Roger Anger: Research on Beauty/Recherche Sur La Beauté* (Berlin: Jovis Verlag GmbH, 2009), 176.

29. The Mother, *Words of the Mother—I*, 193–94; David J. Lorenzo, *Tradition and the Rhetoric of Right: Popular Political Argument in the Aurobindo Movement* (Madison, NJ: Fairleigh Dickinson University Press, 1999), 99–100.

30. For a concise description of the restoration methods improvised by early Aurovillians, see the case study for the United Nations Environment Programme World Conservation Monitoring Center written by Paul Blanchflower, an Aurovillian, "Restoration of the Tropical Dry Evergreen Forest of Southern India in the Auroville Township and its Bioregion" (Cambridge, UK: United Nations Environment Programme, World Conservation Monitoring Center). Available at http://www.unep-wcmc.org/restoration-of-the-tropical-dry-evergreen-forest-of-southern-india-in-the-auroville-township-and-its-bioregion_834.html (accessed September 6, 2012).

31. "The Sri Aurobindo Society accepted the growing financial support for Auroville from organizations in India and abroad. Indian state governments contributed Rs. 6,650,000 and the Central government Rs. 2,614,000. UNESCO contributed

less than Rs. 40,000." Minor, *Auroville and Secular India*, 59. "Because the land-scape was heavily eroded and deforested, the first projects attempted were soil conservation, reforestation, and refertilization projects. They were in full swing by 1972 and consumed the largest percentage of Auroville's resources." Minor, *Auroville and Secular India*, 61.

32. Jan Allen, "Fertile Memories," http://www.auroville.org/environment/fertile/fertile.htm (accessed April 20, 2010).

33. Radio Team, "Newcomer Reception #3," [Joss Brooks addresses the Newcomer Reception on 21 March 2009], recorded for Auroville Radio, http://www.aurovilleradio.org/component/content/article/1149-Newcomer%20Reception%20#3 (accessed May 26, 2010).

34. Lorenzo, *Tradition and the Rhetoric of Right*, 93 n79. See also the account of an American settler, Savitra, *Auroville: Sunword Rising/A Trust for the Earth* (Auroville: Community of Auroville, 1980), 11–15.

35. In another example, Brooks describes his work constructing a video-recording studio out of casuarina poles with palm leaf thatch for a roof. From the min-ute she was introduced by disciples to the then-brand-new technology of video recording, the Mother was fascinated by it. Abstract, mandala-like images pro-duced by video cameras when they are directed toward a screen appeared to her like clear manifestations of the new consciousness. The video studio she commissioned in Auroville was designed to broadcast performances of Sri Aurobindo's epic poem, *Savitri*, to villagers all over India as a fledgling—and audacious—experiment in distance education for rural India.

36. See, for example, her interpretation of a great cyclone that on the night of December 5, 1972 destroyed many of the buildings erected with so much effort by Aurovillians: "It is a warning that nature is giving, that those who do not have the true spirit of Auroville will have to change or to go if they do not want to change." *Words of the Mother—I*, 218.

37. Anonymous, *References to Auroville in Mother's Agenda*, 211, 220–23.

38. Lorenzo, *Tradition and the Rhetoric of Right*; Minor, *Auroville and Secular India*; Shinn, "Religious Vision and Social Consequences in a South Indian Utopian Community," 239–53.

39. It is difficult, and somewhat controversial, to estimate the population of the Auroville plateau at the time of its founding. While Robert Minor cites the rather high figure of 30,000 local Tamil villagers *using* the land (*Auroville and Secular India*, 55), the current master plan, written in 2001, enumerates six Tamil vil-lages lying within the designated area of the township (Edayanchavadi, Irumbai, Kottakarai, Rayapudupakkam, Pettai, and Alankuppam), with three more on its border (Kuilapalayam, Acharampattu, and Oddampalayam). In 2001, the nine villages had a population of only 11,000 persons, http://www.auroville.info/ACUR/masterplan/location.htm (accessed 6 July 2011).

40. *Words of the Mother—I*, 243 (September/October 1969).

41. Jan Allen, Fertile Memories.

42. *Words of the Mother—I*, 241–42.

43. Ibid., 234.

44. Joss Brooks, "Auroville—Reaching Out," Conference Proceedings, IPC-IV Designing for a Sustainable Future (Permaculture Association of Western Australia, 1997), http://permaculturewest.org.au/ipc6/ch02/brooks/index.html (accessed June 29, 2010).

45. Auroville Master Plan, "Demographic Characteristics," http://www.auroville.info/ACUR/masterplan/demographic.htm.

46. Priya Sundaravalli, "The Hidden World of Ammas," *Auroville Today*, December 2006, http://www.auroville.org/journals&media/avtoday/archive/2004–2009/2006–12/ammas.htm (accessed May 25, 2010).

47. *Words of the Mother—I*, 243–44.

48. Interview with Ramadasan (pseudonym), Auroville, December 28, 2006.

49. Census, Auroville Population, April 2012. Available at http://www.auroville.org/society/av_population.htm (accessed September 7, 2012).

50. For a sharply critical assessment of what Amita Baviskar calls urban bourgeois environmentalists' efforts to "green" Indian cities at the expense of poor slum-dwellers, see her article, "The Politics of the City." *Seminar* 516 (2002), http://www.india-seminar.com/2002/516/516%20amita%20baviskar.htm (accessed July 29, 2010). See also Mary E. Hancock, *The Politics of Heritage from Madras to Chennai* (Bloomington: Indiana University Press, 2008).

51. Vandana Shiva, *Biopiracy : The Plunder of Nature and Knowledge* (Boston: South End Press, 1997).

52. Interview with P. M. Unnikrishnan, Foundation for the Revitalisation of Local Health Traditions, Ananda Nagar, Bangalore, July 25, 2001.

53. Darshan Shankar, "Conserving the Medicinal Plants of India: The Need for a Biocultural Perspective," *The Journal of Alternative and Complementary Medicine* 2, no. 3 (1996): 349–58.

54. Interview with Joss Brooks and Anita Brooks, Pitchandikulam, Auroville, July 13, 2004.

55. Cf. David Dean Shulman, *Tamil Temple Myths: Sacrifice and Divine Marriage in the South Indian Saiva Tradition* (Princeton, NJ: Princeton University Press, 1980).

56. Kelly D. Alley, *On the Banks of the Ganga: When Wastewater Meets a Sacred River* (Ann Arbor: University of Michigan Press, 2002).

57. Interview with Veeradasan (pseudonym), Kizhputtupattu Forest, December 26, 2006.

58. R. Venkateswaran and N. Parthasarathy, "Tropical Dry Evergreen Forests on the Coromandel Coast of India: Structure, Composition and Human Disturbance," *Ecotropica* 9 (2003): 55.

59. See Diane Mines on the importance of density as a signal of increase that is translated into an index of value (signifying abundance, fertility, and "bigness"

or high social status and influence) by Hindu festival participants. Mines, *Fierce Gods*, 162–67.

60. Interview with Ramesh, Kizhputtupattu Forest, July 12, 2004. I have transcribed Ramesh's words exactly as they were recorded and did not translate his idiomatic Indian English into standard American English.

61. Peter Tomkins and Christopher Bird, *The Secret Life of Plants* (New York: Harper and Row, 1973). Also see the work of Grover Cleaveland "Cleve" Backster, a pioneer in the use of polygraph tests to detect lying, who later turned his attention to human–plant communication. Cleve Backster, *Primary Perception: Biocommunication with Plants, Living Foods, and Human Cells* (Anza, CA: White Rose Millennium Press, 2003).

62. Interview with Veeradasan (pseudonym), Kizhputtupattu Forest, December 26, 2006.

63. Interview with Joss Brooks and Anita Brooks, Pitchandikulam, Auroville, July 13, 2004.

64. Arjun Appadurai and Carole A. Breckenridge, "The South Indian Temple: Authority, Honour and Redistribution," *Contributions to Indian Sociology* (n.s.) 10, no. 2 (1976): 187–211.

65. "The Work of Autoville in Nadukuppam," *Auroville Today*, December 2008, http://www.auroville.org/journals&media/avtoday/archive/2004-2009/2008-12/Nadukuppam.htm (accessed September 7, 2012).

66. Other difficulties that may have arisen in the course of the FRLHT–Pitchandikulam initiative at Puttupattu may be surmised in light of a similar but unsuccessful collaboration attempted in Urani. As described in the previous chapter, like Puttupattu, the village of Urani is located on the East Coast Road. However, here a village association of elders runs the forested shrine rather than the Tamil Nadu HRCE. While elderly widows associated with the dominant lineage in the village expressed regret that the project was never initiated, the current Nattanmai (village traditional leader) offered a jumbled account of a scheme ripe for fraud and deception narrowly averted by his staunch refusal to participate. Meanwhile, I heard stray remarks from members of the Pitchandikulam team about their having been rebuked for arriving at village meetings in "short pants" (i.e., shorts, which, though favored by both Indian and Western Aurovillians, are considered unsuitable attire for grown men by conservative Tamils). These suggest that Aurovillians may have been less than sensitive to the cultural sensibilities of villagers, while villagers were, for their part, suspicious and unwilling to overlook such cultural differences in the interest of collaboration.

67. Ramachandra Guha and Juan Martinez-Alier, *Varieties of Environmentalism: Essays North and South* (London: Earthscan Publications, 1997).

68. Ramachandra Guha, "Ideological Trends in Indian Environmentalism," *Economic and Political Weekly* 23, no. 49 (1988): 2578–81.

69. Amita Baviskar, "Vanishing Forests, Sacred Trees: A Hindu Perspective on Eco-Consciousness." *Asian Geographer* 18, no. 1–2 (1999): 24.

70. Ibid, 24.

71. Subir Sinha, Shubhra Gururani, and Brian Greenberg, "The 'New Traditionalist' Discourse of Indian Environmentalism," *Journal of Peasant Studies* 24, no. 3 (1997): 65–99.

72. Emma Tomalin, *Biodivinity and Biodiversity: The Limits to Religious Environmentalism* (Burlington, VT: Ashgate, 2009), 148–49.

73. Ibid., 161.

74. Tomalin is clear that her use of the modifiers "weak" and "strong" are not meant to pass judgment on the efficacy or value of either type, and I would concur. I would add, though, that a shortcoming of weak environmentalism is a tendency to represent the religious aspects of a phenomena in a somewhat narrow or superficial manner, insofar as the environmentalist's primary concern is with its ecological rather than religious aspects. Such a tendency is evident in the FRLHT–Pitchandikulam discourse at Puttupattu in, for example, the lack of attention to purity/pollution beliefs and their influence on pilgrim's behavior in the grove and its neglect of the beliefs and practices surrounding Ayyanarappan and Veerabhadran considered as lineage deities in favor of viewing them as Brahmanical gods.

75. David Haberman, *River of Love in an Age of Pollution: The Yamuna River of Northern India* (Berkeley: University of California Press, 2006), 178–79.

76. Tomalin's examples of strong religious environmentalism in India include the Vrindavan Conservation Project (funded by the World Wildlife Fund for Nature, the Alliance for Religion and Conservation, and the UK-based charity Friends of Vrindavan); a gathering of a loose global network of progressive, anarchistic environmental direct activists called the Rainbows in the Himalayan foothills; sacred grove preservation advocates in urban centers from Delhi to Bangalore; and sacred river restoration advocates in north India.

77. Interview with Joss Brooks, Otteri, Chennai, December 21, 2006.

78. Interview with N. Loganathan, Urani, July 12, 2004.

79. One must distinguish between Loganathan's and Brooks's expansive epistemology that embraces the truths of both science and religion from Madhav Gadgil and V. D. Vartak's confidence that "behind" the practice of sacred grove preservation there is some nascent or proto-scientific understanding of their ecological benefit, as discussed in chapter 3. Gadgil and Vartak's ultimately rationalist bias leads them to predict that when the scientific value of sacred groves, for example, are made clear to people, the epiphenomenal religious beliefs attributed to them will drop away. This bias finds its most extreme expression in critics like Meera Nanda, who abhor discourse synthesizing religious and scientific forms of knowledge as intellectually corrosive pseudo-science.

80. Interview with N. Loganathan, Urani, July 12, 2004.

81. Radio Team, "Newcomer Reception #3."

CHAPTER 5

1. Subir Sinha, Shubhra Gururani, and Brian Greenberg, "The 'New Traditionalist' Discourse of Indian Environmentalism," *Journal of Peasant Studies* 24, no. 3 (1997): 89.

2. Emma Mawdsley, "Hindu Nationalism, Neo-Traditionalism, and Environmental Discourses in India," *Geoforum* 37 (2006): 383.

3. For other examples see Emma Mawdsley, "The Abuse of Religion and Ecology: The Vishva Hindu Parishad and Tehri Dam," *Worldviews: Environment, Culture, Religion* 8, no. 2 (2006): 1–24; Mukul Sharma, "Saffronising Green," *Seminar* 516 (2002).

4. Savitha Gautam, "Nanditha Krishna and P.C. Ramachandran Share Memories," *The Hindu*, December 14, 2004, http://www.thehindu.com/thehindu/ mp/2004/12/14/stories/2004121400420100.htm (accessed June 15, 2010).

5. See the organization's website at http://cpreec.org/.

6. The following is based on interviews I conducted in July 2001 at the CPREEC headquarters in Chennai and on their publications, principally Nanditha Krishna and Javanti Prabhakaran, eds., *The Ecological Traditions of Tamilnadu* (Chennai, India: CPR Environmental Education Centre, 1997), and M. Amrithalingam, *Sacred Groves of Tamilnadu—A Survey* (Chennai, India: CPR Environmental Education Centre, 1998).

7. Interview with P. Sudhakar, CPR Foundation, Alwarpet, Chennai, July 18, 2001.

8. Interview with Nanditha Krishna, CPR Foundation, Alwarpet, Chennai, July 5, 2004.

9. Correspondent, "The Nenmeli Experience," *Madras Musings*, June 16–30, 2002, 4; P. Oppili, "A Barren Area Transformed into Garden," *The Hindu*, June 6, 2002; "Nenmeli Eco-Village," *Success Stories*, CPR Environmental Education Centre, 2007, http://cpreec.org/success.htm#2; Sharon St. Joan, *Nenmeli: Where the Trees Are Happy* (Kanab, UT: Best Friends Animal Society, 2010. Available from http://network.bestfriends.org/golocal/india/14864/ news.aspx (accessed June 15, 2010).

10. Interview with Nenmeli residents, Nenmeli Muttumariyamman temple, Kanchipuram District, July 9, 2004.

11. Interview with M. Amrithalingam, Nenmeli, Kanchipuram District, July 9, 2004.

12. Interview with Nanditha Krishna, CPR Foundation, Alwarpet, Chennai, July 19, 2004. In addition, Dr. Krishna stated that the CPREEC had obtained a written agreement from village leaders promising not to participate in animal sacrifice, and explained that while some "bad characters" in the village might still bring goats to the temple festival, at least the temple administration knows they should not.

13. A host of excellent scholarship has examined the history and dynamics of Hindu nationalism in India. See, for example, Thomas Blom Hansen, *The Saffron Wave: Democracy and Hindu Nationalism in Modern India* (Princeton, NJ: Princeton

University Press, 1999); Christophe Jaffrelot, *The Hindu Nationalist Movement in India* (New York: Columbia University Press, 1996); David Ludden, ed. *Contesting the Nation: Religion, Community and the Politics of Democracy in India* (Philadelphia: University of Pennsylvania Press, 1996).

14. S. Viswanathan, "A Decree on Animal Sacrifice," *Frontline*, October 13, 2003.

15. Interview with Nanditha Krishna, CPR Foundation, Alwarpet, Chennai, July 18, 2001.

16. Nanditha Krishna, "Blood on Our Hands," *The New Indian Express*, September 14, 2003.

17. Ibid.

18. Ibid.

19. P. Sudhakar, "Ban on Animal Sacrifice Has Divided Communities: A Survey," *The Hindu*, September 15, 2003, http://www.thehindu.com/2003/09/15/stories/2003091504490400.htm (accessed June 10, 2010); S. Dorairaj, "Sacrificing Age-Old Practice," *The Hindu*, September 8, 2003, http://www.thehindu.com/thehindu/mp/2003/09/08/stories/2003090800700100.htm (accessed June 15, 2010).

20. Sudhakar, "Ban on Animal Sacrifice Has Divided Communities: A Survey."

21. Nanditha Krishna, "Who Is an Aryan?" *The New Indian Express*, October 26. 2003.

22. Ibid.

23. Nanditha Krishna, "Winds of Change," *The New Indian Express*, April 4, 2004.

24. Ibid.

25. "Religious Conversions Single Largest Threat to Ecology," Arise India Forum website http://www.ariseindiaforum.org/religious-conversions-single-largest-threat-ecology/ (accessed September 7, 2012), citing *Deccan Chronicle*, Chennai, January 8, 2011. See also similar remarks Krishna made on December 7, 2005, at a one-day seminar on "Ecological Traditions of Kerala" in Tiruvananthapuram, http://ecoheritage.webindia.com/viewdetails.php?$mFJ (accessed September 7, 2012).

26. Krishna, "Winds of Change."

27. Mawdsley, "The Abuse of Religion and Ecology: The Vishva Hindu Parishad and Tehri Dam, 1–24;" Sharma, "Saffronising Green."

AFTERWORD

1. One should not, however, exaggerate the successes of ecological restoration. As Robert Elliot has argued, too sanguine a view of the potential for ecological regeneration can encourage mining and other companies to despoil wilderness areas with the argument that they can be restored to "natural" levels afterwards. Robert Elliott, *Faking Nature: The Ethics of Environmental Restoration* (New York: Routledge, 1997).

2. Cf. Gautam Gajula, "Sacred Grove Lore and Laws: On the Beliefs of Ecologists, Environmentalist-Historians and Others," *Indian Folklife* 26 (2007): 19–24.

3. William R. Jordan, III, *The Sunflower Forest: Ecological Restoration and the New Communion with Nature* (Berkeley: University of California Press, 2003), 19.

4. William K. Stevens, *Miracle Under the Oaks: The Revival of Nature in America* (New York: Pocket Books, 1995).

Bibliography

Adiga, Aravind. *The White Tiger: A Novel*. New York: The Free Press, 2008.

Agarwal, Bina. "Participatory Exclusions, Community Forestry and Gender: An Analysis for South Asia and Conceptual Framework." *World Development* 29, no. 10 (2001): 1623–48.

Allen, Jan. "Fertile Memories." *Auroville: A Universal City in the Making*. Accessed February 14, 2012: http://www.auroville.org/environment/fertile/fertile.htm.

Alley, Kelly D. *On the Banks of the Ganga: When Wastewater Meets a Sacred River*. Ann Arbor: University of Michigan Press, 2002.

Allocco, Amy L. "Snake Goddesses and Anthills: Modern Challenges and Women's Ritual Responses in Contemporary South India." Ph.D. diss., Emory University, Atlanta, 2009.

Amrithalingam, M. *Sacred Groves of Tamilnadu: A Survey*. Chennai, India: CPR Environmental Education Center, 1998.

Anonymous. "The Mother as an Artist: Some Biographical Details." In *Mirra Alfassa, Paintings and Drawings*. Pondicherry, India: Sri Aurobindo Press, 1992.

Anonymous. *References to Auroville in Mother's Agenda*. Auroville, India: Auroville Press, n.d.

Apffel-Marglin, Frederique, and Pramod Parajuli. "'Sacred Grove' and Ecology: Ritual and Science." In *Hinduism and Ecology: The Intersection of Earth, Sky, and Water*, Edited by Christopher Key Chapple and Mary Evelyn Tucker, 291–316. Cambridge, MA: Harvard University Press, 2000.

Appadurai, Arjun, and Carol A. Breckenridge. "The South Indian Temple: Authority, Honour and Redistribution." *Contributions to Indian Sociology* (n.s.) 10, no. 2 (July 1976): 187–211.

Auroville Master Plan. *Auroville: A Universal City in the Making*. Accessed February 14, 2012: http://www.auroville.info/ACUR/masterplan/menu1.htm.

Babb, Lawrence A. *The Divine Hierarchy: Popular Hinduism in Central India*. New York: Columbia University Press, 1975.

Backster, Cleve. *Primary Perception: Biocommunication with Plants, Living Foods, and Human Cells*. Anza, CA: White Rose Millennium Press, 2003.

Baviskar, Amita. *In the Belly of the River: Tribal Conflicts over Development in the Narmada Valley.* New York: Oxford University Press, 1995.

Baviskar, Amita. "Tribal Politics and the Discourses of Environmentalism." *Contributions to Indian Sociology* 31, no. 2 (1997): 195–224.

Baviskar, Amita. "Vanishing Forests, Sacred Trees: A Hindu Perspective on Eco-Consciousness." *Asian Geographer* 18, nos. 1–2 (1999): 21–31.

Baviskar, Amita. "The Politics of the City." *Seminar* 516 (2002). Accessed February 14, 2012: http://www.india-seminar.com/2002/516/516%20amita%20obaviskar.htm.

Beck, Brenda. "Colour and Heat in South Indian Ritual." *Man (n.s.)* 4, no. 4 (1969): 553–72.

Blackburn, Stuart H. "The Kallars: A Tamil 'Criminal Tribe' Reconsidered." *South Asia (n.s.)* 1, no. 1 (1978): 38–51.

Blanchflower, Paul. "Restoration of the Tropical Dry Evergreen Forest of Southern India in the Auroville Township and its Bioregion." Cambridge, UK: United Nations Environment Programme, World Conservation Monitoring Center. Accessed September 6, 2012: http://www.unep-wcmc.org/restoration-of-the-tropical-dry-evergreen-forest-of-southern-india-in-the-auroville-township-and-its-bioregion_834.html.

Brandis, Dietrich. *Indian Forestry.* Woking, UK: Oriental University Institute, 1897.

Brooks, Joss. "Auroville—Reaching Out." In *Conference Proceedings, IPC-IV Designing for a Sustainable Future.* Permaculture Association of Western Australia, 1997. Accessed June 29, 2010: http://permaculturewest.org.au/ipc6/cho2/brooks/index.html.

Brosius, Peter. "Analyses and Interventions: Anthropological Engagements with Environmentalism." *Current Anthropology* 40, no. 3 (1999): 245–69.

Brubaker, Richard L. "The Ambivalent Mistress: A Study of South Indian Village Goddess and their Religious Meaning." Ph.D. diss., University of Chicago, 1978.

Burman, J. J. Roy. *Sacred Groves among Communities: The Mahadeo Kolis and the Kunbis of the Western Ghats.* New Delhi: Mittal Publications, 2003.

Cederlof, Gunnel, and K. Sivaramakrishna, eds. *Ecological Nationalisms: Nature, Livelihoods and Identities in South Asia.* Seattle: University of Washington, 2006.

Chandran, M. D. Subhash, and J. Donald J. Hughes. "The Sacred Groves of South India: Ecology, Traditional Communities and Religious Change." *Social Compass* 44, no.3 (1997): 413–27.

Chandran, M. D. Subhash, and J. D. Hughes. "Sacred Groves and Conservation: The Comparative History of Traditional Reserves in the Mediterranean Area and in South India." *Environment and History* 6, no. 2 (May 2000): 169–86.

Chapple, Christopher Key, and Mary Evelyn Tucker, eds. *Hinduism and Ecology: The Intersection of Earth, Sky, and Water.* Cambridge, MA: Harvard University Press, 2000.

Clark-Decés, Isabelle. *The Encounter Never Ends: A Return to the Field of Tamil Rituals.* Albany: State University of New York Press, 2007.

Correspondent. "The Nenmeli Experience." *Madras Musings* (Chennai), June 16–30, 2002.

CPR Environmental Education Center. Accessed February 14, 2012: http://cpreec. org/.

Daniel, E. Valentine. *Fluid Signs: Being a Person the Tamil Way.* Berkeley: University of California Press, 1984.

Dirks, Nicholas B. "The Pasts of a Palaiyakkarar: The Ethnohistory of a South Indian Little King." *The Journal of Asian Studies* 41, no. 4 (1982): 655–83.

Dirks, Nicholas B. *The Hollow Crown: Ethnohistory of a Little Kingdom in South India.* Cambridge, UK: Cambridge University Press, 1987.

Dirks, Nicholas B. *Castes of Mind: Colonialism and the Making of Modern India.* Princeton, NJ: Princeton University Press, 2001.

Dixon, Joy. *Divine Feminine: Theosophy and Feminism in England.* Baltimore: Johns Hopkins University Press, 2001.

Dorairaj, S. "Sacrificing Age-Old Practice." *The Hindu,* September 8, 2003. Accessed June 15, 2010: http://www.thehindu.com/thehindu/mp/2003/09/08/sto-ries/2003090800700100.htm.

Dumont, Louis. "A Structural Definition of Folk Deity of Tamil Nad: Aiyanar the Lord." *Contributions to Indian Sociology* 3 (1959): 75–87.

Dumont, Louis. *A South Indian Subcaste: Social Organization and Religion of the Pramalai Kallar.* Translated by Michael Moffatt. Delhi: Oxford University Press, 1986.

Durkheim, Émile. *Elementary Forms of the Religious Life.* Translated by Karen E. Fields. New York: Free Press, 1995. (Originally published 1915)

East Coast Road, Tamil Nadu, India Case Study (Transportation). Accessed April 20, 2010: http://ncppp.org/undp/eastcoastroad.html.

Elliot, Robert. *Faking Nature: The Ethics of Environmental Restoration.* New York: Routledge, 1997.

Elison, William. "'Bonafide Tribals': Religion and Recognition among Denizens of Mumbai's Forest Frontier." *Journal for the Study of Religion, Nature and Culture* 4, no. 2 (2010): 191–212.

Finnis, Elizabeth. "Why Grow Cash Crops? Subsistence Farming and Crop Commercialization in the Kolli Hills, South India." *American Anthropologist* 108, no. 2 (June 2006): 363–69.

Fortier, Jana. *Kings of the Forest: Cultural Resilience of Himalayan Hunter-Gatherers.* Honolulu: University of Hawaiʻi Press, 2009.

Foulston, Lynn. *At the Feet of the Goddess: The Divine Feminine in Local Hindu Religion.* Portland, OR: Sussex Academic Press, 2002.

Francis, W. *Madras District Gazetteers: Madura.* Vol. 1. Madras: Madras Government Press, 1914.

Francis, W. *Madras District Gazetteers: South Arcot*. Vol. 1. Madras: Superintendent Government Press, 1906.

Freeman, Rich [J. R.] *Forests and the Folk: Perceptions of Nature in the Swidden Regimes of Highland Malabar*. Pondy Papers in Social Sciences 15. Pondicherry, India: Institut Français de Pondichéry, 1994.

Freeman, Rich [J. R]. "Gods, Groves and the Culture of Nature in Kerala." *Modern Asian Studies* 33, no. 2 (1999): 257–302.

Frykenberg, Robert E. "On Roads and Riots in Tinnevelly: Radical Change and Ideology in Madras Presidency During the 19th Century." *South Asia* 2 (1982): 34–52.

Fuller, C. J. *The Camphor Flame: Popular Hinduism and Society in India*. Princeton, NJ: Princeton University Press, 1992.

Gadgil, Madhav, and Ramachandra Guha. *This Fissured Land: An Ecological History of India*. New Delhi: Oxford University Press, 1999.

Gadgil, Madhav, and V. D. Vartak. "Sacred Groves of India: A Plea for Continued Conservation." *The Journal of Bombay Natural History Society* 72 (1975): 314–20.

Gadgil, Madhav, and V. D. Vartak. "Groves Dedicated to the Gods." *The Illustrated Weekly of India*, September 1973, 19–21.

Gajula, Gautam. "Sacred Grove Lore and Laws: On the Beliefs of Ecologists, Environmentalist-Historians and Others." *Indian Folklife* 26 (July 2007): 19–24.

Garcia, Claude, and J. P. Pascal. "Sacred Forests of Kodagu: Ecological Value and Social Role." In *Ecological Nationalisms: Nature, Livelihoods and Identities in South Asia*. Edited by Gunnel Cederlof and K Sivaramakrishna, 199–230. Seattle: University of Washington, 2006.

Gautam, Savitha. "Nanditha Krishan and P. C. Ramachandran Share Memories." *The Hindu*, December 14, 2004. Accessed June 15, 2010: http://www.thehindu.com/thehindu/mp/2004/12/14/stories/2004121400420100.htm.

Ghose, Aurobindo. *The Life Divine*, Sri Aurobindo Birth Centenary Library, Vol. 18. Auroville, India: Sri Aurobindo Ashram, 1972.

Ghosh, Amitav. *The Hungry Tide*. Boston: Houghton Mifflin, 2005.

Gold, Ann Grodzins. "Why Sacred Groves Matter: Post-Romantic Claims." In *Village Matters: Relocating Villages in the Contemporary Anthropology of India*. Edited by Diane Mines and Nicolas Yazgi, 107–29. New York: Oxford University Press, 2010.

Gold, Ann Grodzins, and Bhoju Ram Gujar. "Of Gods, Trees and Boundaries: Divine Conservation in Rajasthan." *Asian Folklore Studies* 48 (1989): 211–29.

Gold, Ann Grodzins, and Bhoju Ram Gujar. *In the Time of Trees and Sorrows: Nature, Power and Memory in Rajasthan*. Durham, NC: Duke University Press, 2002.

Gold, Ann Grodzins, and Bhoju Ram Gujar. "Malaji's Hill: Divine Sanction, Community Action." *Indian Folklife* 26 (July 2007): 9–14.

Guha, Ramachandra, and Juan Martinez-Alier. *Varieties of Environmentalism: Essays North and South*. London: Earthscan, 1997.

Guha, Ramachandra. "Ideological Trends in Indian Environmentalism." *Economic and Political Weekly* 23, no. 49 (1988): 2578–81.

Guha, Sumit. *Ecology and Ethnicity in India, c. 1200–1991.* Cambridge, UK: Cambridge University Press, 1999.

Haberman, David. *River of Love in an Age of Pollution: The Yamuna River of Northern India.* Berkeley: University of California Press, 2006.

Hancock, Mary E. *The Politics of Heritage from Madras to Chennai.* Bloomington: Indiana University Press, 2008.

Hansen, Thomas Blom. *The Saffron Wave: Democracy and Hindu Nationalism in Modern India.* Princeton, NJ: Princeton University Press, 1999.

Hardgrave, Robert L. *The Nadars of Tamilnad: The Political Culture of a Community in Change.* Berkeley: University of California Press, 1969.

Hart, George. *Poems of Ancient Tamil: Their Milieu and their Sanskrit Counterparts.* Berkeley: University of California Press, 1975.

Hart, George L. "Introduction." In *The Four Hundred Songs of War and Wisdom: An Anthology of Poems from Classical Tamil: The Purananuru.* Edited and translated by George L. Hart and Hank Heifetz, xv–xxxvii. New York: Columbia University Press, 1999.

Hart, George L. and Hank Heifetz, eds. *The Four Hundred Songs of War and Wisdom: An Anthology of Poems from Classical Tamil: The Purananuru.* New York: Columbia University Press, 1999.

Heehs, Peter. *Sri Aurobindo: A Brief Biography.* New Delhi: Oxford University Press, 1989.

Heehs, Peter. *The Lives of Sri Aurobindo.* New York: Columbia University Press, 2008.

Herring, Ronald, and Subir Sinha. "Common Property, Collective Action, and Ecology." *Economic and Political Weekly* 28, nos. 27–28 (July 1993): 1425–32.

Hiltebeitel, Alf, ed. *Criminal Gods and Demon Devotees: Essays on the Guardians of Popular Hinduism.* Albany: State University of New York Press, 1989.

Imperial Gazetteer of India: Provincial Series. Madras II: The Southern and West Coast Districts, Native States and French Possessions. Calcutta: Superintendent of Government Printing, 1908.

"India: State of Forest 2009." Forest Surveys of India. Dehradun, India: Ministry of Environment and Forests, Government of India, 2009.

Jaffelot, Christophe. *The Hindu Nationalist Movement in India.* New York: Columbia University Press, 1966.

Jain, Pankaj. *Dharma and the Ecology of Hindu Communities: Sustenance and Sustainability.* Burlington, VT: Ashgate Publishing Company, 2011.

Jordan, William R. *The Sunflower Forest: Ecological Restoration and the New Communion with Nature.* Berkeley: University of California Press, 2003.

Kalam, M. A. *Sacred Groves in Kodagu District of Karnataka (South India): A Socio-Historical Study.* Pondy Papers in Social Sciences 21. Pondicherry, India: Institut Français de Pondichéry, 2001.

Kapadia, Karin. *Siva and Her Sisters: Gender, Caste, and Class in Rural South India.* Boulder, CO: Westview Press, 1995.

Kent, Eliza F. "A Road Runs through It: Changing Meanings in a Sacred Grove in Tiruvannamalai, Tamil Nadu." *Journal for the Study of Religion, Nature and Culture* 4, no. 2 (June 2010): 213–31.

Kent, Eliza F. "Forests of Belonging: The Contested Meanings of Trees and Forests in Indian Hinduism." *Journal for the Study of Religion, Nature and Culture* 4, no. 2 (June 2010): 129–38.

Kent, Eliza F. "Sacred Groves and Local Gods: Religion and Environmentalism in South India." *Worldviews: Global Religions, Culture, and Ecology* 13, no. 1 (April 2009): 1–39.

Kent, Eliza F., and M. P. Ramanujam. "Fierce Gods and Dense Forest: Sacred Groves in Coromandel." *Indian Folklife* 26 (July 2007): 14–19.

Kinsley, David R. *Hindu Goddesses: Visions of the Divine Feminine in the Hindu Religious Tradition.* Berkeley: University of California Press, 1988.

Kjaerholm, Lars. "Aiyanar and Aiyappan in Tamil Nadu: Change and Continuity in South Indian Hinduism." *Folk. Dansk Ethnografisk Tidsskrift Kobenhavn* 26 (1984): 67–92. Accessed August 10, 2010: http://www.hindu.dk/1d/ar/Ai-Ai1200.pdf.

Krishna, Nanditha. "Blood on Our Hands." *The New Indian Express*, September 14, 2003.

Krishna, Nanditha. "Who is an Aryan?" *New Indian Express*, October 26, 2003.

Krishna, Nanditha. "Winds of Change." *New Indian Express*, April 4, 2004.

Krishna, Nanditha, and Javanti Prabhakaran, eds. *The Ecological Traditions of Tamilnadu.* Chennai, India: CPR Environmental Education Centre, 1997.

Kundoo, Anupama. *Roger Anger: Research on Beauty/Recherche Sur La Beaute.* Berlin: Jovis Verlag GmbH, 2009.

Lawbuary, Jo. "Eucalyptus Planting in 'Social Forestry' in India: Boon or Curse?" *Ganesha.* Accessed August 9, 2010: http://www.ganesha.co.uk/articles.htm.

Lorenzo, David J. *Tradition and the Rhetoric of Right: Popular Political Argument in the Aurobindo Movement.* Madison, NJ: Fairleigh Dickinson University Press, 1999.

Ludden, David. *Peasant History in South India.* Princeton: Princeton University Press, 1985.

Ludden, David, ed. *Contesting the Nation: Religion, Community and the Politics of Democracy in India.* Philadelphia: University of Pennsylvania Press, 1996.

Lutgendorf, Philip. "City, Forest, and Cosmos: Ecological Perspectives from the Sanskrit Epic." In *Hinduism and Ecology: The Intersection of Earth, Sky, and Water.* Edited by Christopher Key Chapple and Mary Evelyn Tucker, 269–89. Cambridge, MA: Center for the Study of World Religions, 2000.

Masilamani-Meyer, Eveline. *Guardians of Tamilnadu: Folk Deities, Folk Religion, Hindu Themes. Neue Hallesche Berichte* 5. Halle, Germany: Franckesche Stiftungen zu Halle, 2004.

Mawdsley, Emma. "Hindu Nationalism, Neo-Traditionalism, and Environmental Discourses in India." *Geoforum* 27, no. 3 (2006): 380–90.

Mawdsley, Emma. "The Abuse of Religion and Ecology: The Vishva Hindu Parishad and Tehri Dam." *Worldviews: Environment, Culture, Religion* 8, no. 2 (2006): 1–24.

McDermott, Robert. *The Essential Aurobindo: The Writings of Sri Aurobindo.* Great Barrington, MA: Lindisfarne Books, 2001.

Meher-Homji, V. M. "Puttupet: A Sacred Termit-Mound Protects a Forest." *Blackbuck* 2, no. 4 (1986): 1–4.

Menzies, Robert. "Forest Paradigms in Vrat Kathas." *Journal for the Study of Religion, Nature and Culture* 4, no. 2 (June 2010): 140–49.

Milton, Kay. *Environmentalism and Cultural Theory: The Role of Anthropology in Environmental Discourse.* New York: Routledge, 1996.

Mines, Diane P. *Fierce Gods: Inequality, Ritual, and the Politics of Dignity in a South Indian Village.* Bloomington: Indiana University Press, 2005.

Mines, Diane and Nicolas Yazgi, eds. *Village Matters: Relocating Villages in the Contemporary Anthropology of India.* New York: Oxford University Press, 2010

Minor, Robert. *The Religious, the Spiritual and the Secular: Auroville and Secular India. SUNY Series in Religious Studies.* Edited by Harold Coward. Albany: State University of New York Press, 1999.

Mohanakrishnan, A. *History of the Periyar Dam with Century Long Performance.* New Delhi: Central Board of Irrigation and Power, 1997.

Mother, The (aka Mirra Alfassa Richards). *Flowers—Their Spiritual Significance.* Edited by Vijay. Pondicherry, India: Sri Aurobindo Society, 1988.

Mother, The. *Mirra Alfassa, Paintings and Drawings.* Pondicherry, India: Sri Aurobindo Press, 1992.

Mother, The. *Words of the Mother—I.* Vol. 13 of *Collected Works of the Mother.* Edited by Sri Aurobindo Trust. Pondicherry, India: Sri Aurobindo Ashram Press, 2004.

Muir, John. "The Forests of the Yosemite Park." In *Nature Writings.* By John Muir, 767–89. New York: Library Classics, 1997.

Mukhim, Patricia. "Grappling with Tradition." *Statesman* (Calcutta and New Delhi), October 14, 2008.

Nair, S. M. "Enchanted Gardens: Rich Pockets of Green." *The Hindu,* Sunday Magazine, June 4, 2000.

Nair, S. M. "Groves that Conserve Ecology." *The Hindu,* May 1, 2003.

Nanda, Meera. *Prophets Facing Backward: Postmodern Critiques of Science and Hindu Nationalism in India.* Piscataway, NJ: Rutgers University Press, 2003.

Nanda, Meera. *The Wrongs of the Religious Right: Reflections on Science, Secularism and Hindutva.* Delhi: Three Essays Collective, 2005.

Nazeer, Mohamed. "Vanishing Sacred Groves." *The Hindu,* September 25, 2004.

"Nenmeli Eco-Village." CPR Environmental Education Centre: Success Stories (2007). Accessed February 14, 2012: http://cpreec.org/success.htm#1.

Nesmith, Cathy. "Gender Trees, and Fuel: Social Forestry in West Bengal." *Human Organisation* 50, no. 4 (1991): 337–48.

Nugteren, Albertina. *Belief, Beauty, and Bounty: Rituals around Sacred Trees in India.* Leiden: Brill, 2005.

Odum, Eugene P. "The Strategy of Ecosystem Development." *Science* (n.s.) 164, n.s., no. 3877 (April 1969): 262–70.

Office of the Register General and Census Commissioner. "Data Highlights: The Scheduled Tribes." *Census of India 2001.* Delhi, India: Office of the Register General, 2001, 2. Accessed September 6, 2012: http:// http://censusindia.gov.in/default.aspx.

"Operational Guidelines for the Centrally Sponsored Scheme: 'Intensification of Forest Management.'" Dehradun, India: Forest Protection Division, Ministry of Environment and Forests, Government of India, 2009. Accessed August 31, 2012: moef.nic.in/divisions/forprt/OPERATIONAL.pdf.

Oppili, P. "A Barren Area Transformed into Garden." *The Hindu,* June 6, 2002.

Pain, Paromita. "Sacred Wealth." *The Hindu,* May 24, 2003.

Pandian, Anand. "Securing the Rural Citizen: The Anti-Kallar Movement of 1896." *Indian Economic and Social History Review* 42, no. 1 (2005): 1–39.

Pandian, Anand. *Crooked Stalks: Cultivating Virtue in South India.* Durham, NC: Duke University Press, 2009.

Parthasarathy, N., and Pia Sethi. "Trees and Liana Species Diversity and Population Structure in a Tropical Dry Evergreen Forest in South India." *Tropical Ecology* 38, no. 1 (1997): 19–30.

Parthasarathy, N., and R. Karthikeyan. "Plant Biodiversity Inventory and Conservation of Two Tropical Dry Evergreen Forests on the Coromandel Coast, South India." *Biodiversity and Conservation* 6, no. 8 (1996): 1063–83.

Parthasarathy, R., ed. and trans. *The Cilapatikaram of Ilanko Atikal: An Epic of South India.* New York: Columbia University Press, 1993.

Patton, Laurie L. "Nature, Romanticism, and Sacrifice in Rigvedic Interpretation." In *Hinduism and Ecology: The Intersection of Earth, Sky, and Water.* Edited by Christopher Key Chapple and Mary Evelyn Tucker, 39–58. Cambridge, MA: Harvard University Press, 2000.

Pillai, P. P. "Iron and Steel Production in India." *Economica* 7 (January 1923): 55–66.

Prabhakar, V. K. *Social and Community Forestry.* New Delhi: Satish Garg, 1998.

Price, Pamela G. *Kingship and Political Practice in Colonial India.* University of Cambridge Oriental Publications 51. Cambridge, UK: Cambridge University Press, 1996.

Radhakrishnan, K. N. *Thirumalinrunjolai: Sri Alagar Koil Stala Purana.* Madurai, India: Sri Kallalagar Devastanam, 1942.

Radio Team. "Newcomer Reception #3" [Joss Brooks's addresses the Newcomer Reception on March 21, 2009]. Auroville Radio. Accessed May 26, 2010: http:// www.aurovilleradio.org/component/content/article/1149-Newcomer%20 Reception%20#3.

Ramakrishnan, P. S., K. G. Saxena, and U. M. Chandrashekara, eds. *Conserving the Sacred for Biodiversity Management.* Enfield, NH: Science Publishers, 1998.

Ramanujam, M. P., and D. Kadamban. "Plant Biodiversity of Two Tropical Dry Evergreen Forests in the Pondicherry Region of South India and the Role of Belief Systems in their Conservation." *Biodiversity and Conservation* 10 (2001): 1203–17.

"Religious Conversions Single Largest Threat to Ecology." Arise India Forum website. Accessed September 7, 2012: http://www.ariseindiaforum.org/religious-conversions-single-largest-threat-ecology/.

Saravanan, Velayutham. "Colonialism and Coffee Plantations: Decline of Environment and Tribals in Madras Presidency during the Nineteenth Century." *The Indian Economic and Social History Review* 41, no. 4 (2004): 469–70.

Saravanan, Velayutham. "Colonial Agrarian Policies in the Tribal Areas of Madras Presidency: 1872–1947." *South Asia Research* 26, no. 1 (2006): 63–85.

Savitra. *Auroville: Sunword Rising/A Trust for the Earth.* Auroville, India: Community of Auroville, 1980.

Shankar, Darshan. "Conserving the Medicinal Plants of India: The Need for A Biocultural Perspective." *The Journal of Alternative and Complementary Medicine* 2, no. 3 (1996): 349–58.

Sharma, Mukul. "Saffronising Green." *Seminar* 516 (2002). Accessed February 14, 2012: http://www.india-seminar.com/2002/516/516%20mukul%20sharma.htm.

Shinn, Larry. "Religious Vision and Social Consequences in a South Indian Utopian Community." *Religious Studies* 20, no. 2 (June 1984): 239–53.

Shiva, Vandana. *Staying Alive: Women, Ecology and Survival in India.* New Delhi: Zed Press, 1988.

Shiva, Vandana. *Biopiracy: The Plunder of Nature and Knowledge.* Boston: South End Press, 1997.

Shulman, David Dean. *Tamil Temple Myths: Sacrifice and Divine Marriage in the South Indian Saiva Tradition.* Princeton, NJ: Princeton University Press, 1980.

Shulman, David Dean. *The King and the Clown in South Indian Myth and Poetry.* Princeton, NJ: Princeton University Press, 1985.

Siebert, Charles. "Elephant Crackup." *The New York Times Magazine,* October 8, 2006. http://www.nytimes.com/2006/10/08/magazine/08elephant.html

Singh, Rachna. "Forest Dept. Launches Initiative to Conserve Sacred Groves." *Times of India* (Mumbai), September 5, 2008.

Sinha, Subir, Shubhra Gururani, and Brian Greenberg. "The 'New Traditionalist' Discourse of Indian Environmentalism." *Journal of Peasant Studies* 24, no. 3 (1997): 65–99.

Skaria, Ajay. *Hybrid Histories: Forests, Frontiers, and Wildness in Western India.* New Delhi: Oxford University Press, 1999.

St. Joan, Sharon. "Nenmeli: Where the Trees Are Happy." Kanab, UT: Best Friends Animal Society, 2010. Accessed June 15, 2010: http://network.bestfriends.org/golocal/india/14864/news.aspx.

Stevens, William K. *Miracle Under the Oaks: The Revival of Nature in America.* New York: Pocket Books, 1995.

Stuckrad, Kocku von. "Finding Data: Some Reflections on Ontologies and Normativities." *Journal for the Study of Religion and Culture* 1, no. 1 (2007): 39–46.

Subramanyam, Sanjay. *Penumbral Visions: Making Polities in Early Modern South India.* Ann Arbor: University of Michigan Press, 2001.

Sudanandha, D. Samuel. "The Making of a Muttaraiyar Cati." Ph.D. diss., University of Washington, Seattle, 1996.

Sudhakar, P. "Ban on Animal Sacrifice Has Divided Communities: A Survey." *The Hindu,* September 15, 2003. Accessed June 10, 2010: http://www.thehindu. com/2003/09/15/stories/2003091504490400.htm.

Sundaravalli, Priya. "The Hidden World of Ammas." *Auroville Today,* December 2006. Accessed September 7, 2012: http://www.auroville.org/journals&media/ avtoday/archive/2004-2009/2006-12/ammas.htm.

"The Work of Auroville in Nadukuppam." *Auroville Today,* December 2008. Accessed September 7, 2012: http://www.auroville.org/journals&media/avto-day/archive/2004-2009/2008-12/Nadukuppam.htm

Thirunavukkarasu, S. *Land Reforms and Tribal Development: A Case Study of Kalrayan Hills Tamil Nadu.* Delhi: Kalpaz Publications, 2006.

Thurston, Edgar, and K. Rangachari. *Castes and Tribes of Southern India,* Vol. 1–7. Madras: Government of Madras, 1909.

Tomalin, Emma. "Bio-Divinity and Biodiversity: Perspectives on Religion and Environmental Conservation in India." *Numen* 51 (2004): 265–95.

Tomalin, Emma. *Biodivinity and Biodiversity: The Limits to Religious Environmentalism.* Burlington, VT: Ashgate, 2009.

Tomkins, Peter, and Christopher Bird. *The Secret Life of Plants.* New York: Harper & Row, 1973.

Venkateswaran, R., and N. Parthasarathy. "Tropical Dry Evergreen Forests on the Coromandel Coast of India: Structure, Composition and Human Disturbance." *Ecotropica* 9 (2003): 45–58.

Visalakshi, N. "Vegetation Analysis of Two Tropical Dry Evergreen Forests in Southern India." *Tropical Ecology* 36, no. 1, (1995): 117–27.

Viswanathan, S. "A Decree on Animal Sacrifice." *Frontline,* October 13, 2003.

Waghorne, Joanne Punzo. *The Raja's Magic Clothes: Re-Visioning Kingship and Divinity in England's India.* University Park: Pennsylvania State University Press, 1994.

Wall, Derek. *Earth First! And the Anti-Roads Movement.* London: Routledge, 1999.

Wedding of the Goddess. Directed by Mira Reyhm Binford and Michael Camerini. Madison: University of Wisconsin at Madison South Asia Center, 1976. DVD.

Whitehead, Henry. *The Village Gods of South India.* Calcutta: Association Press, 1921. (Originally published 1916)

Worster, Donald. *Nature's Economy: A History of Ecological Ideas.* 2d ed. New York: Cambridge University Press, 1984.

Zimmerman, Francis. *The Jungle and the Aroma of Meats: An Ecological Theme in Hindu Medicine.* Comparative Studies of Health Systems and Medical Care 20. Berkeley: University of California Press, 1988.

Index

CPSIA information can be obtained
at www.ICGtesting.com
Printed in the USA
LVHW111434130920
665857LV00002B/183